**WHAT THE CRITICS SAY:**

SO-CWS-948

*A very worthwhile addition to any travel library.* —**WCBS Newsradio**

*Armed with these guides, you may never again stay in a conventional hotel.*
—**Travelore Report**

*Easily carried ... neatly organized ... wonderful. A helpful addition to my travel library. The authors wax as enthusiastically as I do about the almost too-quaint-to-believe Country Inns.* —**San Francisco Chronicle**

*One can only welcome such guide books and wish them long, happy, and healthy lives in print.* —**Wichita Kansas Eagle**

*This series of pocket-sized paperbacks will guide travelers to hundreds of little known and out of the way inns, lodges, and historic hotels.... a thorough menu.*
—**(House Beautiful's) Colonial Homes**

*Charming, extremely informative, clear and easy to read; excellent travelling companions.* —**Books-Across-The-Sea** *(The English Speaking Union)*

*...a fine selection of inviting places to stay... provide excellent guidance....*
—**Blair & Ketchum's Country Journal**

*Obviously designed for our kind of travel.... [the authors] have our kind of taste.*
—**Daily Oklahoman**

*The first guidebook was so successful that they have now taken on the whole nation.... Inns are chosen for charm, architectural style, location, furnishings and history.* —**Portland Oregonian**

*Many quaint and comfy country inns throughout the United States... The authors have a grasp of history and legend.* —**Dallas (Tx.) News**

*Very fine travel guides.* —**Santa Ana (Calif.) Register**

*A wonderful source for planning trips.* —**Northampton (Mass.) Gazette**

*...pocketsize books full of facts.... attractively made and illustrated.*
—**New York Times Book Review**

*Hundreds of lovely country inns reflecting the charm and hospitality of various areas throughout the U.S.* —**Youngstown (Ohio) Vindicator**

*Some genius must have measured the average American dashboard, because the Compleat Traveler's Companions fit right between the tissues and bananas on our last trip.... These are good-looking books with good-looking photographs.... very useful.*

—**East Hampton (N.Y.) Star**

## ALSO AVAILABLE IN THE COMPLEAT TRAVELER SERIES

If your local bookseller, gift shop, or country inn does not stock a particular title, ask them to order directly from Burt Franklin & Co., Inc., 235 East 44th Street, New York, New York 10017, U.S.A. Telephone orders are accepted from recognized retailers and credit card holders. In the United States, call, toll free, 1-800-223-0766 during regular business hours. (In New York State, call 212-687-5250.)

THE COMPLEAT TRAVELER'S COMPANION

# Country New England Inns

*by*

**Anthony Hitchcock**

*and*

**Jean Lindgren**

**BURT FRANKLIN & CO.**

Published by Burt Franklin & Company
235 East Forty-fourth Street
New York, New York 10017

SIXTH EDITION

**Library of Congress Cataloging in Publication Data**

Hitchcock, Anthony
Country New England inns.

(The compleat traveler's companion)
Includes index.
1.  Hotels, taverns, etc. — New England — Direct-
ories.   I. Lindgren, Jean, joint author.
II. Title.   III. Series: Compleat traveler's
companion.
TX907.H55     1983     647′.947401
0-89102-270-8

Printed in the United States of America


3 5 4 2

# Contents

# Introduction

PEOPLE ARE DRAWN to New England for many reasons. Some are attracted by the long coastline with its variety of beaches. Others love the inland areas with their myriad lakes, forests, rolling hills, and mountains. Sportsmen enjoy New England the year round for its hunting, fishing, boating, skiing, swimming, mountain climbing, or hiking. Artists come to paint; writers, to write. Theater-lovers come for summer theater, and history buffs come to observe the lessons of the past represented in the thousands of museums, historical societies, and historic sites that are found in every corner of these states. For our part, we find ourselves drawn back by some even more deeply rooted force, perhaps from our childhood. One of us was born and has spent the better part of his youth in New England, and the other has summered there for many years. For whatever reason and in whatever season, you will find New England a most compelling place. It is unlikely that you will fail to return. Many never leave.

If you have decided to go, here are some helpful suggestions. First, choose your season and area with care. If you cannot cope with snow, you will certainly know not to select a winter weekend. It is not so well known, however, that the early-spring mud season makes travel on back roads in the three most northerly states trying at best. If you plan an April trip to a remote inn, be sure to ask if local travel will be a problem.

We also suggest you write early for literature about inns that interest you. We have deliberately omitted a rating system, because tastes in old inns vary widely from the very informal to the elegantly formal. Read the brochures, look at the pictures, check the maps, and determine if the inns will actually meet your needs. Inns are not at all like motels. Each has special qualities that can be one's personal pleasure but not necessarily another's. Do not hesitate to call an innkeeper and discuss your requirements. Most innkeepers are highly understanding of the needs of their guests. If you are seeking an old-fashioned, small country inn that is secluded, with few outside distractions, ask before you go. We have purposely included a wide range of inns, from the simplest to small resorts.

In this new edition, we have quoted the most recent room rates in a combined rate chart and index at the end of the book. Readers should note that the listed rates are *subject to change.* While the quoted rates are for double occupancy in most cases, single travelers as well as larger groups should inquire about special rates. We list daily room rates as based on the American Plan (AP, all three meals included), Modified American Plan (MAP, breakfast and dinner included), Bed and Breakfast (BB, either full or Continental breakfast included), or European Plan (EP, no meals). In many cases a tax and a service charge will be added. Be sure to ask. Children and pets present special problems for many inns. If either is *not* welcome at an inn it is noted in the description. These regulations also often change, and it is imperative that families traveling with either inquire in advance. Though many inns state they are open all year, we find that many close during slow periods. Call first to confirm your room reservations.

A wealth of travel information can be obtained free of charge from the highly organized state and local chambers of commerce. The single best source of state information in compact form is on the back of each state's official road map. These are issued by the respective state departments of transportation but are usually shipped by the state tourism office of the division of commerce and development in each state capital.

The inns described in this book were chosen for their inherent charm, based partially on their architectural style, location, furnishings, and history. We have made every effort to provide information as carefully and accurately as possible, but we remind readers that all listed rates and schedules are subject to change. Further, we have neither solicited nor accepted any fees or gratuities for being included in this book or any of the other books in this series. We have tried to be responsive to reader suggestions arising out of earlier editions of this book. Should readers wish to offer suggestions for future editions, we welcome their correspondence. Please write to us in care of our publishers: Burt Franklin and Company, 235 East Forty-fourth Street, New York, NY 10017.

JEAN LINDGREN
ANTHONY HITCHCOCK

# Country
# New England
# Inns

# Connecticut

## *East Haddam, Connecticut*

### BISHOP'S GATE

Route 151, East Haddam, CT 06423. 203-873-1677. *Innkeeper:* Julie Bishop. Open all year.

Bishop's Gate offers visitors a chance to experience New England at its best. The 1817 Greek Revival house is set behind a prim white picket fence in a historic town on the Connecticut River. The beautifully restored house is decorated throughout with nineteenth-century antiques and Oriental rugs on wide-board floors.

This is the home and inn of Julie Bishop, whom most guests consider one of the nicest things about staying here. As an opera fan and past president of the Goodspeed Opera House Guild, Julie chose the inn for its proximity to the renowned playhouse. The walls of her kitchen, the true heart of the inn, are covered with autographed photos of performers. Breakfast is served here at the harvest table, and soft chairs and a couch are grouped around a wood-burning fireplace. It is almost impossible to choose a favorite guest room. Three have fireplaces, and all have antique furnishings. The Jenny Lind Room has a four-poster complete with fishnet-lace canopy.

*Accommodations:* 5 rooms with shared bath. *Pets:* Not permitted. *Children:* Under six not permitted. *Driving Instructions:* From Route 9, take exit 7 to East Haddam. Follow Route 82 for 1 mile. Turn left at Route 151 and go 1 mile.

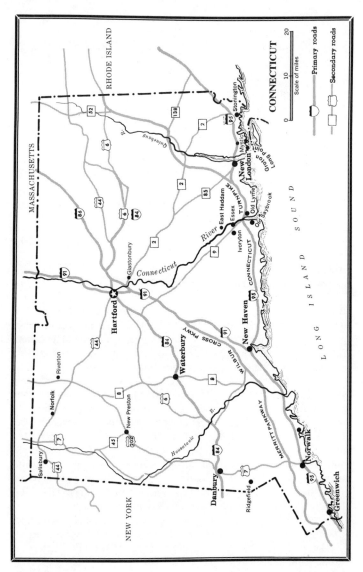

CONNECTICUT

Scale of miles

Primary roads
Secondary roads

0      10      20

RHODE ISLAND

MASSACHUSETTS

Quinebaug R.

52

138

2

95

Stonington

Mystic

New London

Groton

Long Point

TURNPIKE

6

84

86

44

6

85

2

East Haddam

Essex

Ivoryton

Old Lyme

Old Saybrook

River

Connecticut

9

95

CONNECTICUT

2

Glastonbury

91

91

Hartford

LONG

ISLAND

SOUND

44

Riverton

Norfolk

New Preston

8

84

Waterbury

6

WILBUR CROSS PKWY

8

91

New Haven

7

45

202

Housatonic R.

MERRITT PARKWAY

84

Salisbury

44

Danbury

Ridgefield

7

Norwalk

95

Greenwich

NEW YORK

*Essex, Connecticut*

## GRISWOLD INN

Essex, CT 06426. 203-767-0991. *Innkeeper:* William Winterer. Open all year except Christmas Eve and Christmas.

The Griswold Inn has been in continuous operation since 1776 and has been carefully renovated over the years, with an overall effect which continues to be among the more pleasing in the state. The Griswold contains fine guest and dining facilities, and a fascinating collection of marine art is displayed on its walls. An extensive library houses a collection of reference material concerning the history of firearms.

Perhaps the most famous room in the inn is the Tap-Room, a paneled room with a pot-bellied stove that has a fire during the winter months. The room was built in 1738 as an early schoolhouse in Essex. It was rolled to the Griswold in the late eighteenth century on a bed of logs. Food is served in seven dining rooms, including the Covered Bridge Room, constructed from components of an abandoned New Hampshire covered bridge. The room's decorations include a collection of Currier and Ives steamboat prints and a number of temperance banners. The menu features a choice of six appetizers and a large number of seafood, meat, and poultry entrées.

The twenty guest rooms are decorated with equal care and include many brass beds and attractive wallpapers. Air conditioning has been added in deference to some modern tastes, but never will a telephone or television jar you from your sleep. Personal touches are the rule here; do not hesitate to ask for an extra pillow or two if you wish.

*Accommodations:* 20 rooms, most with bath. *Driving Instructions:* Take exit 3 from Route 9 (exit 69 on the Connecticut Turnpike) to Essex Village.

# Glastonbury, Connecticut

## BUTTERNUT FARM

1654 Main Street, Glastonbury, CT 06033. 203-633-7197.*Innkeeper:* Donald B. Reid. Open all year.

Butternut Farm is a treasure house of antiquities. To the best of our knowledge this handsome home is without peer among New England guest houses with respect to its collection of antiques and the architectural richness of the homestead. Butternut Farm was built in two stages by Jonathan Hale, beginning in 1720, the year of his marriage. The interior of this classic Colonial house was painstakingly restored to its original condition by innkeeper Donald Reid by exposing the original wide brick fireplaces, uncovering the broad pumpkin-pine floorboards, and removing paint from the paneling on many of the rooms' walls. Hand-hammered hinges, paneled fireplaces, handsome summer beams (in both sitting and guest rooms), and cornice detailing are but a few of the features of this guest house. Many visitors come to Butternut Farm simply to see its collection of eighteenth-century Connecticut antiques. A cherry highboy, a cherry six-board chest, ball-foot "hired man" beds, a pencilpost cherry bed, a pine-and-oak gateleg table, early eighteenth-century bannister-back chairs, and a fine collection of English Delft are but a representative sampling of the richness of Mr. Reid's collection. Some guests come to see his herb gardens — a hobby that has grown into a modest herb-farm business.

Overnight accommodations are in rooms furnished in keeping with the Colonial period. Even the modern bathrooms that were added are unobtrusive. Breakfast is served to guests in the former kitchen, which Jonathan Hale converted to his dining room when he added the rear section to his original building in 1743.

*Accommodations:* 4 rooms with private bath. *Driving Instructions:* Take I-91 or Route 2 to Glastonbury. From the center of town drive south 1.6 miles to the inn. Enter from Whapley Road.

## THE HOMESTEAD INN

420 Field Point Road, Greenwich, CT 06830. 203-869-7500. *Innkeepers:* Nancy Smith and Lessie Davison. Open all year.

The Homestead has been restored with a capital "R." The two innkeepers, Nancy Smith and Lessie Davison, teamed up with interior designer John Saladino and transformed the old house into a period inn. The Homestead, as it has always been called, began in 1799 as the home of Augustus Mead, a judge and gentleman farmer. It was remodeled over the years in the distinctive "Carpenter Gothic" Victorian style it displays today. The interior has been redone stem to stern. One attractive little bedroom with exposed beams was stripped of many layers of wallpaper to reveal its surprise — delicate, original stenciling of robins; hence its name, the Robin Room. The snug Poppy Room is all tans and reds, while the large Butterfly Room is bright and sunny.

The inn is furnished throughout with a fine collection of antiques. Its classic French restaurant, La Grange, is a festival for the senses. House specialties at the evening meal are escalopes de ris de veau aux chanterelles, crab "Belle Haven," a cassolette d'escargots, and a rich chocolate cake. The blue and white Wedgwood plates and formal settings contrast grandly with the rugged barn siding and ancient chestnut beams hung with bunches of dried herbs. A fire burns in the brick hearth on cool evenings.

A favorite retreat for guests is the intimate library with its lush furnishings and working hearth. The best entertainment at the Homestead is investigating the rooms and narrow staircases. In warm weather the veranda, overlooking the hilly lawn and shade trees, is set up with plenty of antique wicker for relaxing in turn-of-the-century style. Be sure to make room and dinner reservations well in advance; the secret of the Homestead is out.

*Accommodations:* 13 rooms with private bath. Complimentary breakfast is included. *Pets:* Not permitted. *Driving Instructions:* Take Route I-95 to exit 3. Turn west toward the railroad bridge, and take a left onto Horseneck Lane. Drive to the end, and turn left onto Field Point Road. The inn is a quarter of a mile uphill on the right.

## *Groton Long Point, Connecticut*

### SHORE INNE

54 East Shore Road, Groton Long Point, CT 06340. 203-536-1180.

*Innkeeper:* Helen Ellison. Open April through mid-November.

In the Roaring Twenties a popular show-business couple found themselves unable to handle the many guests flocking to their waterside home, so they built a guest house right next door. The gregarious entertainers are gone now, but the little guest house is still going strong as the Shore Inne. Its situation is unique, thanks to a "grandfather clause" that has enabled the business to continue even though the neighborhood has turned strictly residential. A large copper beech tree shades the lawn, which leads down to the shore. From its picture windows, the living room offers views of Fisher's Island Sound and Mouse Island. Its white wicker furnishings have cushions covered with fabrics of greens, yellows, and bittersweets. The guest rooms are simply and comfortably decorated in the manner of a seaside summer house; homemade patchwork coverlets brighten the beds. Most rooms have views of the water.

The guest house is convenient to the many tourist attractions in the area including Mystic Seaport and Mystic Aquarium.

*Accommodations:* 7 rooms, 5 with private bath. *Pets:* Not permitted. *Driving Instructions:* Take I-95 exit 88 or 89 to Route 1, continue to Route 215. Take Route 215 to Groton Long Point Road. The East Shore Road is the first left turn after the Yankee Fisherman Restaurant. The inn is in the Mystic–New London area.

## *Ivoryton, Connecticut*

## COPPER BEECH INN

Main Street, Ivoryton, CT 06442. 203-767-0330. *Innkeepers:* Paul and Louise Ebeltoft. Open all year, closed Mondays.

The Copper Beech Inn is renowned for its restaurant, a recipient of praise from nearly all of the major magazines and newspapers that cover Connecticut. For several years it has been named the best restaurant in the state by the readers of *Connecticut Magazine.*

This Victorian mansion, dating from 1898, has gained a reputation for its unusually large menu, which can best be described as country-French classical. Meals are served in three well-appointed dining rooms: the Queen Anne Ivoryton Room, the Chippendale Comstock Room, and the Empire Copper Beech Room. Candlelit dining at the Copper Beech features formal service, hand-blown stemware, and silver. Before dinner, guests may enjoy drinks in the mansion's former greenhouse. Among the dining rooms' specialties are rack of lamb carved at the table, baby pheasant, Long Island duckling, fresh native fish, lobster bisque, hot country pâté, medallions of veal chasseur, and sweetbreads served in brioche in cream sauce. Beef Wellington is served in a truffle sauce. After the meal, guests may retire to one of the guest rooms, furnished in colonial motif. Each has retained its original cast-iron claw-footed bathtub.

*Accommodations:* 5 rooms with private bath. *Pets:* Not permitted. *Children:* Inquire before bringing. *Driving Instructions:* The inn is on Main Street, 1½ miles west of Route 9, exit 3 or 4.

## 1833 HOUSE

33 Greenmanville Avenue (Route 27), Mystic, CT 06355. 203-572-0633. *Innkeeper:* Joan Brownell Smith. Open all year except Christmastime.

This old New England guest house was built, as the name implies, in 1833 and is just next door to the historic Mystic Seaport Museum. The old seaport and the masts of the tall ships can be seen from some of the guest-room windows. The inn is a small, comfortable place with a friendly atmosphere enhanced by Mrs. Smith's furnishings — a blend of period Victorian pieces and family furniture. The most popular spot in the house is Joan's big, sunny kitchen where guests congregate for hot coffee with their Continental breakfasts.

In warm weather one can watch the sails being set on the whaling ship *Morgan* while sitting under a tree in the spacious yard. It is only a short walk from here to the South Gate of the seaport, and in season the courtesy bus stops almost at the door. Mrs. Smith is a mine of information on the seaport, having spent many hours as a volunteer at the Tourist Center. She is also glad to pick guests up at the Amtrak railroad station nearby. Whether guests arrive on foot or by car, they are certain to be greeted by the inn's pets, Thumper and Po' Baby.

*Accommodations:* 4 rooms, 2 with private bath. *Pets:* Welcome. *Driving Instructions:* Leave I-95 at exit 90 and go 1 mile south on Route 27 toward Mystic Seaport. The guest house is just past it.

## THE INN AT MYSTIC

Routes 1 and 27, Mystic, CT 06355. 203-536-9604. *Innkeeper:* Jody Dyer. Open all year.

On 15 acres of land in historic Mystic Seaport is a complex of buildings the jewel of which is a Colonial Revival mansion built in 1904 that overlooks the harbor and Pequoitsepois Cove. It was bought by the innkeepers of the Mystic Motor Inn and Flood Tide Restaurant, a new and highly rated establishment built in an old peach orchard. The inn adjoins this property and sits amid 8 acres of attractive formal gardens. Wide porches with towering columns offer views of the sea and gardens.

The guest rooms at the inn are decorated with Victorian furnishings, and some have canopied beds and working fireplaces. The

English pine-paneled drawing room with its baby grand piano also offers somewhat formal Victorian charms. Bathrooms at the inn are sheer self-indulgence with luxurious whirlpool soaking tubs and "thermacuzzi" spas.

In the winter there is bed-and-breakfast service at the inn. The formal dining room, drawing room, and gardens are popular for weddings and formal functions, and the grounds offer swimming, boating, and tennis.

In addition to the five period guest rooms in the inn, there are four rooms in the Gatehouse. Built in the early 1950s as a guest house, this building has English paneling, fireplaces, imported mantels, and a quiet setting overlooking the orchard. All other accommodations in the Inn at Mystic are modern motel rooms.

*Accommodations:* 70 rooms with private bath. *Pets and children:* Not permitted in the inn or Gatehouse. *Driving Instructions:* The inn is at the corner at Routes 1 and 27.

## BOULDERS INN

Route 45, Lake Waramaug, New Preston, CT 06777. 203-868-7918. *Innkeepers:* Carolyn and Jim Woolen. Open all year.

Up in the Berkshire Hills, on 30 acres of woods and lake frontage, is the Boulders Inn. Oxen dragged granite lintels and fieldstones like boulders to the building site in 1895. The inn overlooks the hills and Lake Waramaug, which provides year-round scenic interest and offers guests many recreational opportunities. In summer there are swimming, fishing, sailing, and canoeing; with winter comes the ice for skating and ice fishing. The hills are crisscrossed with trails that beckon hikers, horseback riders, and cross-country skiers. The Woolens stock ski equipment for guests.

The inn was a private home up until thirty-five years ago and has been a hostelry ever since. Its den and living room, both with fireplaces, are furnished with family antiques and upholstered chairs in groupings by picture windows. The terrace with its lake vistas is popular in warm weather for dining and for viewing the sunsets at the cocktail hour. Meals at Boulders offer traditional American and Continental fare, such as steaks, baked chicken, duckling, and shrimp.

The six spacious guest rooms have a blend of antiques and comfortable furniture. Cottages scattered about the inn's grounds are winterized, each has its own deck, and some have fireplaces.

*Accommodations:* 6 rooms with bath in the inn, several in the cottages. *Driving Instructions:* Take Route 202 to Route 45 North. The inn is 1½ miles up the road on the right.

## *Norwalk, Connecticut*

### SILVERMINE TAVERN

Perry Avenue and Silvermine Avenue, Norwalk, CT 06850. 203-847-4558. *Innkeeper:* Francis Whitman, Jr. Open all year, except Tuesdays from September to May.

Four buildings make up the Tavern group — the Coach House, the Old Mill, the Country Store, and the Tavern itself. The buildings are furnished in antiques, Oriental rugs, and primitive paintings. Each guest room has authentic antique beds (three have canopies). Several rooms have balconies overlooking the millpond. A waterfall contributes to the charm of the 200-year-old building called the Old Mill. Fireplaces going in winter, shade trees in summer, and colorful foliage in autumn create an atmosphere of New England hospitality.

The Tavern has several dining rooms overlooking the swans on the millpond and the wooded banks of the Silvermine River. Decorated with unusual kitchen utensils and primitive portraits, it is very popular with tourists. The menu features traditional New England fare: shore dinners, Boston scrod, steaks, and chicken. The Tavern is particularly proud of its Indian pudding.

*Accommodations:* 10 rooms with private bath. *Driving Instructions:* Take exit 39 on the Merritt Parkway (Route 15). Proceed south on Route 7 to the first traffic light, then turn right on Perry Avenue. Follow Perry for 1½ miles to the inn.

## Old Lyme, Connecticut

### BEE AND THISTLE INN

100 Lyme Street, Old Lyme, CT 06371. 203-434-1667. *Innkeepers:*
Bob and Penny Nelson. Open all year.

The Bee and Thistle Inn is on 5½ acres along the Lieutenant River in
the historic district of Old Lyme. Its bordering stone walls, sunlit
porches, inviting parlors, and formal gardens capture the feeling of a
traditional New England home. Built in 1756, the inn has many fireplaces, a carved staircase, and antique furnishings typical of the pre-
Federal period. Guest rooms have canopied or four-poster beds
covered with antique quilts or afghans. Nooks abound where one can
curl up with a book or write a letter to a friend.

Breakfast is served on the sunny porches or before the fire in the
dining room. Freshly baked muffins and omelets highlight the morning meal. In the evening, candlelight dining focuses on fresh seafood,
lamb, veal, duckling, and choice steaks. Many of Old Lyme's galleries, museums, gift shops, and antique shops are within walking distance of the inn.

*Accommodations:* 10 rooms, 8 with private bath. *Pets:* Not permitted. *Driving Instructions:* From the south, take I-95 to exit 70,
turn left off the ramp, then right at the stoplight and left at the next
stoplight. From the north, take exit 70 off I-95 and turn right off the
ramp. The inn is the third building on the left.

## Ridgefield, Connecticut

### THE ELMS

500 Main Street, Ridgefield, CT 06877. 203-438-2541. *Innkeepers:* Robert and Violet Scala. Open all year except Wednesdays.

The Elms was built in 1760 by Amos Seymour, a master carpenter of his time. Such were his woodworking skills that he also made every piece of furniture in his home. Forty years later Seymour's house was turned into an inn by one S. A. Rockwell.

The Elms survives with a selection of antiques that makes a visit there reminiscent of a stay at grandmother's house. Perhaps this is most evident in the inn's sitting room, where a large Victorian couch has a set of antimacassars. The guest rooms upstairs all have shuttered doors, an unusual touch. One room we particularly liked has four-poster beds, white walls with blue trim, and an original claw-footed bathtub. A smaller guest room in the back of the inn has pine floors and a Victorian walnut bureau with a marble top.

Downstairs, the bar has exposed beams, a large fireplace, and walls hung with old barometers. Dining is available in two formal dining rooms, one of which has a fine chicken weathervane as part of its decor. A special private dining room, for groups who wish to reserve it, has such luxurious touches as silver candlesticks. The Elms prides itself on its continental cuisine, strongly influenced by French and Italian cooking traditions.

*Accommodations:* 20 rooms with private bath. *Pets:* Not permitted. *Driving Instructions:* The inn is on Main Street (Route 35).

## STONEHENGE

Route 7, Ridgefield, CT 06877. 203-438-6511. *Innkeepers:* David Davis and Douglas Seville. Open all year; restaurant closed Tuesdays.

Stonehenge, an 1832 farmhouse turned country inn, is renowned for its cuisine served in an attractive setting. The white brick and fieldstone house is beside a trout pond with its own waterfall and a number of water fowl including mallards, wild and tame geese, and some swans. On a quiet country side road, the inn is surrounded by lawns, shade trees, and a wooded glen with a scenic footpath that leads around the pond. The house is filled with antiques, and its library–living room is presided over by a grandfather's clock and several old barometers. Two large guest rooms are upstairs in the house, and six are in an annex just across the lawn. All are furnished with antiques, and the two in the farmhouse have fireplaces.

Stonehenge prides itself on its unusual fare. Some of their special offerings are smoked trout, Stonehenge's own smoked sausage with mustard wine sauce, and shrimp in beer batter with pungent fruit sauce. Main-course specialties include fresh brook trout, rack of lamb, and pheasant and venison in season. Stonehenge, just an hour and a half from New York City, is a perfect spot for a weekend getaway.

*Accommodations:* 2 rooms in the house, 6 rooms in the annex. *Pets:* Not permitted. *Driving Instructions:* The inn is on a side road off Route 7. A large sign on the road points the way.

## WEST LANE INN

22 West Lane, Ridgefield, CT 06877. 203-438-7323. *Innkeeper:* Maureen M. Mayer. Open all year.

The West Lane is one of Connecticut's newest old inns. It was first built in the early nineteenth century as the home of one of the wealthy landowners of that era. It has an impressive columned porch running along the entire front with a central bow window on the second floor. The inn is set behind a broad lawn and flowering shrubs framed by a stand of tall maples. Inside, the tone is of quiet elegance, with oak paneling, deep-pile carpeting, and a fire on the hearth in the lobby. Off the lobby on one side is a breakfast room, and on the other side is the office. The rooms are large and have either one king-size or two queen-size beds, as well as climate controls, color television, and radio. Some of the rooms have working fireplaces, and four have kitchenettes.

*Accommodations:* 20 rooms with private bath. *Pets:* Not permitted. *Driving Instructions:* Take Route 35 (West Lane Road) to about a mile west of the center of the village of Ridgefield.

## Riverton, Connecticut

## OLD RIVERTON INN

Route 20, Riverton, CT 06065. 203-379-8678. *Innkeeper:* Mark A. Telford. Open all year; dining room closed Mondays.

The Old Riverton Inn was built in 1796 as a stagecoach stop on the Hartford to Albany Post Road and was completely remodeled in 1940, when a new bridge was constructed in front of it.

The inn's front lounge and dining room have wallpaper by Nancy McClelland, an authority on antique papers. Its design, taken from an old hatbox, is called the "Hampshire Bird." An upstairs lounge where houseguests frequently gather has a paisley design. The room also features a card table and a number of picture puzzles as well as needlepoint chairs to relax in. In the ten upstairs guest rooms, needlepoint is again seen on the luggage racks.

In 1954 the Grindstone Terrace was enclosed to make a room in which about fifty antique wheels make up the floor. The early wheels were mined in Nova Scotia and brought to the mouth of the Connecticut River by boat and subsequently to the inn by ox cart. Other floors in the bar and entrance have polished Vermont flagstone that made the journey from the north on barges down the Connecticut. The Hobby Horse Bar has saddles on wooden kegs. The dining room menu features standard New England fare with a selection of steaks, chops, seafood, and chicken dishes.

*Accommodations:* 10 rooms with private bath. *Driving Instructions:* Take Route 8 north, and turn right on Route 20.

## UNDER MOUNTAIN INN

Undermountain Road (Route 41), Salisbury, CT 06068. 203-435-0242. *Innkeepers:* Al and Lorraine Bard. Open Wednesday through Sunday all year except March.

Under Mountain Inn, set amid Litchfield County's Connecticut Berkshires, is meticulously restored, with a profusion of antiques, attractive wallpapers, and wide-board pine. Under Mountain was fashioned from the ancestral homestead of the Scoville and Fisher families. A large part of the building predates 1740. A clue to its antiquity was found during the restoration; a bundle of very wide pine boards was discovered hidden between the ceiling and attic floorboards. Apparently the result of a pre-Revolutionary silent protest, the boards were probably placed there in disobedience of a colonial law requiring all such lumber to be turned over to the king of England.

The wide pine is now to be seen on the front of the bar in the Tavern Room. This intimate dining room, once the "borning" room of the house, is one of four dining rooms at the inn. When we were there, a fire burned in the hearth, and the aroma of burning pine mingled with that of the food being prepared in the kitchen. The menu posted on the blackboard offered starters of asparagus on artichoke hearts and mushroom caps stuffed with crab. Duckling with a plum glaze is a specialty, and lamb (roast and shanks), sirloin steak, Cornish game hens, and New England meat pies appear with regularity. The inn's comfortable parlor has a blue Oriental rug, rose-colored walls, a profusion of plants, and interesting woodwork around the fireplace. A separate living room is done in soft greens with a rose rug.

The seven bedrooms upstairs are done with equal care. Perhaps the most popular is the one Al Bard laughingly refers to as the "Love Room," because of the size of its claw-footed bathtub and its four-poster bed. A twin-bedded room has old-fashioned rose and blue wallpapers with matching drapes and headboard, a blue woven rug, an antique highboy, and wing chairs. The hall outside the room has a library full of books. Horses graze in a meadow adjoining the inn.

*Accommodations:* 7 rooms with bath. *Pets:* Not permitted. *Driving Instructions:* The inn is on Route 41, just south of the Massachusetts border in the northwestern corner of Connecticut.

## WHITE HART INN

Junction of routes 41 and 44, Salisbury, CT 06068. 203-435-2511. *Innkeeper:* John D. Harney. Open all year.

On the village green in Salisbury, the White Hart Inn was built in 1800 as a private residence but has been in continuous service as a hostelry since 1867. The inn is actually a three-building complex consisting of the original 1800 building, an adjacent annex that was also built as a residence and at one time served as a private girls' school, and a more modern seven-room motor court–type building next to the inn. Guests therefore have a choice of accommodations in several styles. All rooms are comfortable and have private baths and telephones.

The inn employs an Oriental chef, so the menu offers an interesting combination of Oriental, Continental, and American cuisine. Among the many dishes are Buddha's ten-ingredient vegetables, sliced pork with oyster sauce, mixed meats in hot spicy sauce, shrimp with cashews, tea-smoked-flavor duckling, rainbow trout Bretonne, tournedos of beef Bordelaise, and broiled filet mignon.

The inn maintains an old-fashioned country store within the main building, complete with potbelly stove and bayberry candles. Also available for sale are old lamps, maple sugar, cheddar cheese, and more.

*Accommodations:* 20 rooms with private bath. *Driving Instructions:* The inn is on the village green at the junction of routes 44 and 41.

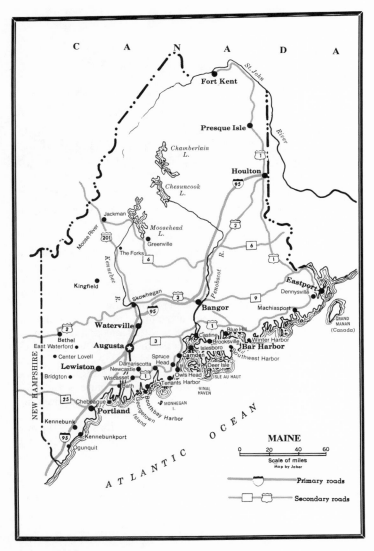

MAINE

Scale of miles
Map by Jaber

0    20    40    60

Primary roads

Secondary roads

# Maine

---

*Bar Harbor, Maine*

## MANOR HOUSE INN

106 West Street, Bar Harbor, ME 04609. 207-288-3759. *Innkeepers:* Jan and Frank Matter. Open mid-April through mid-November.

In the late nineteenth century it was the fashion of the wealthy to build elegant summer cottages at the seashore. Two of the most fashionable summer communities were Newport and Bar Harbor, and it was in the latter that Colonel James Foster built his twenty-two–room Victorian mansion. Listed on the National Register of Historic Places, Foster's "cottage" is now the site of the Manor House Inn. Complete with wraparound veranda, the inn is just across the street from the prestigious Bar Harbor Club, where inn guests may use the facilities for a daily subscription fee.

The Manor House Inn has been decorated with antiques appropriate to Colonel Foster's time. Wallpaper patterns characteristic of the last half of the nineteenth century were chosen, and Oriental rugs, high-backed Victorian beds, marble sinks, and formal upholstered period chairs and sofas are the rule. Breakfasts include warm blue-

berry muffins, coffee, tea, and juices. Guests may request picnic lunches if they wish to explore the countryside all day. Frank is the publisher of *The Islander,* a quarterly magazine about Bar Harbor and the surrounding Mount Desert Island, and it is hard to imagine a question about the area that the Matters will not be able to answer.

*Accommodations:* 9 rooms plus 2 guest cottages, all with private bath. *Pets and Children:* Not permitted. *Driving Instructions:* West Street runs from Route 3 to Main Street, in Bar Harbor.

# THORNHEDGE INN

47 Mount Desert Street, Bar Harbor, ME 04609. 207-388-5398.
*Innkeepers:* Elinor and Alonzo Geel. Open March 1 to November
15.

Thornhedge, a summer "cottage" built in 1900 for a retired Boston publisher, has changed very little over the years. Its three parlors and dining room have their original wall coverings and leaded windows. The furnishing and decor of the rooms is primarily formal turn-of-the-century with old-fashioned floral-print upholstery and matching drapes. The guest rooms are summery with fresh floral wallpapers and organdy tie-backs at the windows. Three of these rooms have working fireplaces, and three others have Franklin stoves. The third-floor rooms are tucked into the sloping eaves, and all the rooms have antique furniture.

Guests are served morning coffee and homemade berry muffins in the sunny dining room. Most houseguests enjoy visiting in the sitting room by the fireside on cool evenings or out on the veranda's wicker chairs. The inn is within walking distance of Bar Harbor shops and restaurants and the shore, and a short drive from Acadia National Park.

*Accommodations:* 14 rooms with private bath. *Pets:* Not permitted.

## Bath, Maine

### GRANE'S FAIRHAVEN INN

North Bath Road, Bath, ME 04530. 207-443-4391. *Innkeepers:*
Jane Wyllie and Gretchen Williams. Open all year.

Grane's Fairhaven Inn stands on the bank of the Kennebec River
surrounded by 27 acres of meadows, lawns, and dark pine woods.
There are outstanding views of the river from its windows. The
colonial structure was built in 1790 by one Pembleton Edgecomb for
his bride and was the Edgecomb family homestead for the next 125
years. In the mid-1900s its back extension was added, and in 1979 the
innkeepers converted it to an inn.

The Fairhaven Inn was an instant success. Its spacious country
rooms are decorated with a blend of antiques and comfortable furnishings. The ceilings are low, befitting an inn of its age, and the
floors are the original pumpkin-pine boards. Colonial colors chosen
for the inn's walls and fires burning in its hearths create an atmosphere of easygoing country tranquility, a result of the extreme care
and hard work lavished on it by the two innkeepers.

It is difficult when here to imagine that the city of Bath with its
well-known Maine Maritime Museum and Performing Arts Center is

only 3 miles away. The inn offers hiking and cross-country skiing on the property.

The inn is renowned for its country breakfasts of juices; fruits in season; eggs served in many styles; and often scrapple, hash browns, or even Finnan haddie. Accompanying all this are homemade breads and muffins with a selection of jams and jellies put up by Gretchen and Jane. Breakfast is the only meal served and is enjoyed by fireside on chilly mornings. The tavern at Fairhaven offers a "bring your own bottle" wet bar, game table, stereo, color television, and piano for friendly get-togethers. There is a library with a large fieldstone fireplace that is just the thing on cold evenings. This is a "get away from it all" place where the guests and the innkeepers alike have a grand time.

*Accommodations:* 9 rooms sharing 4 baths. *Pets:* Permitted with advance notice. *Driving Instructions:* Take Route 1 north from Brunswick and exit at New Meadows. At the top of the exit turn right and go $7/_{10}$ mile to a stop sign. Turn right for one car length, then turn immediately left. Go $7/_{10}$ mile. The road then turns right, and a golf course is on the left. Continue for $9/_{10}$ mile, make a left turn into North Bath Road, and go ½ mile to the inn.

*Bethel, Maine*

## THE BETHEL INN AND COUNTRY CLUB

Broad Street, Bethel, Maine. *Mailing address:* P.O. Box 26, Bethel, ME 04217. 207-824-2175. *Innkeeper:* Richard D. Rasor. Open all year.

If you were traveling through New England and found any one of the buildings that constitute the Bethel Inn you would be more than pleased. This resort-inn has five outstanding buildings dating from the late nineteenth and early twentieth century. It is, in effect, a village of colonial-style guest buildings set on 85 rolling acres interlaced with shaded paths and gardens. The main inn, built in 1913, has a living room, a music room with a Steinway, a library, a dining room, and a lounge. Each of these rooms has its own fireplace, which is kept going on cool fall and winter days.

The main dining room seats 220, a number in keeping with the resort's size. An Oriental rug before the room's formal fireplace creates an atmosphere of quiet elegance enhanced by the painted beams, swag-draped banks of windows, white linen, and Syracuse china service. Typical menu offerings include Maine lobster, sole baked in wine, stuffed shrimp, haddock au gratin, duck à l'orange, and roast prime ribs.

The inn's sixty-five guest rooms are large and airy with carpeting and simple furnishings that include Windsor chairs, lace curtains, and nubbly white bedspreads. Each has a private bath and direct-dial telephones.

The Bethel Inn faces the village common, a National Historic District with the Moses Mason House and Museum directly opposite the inn. The rear of the inn overlooks the resort's acreage and the White Mountains in the distance. Major resort facilities in summer include swimming, golf on a nine-hole course, tennis, and sailing. In winter there is cross-country skiing on the inn's trails, which crisscross the golf course and surrounding woodland. Rentals and instruction are available at the inn's touring center, which also operates a competitive racecourse. Downhill skiers are drawn to the Sunday River Ski Area with its 5,100-foot chair lift and 19 trails up to 3 miles in length.

*Accommodations:* 65 rooms with bath. *Pets:* Not permitted. *Driving Instructions:* Take Route 26 (exit 11 on I-95) to Bethel. From New Hampshire, take Route 2 into the village.

## NORSEMAN INN

Bethel, ME 04217. 207-824-2002. *Innkeepers:* Jakki and Claus Wiese. Open December 26 through skiing season and June through August.

The Norseman Inn has been fashioned out of a Revolutionary War home by its multitalented innkeepers, Jakki and Claus Wiese. It is a welcoming, family-oriented place that is more than simply a skiing inn, even though there is a strong skiing tradition here. The Wieses are avid skiers, and all of their family are experts; Jakki started the first girls' skiing team in New Hampshire. The family's interest in the sport, as well as the inn's proximity to the Sunday River Ski Area (3 miles) and the New Hampshire White Mountain ski areas at Wildcat, Black Mountain, and Tuckerman Ravine (all within half an hour's drive), means that many skiers stay at the Norseman every winter.

There is a decided Scandinavian atmosphere at the Norseman: Claus was born in Oslo, Norway, and Jakki is of Swedish heritage. Claus is a dedicated gardener whose produce appears regularly on the dinner table. His talents extend to carving, and his gnarled bowls are displayed in the inn as is his excellent artwork.

Dining is a special event at the Norseman. Jakki gets to know her

guests and finds out their preferences and special needs. She respects the differences between adults' and children's palates and often serves children's meals designed especially to appeal to them. Meals, served family-style, center around a daily entrée. Depending on the time of year and the cross-section of guests in residence, the entrée might be a roast leg of lamb, a Scandinavian poached fish dinner, or even a complete Swedish smorgasbord. The traditional fish dinner — a recent addition to Jakki's repertoire that guests have greeted enthusiastically — is poached cod with boiled potatoes, drawn-butter sauce, hard-boiled eggs, and pickled cauliflower and other classic accompaniments.

The guest rooms upstairs are simple and comfortable. Each is wallpapered; some have antique furniture and others have sturdy old-fashioned beds. One front room has twin spool-beds. There is an old spinning wheel in the hall upstairs and, on the wall, a striking photographic portrait of Jakki's grandparents. The inn is very much at home with children and has a special recreation room just for younger guests. While here, don't miss nearby Grafton Notch State Park, with its spectacular gorges deeply cut in stone by the river currents.

*Accommodations:* 14 rooms, 1 with bath. *Pets:* Not permitted. *Driving Instructions:* From the south take Route 95 to Route 26, which passes the inn near the center of Bethel. From Montreal take either Route 2 or 26, which lead to the inn.

## ALTENHOFEN HOUSE

Peters Point, Blue Hill, ME 04614. 207-374-2116. *Innkeepers:* Peter and Brigitte Altenhofen. Open all year.

Altenhofen House is a large mansion built in 1810 on a spit of land surrounded by the tidewaters of the Atlantic Ocean and Blue Hill Bay. The handsome Georgian estate sits amid rolling pasturelands dotted with grazing horses. Verandas look out to the sea or out across the swimming pool to distant Maine hills. Miles of carriage paths offer unspoiled cross-country skiing and horse-drawn sleigh rides in winter and hiking or horseback riding in warmer months.

The mansion has been beautifully restored by the Altenhofens. The rooms are furnished with nineteenth-century antiques, and several are highlighted by working fireplaces, including two in guest rooms and two in the library. Peter and Brigitte are from Germany, speak many languages, and traveled all over the world before settling in this piece of Downeast heaven. In addition to the European hospitality found here, guests are offered a single-entrée, five-course dinner. Each evening is devoted to the cuisine of one or another European country. Thus, a Greek dinner might begin with salade Pallas Athene and continue with moussaka followed by crema Kolispera. The German meal could include blumenkohlcreme suppe, sauerbraten, and meringues mit eis und pflaumer.

*Accommodations:* 6 rooms with private bath. *Driving Instructions:* Blue Hill is reached via Route 172 from Ellsworth or Route 15 from Bucksport.

## BLUE HILL INN

Blue Hill, ME 04614. 207-374-2844. *Innkeepers:* Jean and Fred Wakelin. Open all year.

The Blue Hill was built in 1830 and has been serving guests as an inn since 1840. The old building is brick-ended, with white clapboard sides and many chimneys. Large shade trees surround the inn. Window boxes of petunias provide color in the summer months. The inn's central location is a short walk from the park and the harbor.

Inside, the Blue Hill Inn has the atmosphere of a comfortable family home, a feeling enhanced by Fred and Jean Wakelin, who go out of their way to make you feel welcome. The bright rooms are

cooled in the summer by ocean breezes and are warm and intimate in winter. Colonial wallpapers, white curtains, and many-paned windows add a country ambience.

The Wakelins serve a different menu each day, including a Continental or full country breakfast and a home-cooked dinner with their own special chowders and a fish or roast entrée. The public is invited by reservation only. Guests may bring their own liquor, since there is no liquor license at the inn. Blue Hill Country Club extends privileges of tennis, golf, and its beach to guests.

*Accommodations:* 9 rooms with private bath. *Pets:* Not permitted. *Driving Instructions:* Take the Maine Turnpike (I-95) to Augusta. Take Route 3 past Bucksport. Turn right onto Route 15.

## TARRY-A-WHILE RESORT

Ridge Road, Bridgton, ME 04009. 207-647-2522. *Innkeepers:* Hans and Barbara Jenni. Open mid-June to Labor Day.

Intrigued by its old-fashioned name, we were pleased to discover this unusual spot where two historic inn buildings, five cottages, a Swiss chef, and an azure lake are important features.

The resort's oldest building, now called Gasthaus, dates from more than a century ago and was moved to its current spot by sled from a nearby town. The most old-fashioned of the buildings, it has shared hall baths and hot-and-cold-water sinks in each of its eleven rooms, whose furnishings include antique beds. Schloss is a Victorian home built in 1902. Its large rooms also capture the feeling of an earlier era with five-drawer pine chests, natural wood trim, and pine-panel fireplaces. There are five cottages on the 30-acre property, each with a private bath. The grounds of the resort slope gently through the pines to the edge of Highland Lake, which offers canoeing, swimming at two sandy beaches, and rowboats and pedal boats as well as lake fishing, sailing, wind-surfing, and waterskiing. There is a large recreation hall on the grounds where guests frequently gather after dinner to play table tennis and shuffleboard or watch television. Across the street from the inn is the Bridgton Highlands Golf Course.

Tarry-A-While has the definite feel of a Swiss resort. Hans is from Davos, and each summer the Jennis fly in a Swiss chef who prepares specialties of his native land, such as veal and mushrooms in light cream sauce, veal sausage with onions, pork cutlet with ham, tomato, and cheese, rabbit in red wine sauce, or boneless pan-fried trout. One of our Swiss favorites, *raclette* (melted cheese with potatoes and gherkins), is prepared at the table and is a real treat. Swiss wines are featured on the wine list.

*Accommodations:* 39 rooms, 18 with private bath. *Pets:* Not permitted. *Driving Instructions:* Take Route 302 to Bridgton. Pick up Ridge Road at the base of Highland Lake and follow the lake road for 2 miles, just past the Highlands Golf Course.

## BREEZEMERE FARM INN

Route 176, Brooksville, Maine. Mailing address: P.O. Box 290, South Brooksville, ME 04617. 207-326-8628. *Innkeepers:* Joan and Jim Lippke. Open Memorial Day weekend through Columbus Day weekend.

Breezemere has operated as a seacoast farm since the middle of the nineteenth century. In New England style the house is attached to the barn by a series of rooms designed in an earlier time to afford access to the farm livestock in severe weather. In 1917 the farm began to take in guests; by the 1930s the demand for accommodations was so great that eight cottages were built, scattered around the inn. The Lippkes completely redecorated the inn in 1978 and have furnished it with antique early-American furniture. The wallpapers are copies taken from early-American homes.

The first floor consists of a pine-paneled living room, a reading room with a wood-burning Franklin stove, a small dining room, and a dining porch overlooking Orcutt Harbor and the meadow where cows graze. Attractive handmade tables, bent-wood chairs, and hanging plants make this an inviting and comfortable room. A front porch has old wicker furniture. The upper two floors have a total of seven bedrooms and four baths. Rooms have four-poster beds, antique bureaus, and mirrors. White organdy curtains frame their many windows.

In 1948 a recreation lodge was built on the property facing the sea. It has a full-length veranda, a library room, and a recreation room with a large fieldstone fireplace where guests gather to play games, sing, dance, and listen to music.

Breezemere is a friendly, casual place. Guests often spend the day hiking, bicycling, and boating. There are marked trails throughout the inn's 60 acres, and boats are available. The inn has a large blueberry field where guests may pick berries for the next day's breakfast. The Lippkes are happy to point out good spots for clamming, picking mussels, seal-watching, and fishing. Bird-watchers frequently sight bald eagles, blue herons, and loons.

Toward the day's end guests gather at the antique bar for drinks (bring your own liquor), then enjoy five-course dinners centered around organically grown vegetables and home-baked breads. Typical dinners start with choice of appetizer, soup, and salad followed by a choice of two of the inn's specialties, such as coquilles St. Jacques, lemony stuffed cod, bouillabaisse, or sesame-seed glazed chicken. Steak is always an available option.

After dinner you can go outside and peer into the trees with a flashlight. If you are lucky, you will be able to see a porcupine eating an apple in the branches. On Saturday evenings a clambake with lobster and chicken is followed by entertainment in the lodge.

*Accommodations:* 7 inn rooms sharing 4½ baths; 6 cottages with private bath. *Pets:* Permitted in cottages only. *Driving Instructions:* From Bucksport, take Route 175 to Route 176.

## Camden, Maine

### AUBERGINE

6 Belmont Avenue, Camden, ME 04843. 207-236-8053. *Innkeepers:* David and Kerlin Grant. Open May to late fall.

When Aubergine first opened, David and Kerlin Grant put much of their energy into creating the first restaurant in Camden offering "French cuisine the new way." What has emerged since then is all of that and more. Aubergine — very much what its advertising has stressed: a small, romantic inn — is a large silver-gray Victorian home built in 1890 with additions in 1910. A small hand-lettered sign hanging from the horse chestnut tree is the only sign that the house on this quiet back street is actually an inn.

When the Grants purchased Aubergine, they removed some of the modernizing features added in recent decades. In the process they discovered that all of the original lighting fixtures and many of its original furnishings had been stored in the basement. All were restored and re-installed in the house. Aubergine has ninety-nine windows — a fact we are sure the innkeepers knew all too well! Each is leaded in the original (1890) part. The inn's rooms are light, with papers and colors chosen so that the eye travels happily from space to space. An abundance of wicker along with freshly painted white trim give a summery feeling to the navy-blue and white living room–bar. Every evening in the fall there is a fire in both the bar and dining room fireplaces. The latter room is decorated in yellow and gray complemented by white linen, silver, and bouquets of fresh flowers from the inn's garden. The sunny bedrooms are decorated in different color schemes. Each is named for its dominant color, with a single wall of old-fashioned flowered wallpaper surrounded by three painted walls. Furnishings are combinations of family antiques and simply styled contemporary pieces, and there are favorite family prints and paintings on the walls. Outside are several flower and herb gardens, including one planted in pinks and whites for the special enjoyment of those taking an after-dinner stroll.

David is a professional chef trained in France. His menu applies *nouvelle cuisine* techniques to a number of regional foods as well as to more widely available meats and vegetables. There are only a handful of appetizers, such as fish pâté and duck terrine, followed by the choice of main dishes like pasta with sweetbreads and lobster, trout fillets with shrimp, or brochette of lamb braised in Madeira — these offerings change frequently. Reservations for dining are essential. The innkeepers will also prepare picnics for inn guests and will arrange sailing charters.

*Accommodations:* 7 rooms, 3 with private bath. *Pets:* Not permitted. *Driving Instructions:* From the south take Route 1 into Camden, stopping at the blinking light and stop sign. A yellow schoolhouse will be on the right. Turn right and go 1 ½ blocks to Aubergine on the left-hand side. Watch for the sign.

## CAMDEN HARBOUR INN

83 Bayview Street, Camden, ME 04843. 207-236-4200. *Innkeepers:* Jim and Loureen Gilbert. Open all year.

The Camden Harbour Inn has eighteen rooms in a sturdy-looking Victorian (1892) building with an enclosed wraparound porch. Eight of these rooms share baths, while the other ten have private baths — all with the original claw-footed tubs. Comfort here is old-fashioned, without such modern distractions as television or room telephones. The inn's kitchen specializes in steaks, chops, prime-rib roasts, and fresh seafood picked up daily from local suppliers. It features lobster dinners in season. In the summer a full country breakfast is included in the room rate.

*Accommodations:* 18 rooms, 11 with bath. *Driving Instructions:* Take Route 1 to the center of Camden. From the only four-way intersection in town, turn down Bayview Street and follow the harbor three blocks to the inn.

## WHITEHALL INN

52 High Street, Camden, ME 04843. 207-236-3391. *Innkeepers:* Jean and Ed Dewing. Open late May to mid-October.

The Whitehall Inn occupies a commanding position in the center of Camden. Edna St. Vincent Millay was sixteen years old when she first recited her poetry at the inn, which maintains a special room filled with Millay memorabilia. Additions have grown out from a sea captain's house that was built in 1834 and forms the nucleus of the inn's buildings. In keeping with the inn's history, antiques have been used throughout in a pleasing way and add to the feeling that one is a guest in a large but comfortable country home. Coastal Maine is an inviting place for peace and quiet surrounded by the panorama of coastal sealife. The Whitehall is a fine place to enjoy just that.

Meals at the inn feature typical New England food with homemade breads, muffins, pastries, and cakes (frequently with Maine's own famous blueberries), New England chowders, and fresh seafood at the head of a long list of specialties. The innkeepers pride themselves on using local ingredients purchased from the many farmers and fishermen in the Camden area, whenever possible.

*Accommodations:* 41 rooms, 38 with bath. *Pets:* Not permitted. *Driving Instructions:* Take Route 1 North to Warren, Maine. Then take Route 90 to the center of Camden. From northern Maine, take Route 1 South to Camden.

**THE MANOR**

Battle Avenue, Castine, ME 04421. 207-326-4861. *Innkeepers:* Paul and Sara Brouillard. Open all year.

Paul and Sara Brouillard are quick to point out that The Manor is *not* a cute little country inn with fat, lazy cats lounging on braided rugs. The Manor *is* an impressive twenty-eight–room mansion designed by McKim, Mead and built in 1895 by Commodore Fuller of the New York Yacht Club. The Manor sits on a small hill overlooking the little town and distant harbors on the coast. Its turn-of-the-century furnishings and decor are properly formal and elegant. Guests have use of the library, the Victorian billiard room, the formal living and dining rooms, and more. Some of the guest rooms have fireplaces and all have sitting areas, as do the attractive grounds, with their French garden. The street in front of the inn deadends just 200 yards away at the lighthouse.

The Manor's owner-chef, Paul Brouillard, has a fine classical-French culinary background combined with an appreciation of nouvelle cuisine. It is not uncommon for him to receive standing ovations after a meal, which might include, for starters, Belon oysters with periwinkle and caviar sauce or mushrooms stuffed with salmon mousse and bay scallops. It might then proceed to smoked local free-roaming chicken with wild rice and green tomato chutney, or duck breast with chanterelles, Armagnac, and shallots served with a black-currant red-wine reduction. The Brouillards also maintain a private marina for guests, with an oyster bar and lobster pound featuring a variety of fresh and smoked seafood far wider than most offered on any U.S. coast — periwinkles, sea urchin roe, ceviche, and edible seaweeds.

*Accommodations:* 15 rooms with private bath, plus 2 Victorian cottages. *Driving Instructions:* A mile north of Bucksport, take Route 175 to Route 166, which leads to Castine.

## Center Lovell, Maine

## CENTER LOVELL INN

Route 5, Center Lovell, ME 04016. 207-925-1575. *Innkeepers:* Bil
and Susie Mosca. Open late May through Columbus Day and
Christmastime through February.

Part of the appeal of inn-hopping in New England is its "over the river
and through the wood" aspect. Just imagine Grandmother's
house — a dog curled by the fireplace, old-fashioned cabbage-rose
wallpaper, and country-auction furnishings in the rooms — having a
fine Italian chef. Center Lovell Inn has all this and more. This Maine
house is a peaceful, family-oriented country inn at whose heart is a
parlor warmed by a vintage woodbox (1860) stove.

Bil and Susie Mosca were browsing through *Yankee* Magazine in
1974 when an ad for an abandoned farmhouse caught their eye. They
left their small Connecticut apartment, drove all night, took one look
at the White Mountains and meadows stretched out in front of the
gingerbready front porch, and bought the place then and there. For
ten years the two have scraped, papered, painted, and gently coaxed
the old house into the appealing inn it is today. The original structure
was built in 1805; the third floor with its cupola topping was added in
1860; and the old pegged and hand-hewn barn out back dates from
the early nineteenth century.

The primary interest at Center Lovell is Bil's cooking. The Mosca family traces its lineage to Senegalia, a seaside village on the Adriatic. Many of the recipes used at Center Lovell have been passed down through at least five generations of good Italian cooks, with the inn's guests the lucky beneficiaries of this family history. House specialties are the veal dishes and Bil's sauces, although it would be hard to pick a favorite. An order-ahead-of-time treat is lobster fra diavalo, clams and shrimp served with the lobster in a zesty sauce. Guests may order from the extensive menu or choose the preset menu, with a chef's selection of the day, appetizer, and dessert. A typical meal might be fresh fruit in champagne, baked fillet of Maine hake stuffed with shrimp and flavored with special sherry, pasta, a salad, breads, and flan (caramel custard).

Intimate dining rooms with romantic fireplaces serve dinner to guests and public alike. The four guest rooms are furnished in a country manner with views through the surrounding shade trees of some of New England's best scenery. A favorite spot in warmer months is the wraparound porch, which first sold the Moscas on the inn with its view of White Mountain National Park and Lake Kezar. The lake offers excellent fishing, canoeing, and sailing.

*Accommodations:* 4 rooms, 2 with private bath. *Pets:* Not permitted. *Driving Instructions:* From Conway, New Hampshire, take Route 302 to Fryeburg, Maine. From Fryeburg take Route 5 north to Center Lovell.

# THE CHEBEAGUE INN BY-THE-SEA

Chebeague Island, ME 04017. 207-846-9634. *Innkeepers:* Harold and Marye Fuller. Open Memorial Day to Columbus Day.

If you like your country inns luxuriously appointed with myriad activities, then you'd better pass the Chebeague Inn by. But if you'd like to try an island vacation (or even an overnight stay) in a country inn with fine Down East cooking, friendly innkeepers, and fellow guests bent only on unwinding and enjoying the island's natural beauty, then this inn is certainly the place.

The Chebeague has been in the capable hands of the Fullers since early 1979. They have mended its worst scars, painted and papered the guest rooms, and cleaned up the signs of neglect from earlier days. However, they are quick to point out a bulge in the wall here or a broken molding there. Their guests certainly don't mind, and it may even add to the character of the place. The Chebeague has all the lines of a classic Norman Rockwell summer hotel. It is on a knoll out in the open with a view overlooking a couple of fairways of the island's nine-hole golf course and the bay. To get to the inn you first take an hour-and-a-quarter ferry ride from Portland or a twelve-minute water-taxi ride from Cousin's Island.

Inside, the inn has a comfortable family-oriented living room with a large stone fireplace, comfortable wing chairs, and plenty of reading material. The dining room provides three meals daily, with an evening menu about equally divided between fresh seafood and meat dishes. A cocktail lounge opens onto a porch with views of the bay and sunsets.

The inn's twelve guest rooms on the second floor include one room with a small bath and a two-room suite with bath. The rest of the rooms share hall bathrooms and are small but colorful and clean. Each has a lavatory, in the old-fashioned "room with sink" way.

*Accommodations:* 12 rooms, plus a 2-room suite with private bath. *Pets:* Not permitted. *Driving Instructions:* Call the inn to check the latest ferry and water-taxi schedules and to arrange taxi pickup at the dock.

*Clark Island, Maine*

## THE CRAIGNAIR INN

Clark Island Road, Clark Island, ME 04859. 207-594-7644. *Innkeepers:* Terry and Norman Smith. Open March through December.

The Craignair is an unpretentious seaside country inn. Originally built to house quarry workers, the Craignair is at the end of the road that leads to Clark Island. Ospreys nest on the disused quarry poles. Set above the ocean and Clark Island as well as the local cove, the dining room and many of the guest rooms have an unobstructed view of the sea. A deck at the seaside allows guests to relax in the sun while watching the lobster boats at work. Indoors is a sitting room with a fireplace, as well as a library. This plain white, unshuttered building is not an inn with fancy surroundings or myriad resort-style activities. It is likely to appeal to writers, naturalists, artists, beachcombers, and anyone seeking relaxation and an opportunity to reaffirm one's inherent connection with the sea. Dinner is a single-entrée affair, with the meal of the day chosen from a menu that changes daily.

*Accommodations:* 16 rooms with shared baths. *Driving Instructions:* From Thomaston, drive south on Route 131 for 5½ miles to Route 73 East, then 1 mile to Clark Island Road and 1½ miles to the inn.

*Damariscotta, Maine*

## DOWNEASTER INN

Bristol Road, Damariscotta, ME 04543. 207-563-5332.*Innkeepers:* Bob and Mary Colquhoun. Open all year.

The Downeaster Inn has one of the handsomest facades of any inn in Maine. Four fluted Corinthian columns rise two stories at the inn's front. When we first spotted the Downeaster from Route 129, we thought that the building might be of modest proportions; but when we rounded the corner of the house to approach the side door, we found that the inn continued back and back.

The original building was constructed in 1810 by Maine's first justice of the peace. He built it to be his home. Sited to provide a view of the Damariscotta inlet, it is now an inn furnished with Victorian antiques, and it is ably managed by Bob and Mary Colquhoun, who have brought a delightful Scottish atmosphere to the place.

In the front hall, a handsome grandfather clock greets visitors. The inn's 10-foot ceilings have a number of attractive chandeliers, and on one wall of the living room is a mural depicting a winding country road. Several rococo love seats and as many period chairs grace this room as well. A door on one side of the inn has particularly elegant blue etched glass. Upstairs and to the rear of the inn, the light and airy guest rooms are comfortably furnished with twin or double beds.

*Accommodations:* 14 rooms, 8 with private bath. *Pets:* Not permitted. *Driving Instructions:* From Damariscotta, take Route 129 east.

## Deer Isle, Maine

## PILGRIM'S INN

Main Street, Deer Isle, ME 04627. 207-348-6615. *Innkeepers:* Dud and Jean Hendrick. Open mid-May to mid-October.

Built in 1793 and now listed in the National Register of Historic Places, Pilgrim's Inn has a true colonial flavor, with its pumpkin-pine wide-board floors, soft colonial tones on the walls, paneled parlor, and numerous working fireplaces. Guests can sit in the common room and gaze out over the millpond nearby. Before-dinner cocktails and hors d'oeuvres are also served in this room. The inn has eleven guest rooms, all with wood stoves and with electric bedwarmers, and all but three with semiprivate bath.

This is a true restoration in which the original lines and purpose of each room have been altered as little as possible. The result is an almost Shaker-like classic simplicity.

Dining is in the Pilgrim's barn with its freshly whitewashed walls and open beams. Wide screened doors open to views of the fields and pond behind the inn. Antique chairs are drawn to tables set with white cloths and freshly picked flowers.

*Accommodations:* 11 rooms with private or shared bath. *Driving Instructions:* Take Route 1 north of Bucksport and turn south on Route 15 to Deer Isle Village. There, turn right on Main Street (the Sunset Road) and drive one block to the inn on the left side.

## *Dennysville, Maine*

Washington County is the last frontier on the East Coast of the United States. A county of tremendous size, its area is larger than the combined states of Rhode Island and Delaware. It has over 1.5 million acres and includes 133,000 acres of lakes left by the action of three successive glaciers. This is a sportsman's paradise as well as a welcome retreat from the crowds of more southerly Maine. The county produces the largest crop of blueberries annually in the world. There are two cities of note: Calais, pronounced locally as Cal-luss, and Machias, pronounced Mach-EYE-us. Calais is on the Canadian border and has a special bond of friendship with its Canadian sister city, St. Stephen. Calais imports all its drinking water from across the border, and fires in either city are answered by both.

## LINCOLN HOUSE COUNTRY INN

Dennysville, ME 04628. 207-726-3953. *Innkeepers:* Mary Carol and Jerry Haggerty. Open all year.

At the end of the Revolutionary War, Benjamin Lincoln accepted the sword of surrender from General Cornwallis. He then was permitted by General Washington to purchase 10,000 acres of land in northern Maine (at the time, part of Massachusetts). In 1787, General Lincoln built a fine country house of fifteen rooms on the property.

The inn has had a rich history in its 190 years. Indians often received lodging in the summer kitchen of the inn, and John James Audubon was a guest there on his way to Newfoundland. Audubon was so pleased with his two-week stay at the Lincolns' home that he named a sparrow the Lincoln Sparrow.

In late 1976, the Haggertys purchased the old home and began carefully to return it to its former splendor. The process has been a slow one, because Jerry Haggerty, a restorer of antiques, is a perfectionist and insists on restoring rather than renovating.

The result is a simple elegance re-created in a fine country home. There are two dining rooms, a main kitchen and a summer one, and six comfortable guest rooms. From several guest rooms you can see the river below, with its family of nesting eagles. North Atlantic salmon fishing, choice birding, nature trails, tennis, boating, canoeing, and river swimming are all within walking distance.

Mary Carol Haggerty takes great care in supervising the cooking at the inn. Dinners — served to the guests and, with advance reservations, to the public — feature the choice of two or three fine entrées, such as stuffed scallops or roast sirloin, poached salmon or leg of lamb. She always offers a choice of soup, such as brandied pumpkin or she-crab, and a choice of dessert that might include apple crisp, cheesecake, or homemade pie. The entrée includes homemade bread, salad, and vegetables. Folks have been known to drive all the way from Ellsworth, just for Mary Carol's dinner. The dining room is closed in winter.

After dinner, take the time to walk down along the edge of the river to watch for the animals and birds that come at dusk to drink. Return to the inn and curl up by the hearth in the old summer kitchen, and you will know why we consider Lincoln House one of the finest country inns in America.

Recently Jerry went into the woods and found a 4,000-pound elm log, hewed it in half, moved it to their newly refurbished woodshed, and refinished it into the grandest bartop in Washington County. The result is "The Woodshed, A Village Pub," which a wood stove helps keep open all winter long.

*Accommodations:* 6 rooms with shared bath. *Driving Instructions:* The inn is within sight of the intersection of routes 1 and 86.

## THE WATERFORD INNE

Box 49, East Waterford, ME 04233. 207-583-4037. *Innkeepers:* Barbara and Rosalie Vanderzanden. Open all year except March to mid-April.

The Waterford Inne is an old country inn in a postcard setting. At the end of a country lane, part of a former stagecoach route, is an 1825 farmhouse complete with shutters, chimneys jutting out here and there, an old red barn, a farm pond, 10 acres of open fields, and dark Maine woods. Barbara and her mother, Rosalie, bought the house in 1978 and lovingly restored and renovated it. The inn still retains its wide-board pumpkin-pine floors and steep narrow stairways.

Five guest rooms are in the main house; four more were recently added to the ell that formerly served as the woodshed. Each room has special touches giving it its own personality and is decorated with antiques and stenciled wallpapers coordinated with the beds' comforters. Such amenities as fresh flowers in summer or electric blankets in winter add to guests' enjoyment and comfort. The downstairs public rooms are decorated with portraits, pewter, copper, and brass pieces, and old wall sconces.

Breakfasts and dinners are always a treat here. Rosalie and Barbara describe their dinners as "country chic," referring to the extra niceties and the gourmet touch the meals receive, and the attention paid to table settings and locations. A couple might be served in an intimate nook, or a table of four might enjoy dining in the library.

*Accommodations:* 9 rooms, 5 with bath. *Driving Instructions:* From Norway, Maine, take Route 118 West for 8 miles to Route 37. Turn left onto Route 37 and go ½ mile to Springer's General Store; then take an immediate right turn up the hill and continue another ½ mile to the inn.

Georgetown Island is one of many islands and peninsulas that extend from the mainland in southern Maine. Just south of the Bath area, the island is noted for *Reid State Park*, the land for which was donated by the builder of the Grey Havens Inn. The area has several fine beaches, picturesque sights of the local lobstering industry, and an Audubon sanctuary.

## GREY HAVENS INN

Reid Park Road, Georgetown, Maine. Mailing address: Box 82, Five Islands, ME 04546. 207-371-2616. *Innkeepers:* The Hardcastle family. Open June 15 through Columbus Day.

At Grey Havens you can lie in your turret guest room and have a 180-degree panoramic view of the ocean. The inn is on an island that feels remote but is accessible by road and a short drive from Bath. Four of the rooms are in the inn's twin turrets, and six of the rooms have been renovated to have private baths. The inn was built by Walter Reid in 1904. It has 260 feet of deep-water anchorage and its own dock. It is within rowing distance of an island nature preserve, and an Audubon sanctuary is just down the road.

The lounge at Grey Havens has a big rock fireplace and a 12-foot picture window, the glass for which was hauled to the inn by ice barge from Rockland. At the time it was the largest piece of glass in the state. The inn is noted for its huge wraparound porch, where guests can relax and even have breakfast if they wish. The dining room features a selection of Down East cooking including corn and cheddar chowder, pumpkin chowder, fresh broiled and baked seafood, each accompanied by home-baked breads and followed by fresh desserts.

*Accommodations:* 14 rooms, 6 with bath. *Pets:* Generally permitted with advance notice. *Children:* Well-behaved children over twelve permitted. *Driving Instructions:* Just east of Bath take Route 127 South. Drive 10½ miles to Reid Park Road, on the right. The inn is ¼ mile down this road, on the left.

## Islesboro, Maine

## ISLESBORO INN

Islesboro, ME 04848. 207-734-2221. *Innkeeper:* Lauren Abat.
Open mid-June to mid-October.

The Islesboro Inn describes itself as a converted "summer cottage."
This is more than somewhat of an understatement, as this "cottage"
has twelve working fireplaces. Seven of these are in guest rooms, and
the rest are in various public rooms with views of Penobscot Bay.
Even the ride to the island is a treat aboard the *Governor Muskie,* a
24-car, 125-passenger ferry that leaves from the small harbor at
Lincolnville. As you watch the mainland slip away, you are easily con-
vinced that a time of relaxation is ahead.

The inn has a terrace often used for luncheon as well as cocktails
before dinner. There are six guest-moorings for yachts reserved next
door at the nine-hole golf course that is open to the public. The
Islesboro Inn also has a clay-surfaced tennis court. Life here is purposely slow, and the separation of the island from the mainland
means that guests are more likely to be contented with sailing,
bicycling, bird-watching, berry picking, or beachcombing. Day trips
to the mainland and nearby Lincolnville, Camden, and Rockland
provide ample opportunity to go shopping or to explore.

*Accommodations:* 14 guest rooms, 4 with bath. *Pets:* Not
permitted. *Driving Instructions:* Take Route 1 north of Rockland
through Camden and to Lincolnville Beach. Board the ferry there;
upon disembarking on Islesboro Island, take the first three right-hand
turns in a row. There is a sign on the tree at the third right.

*Kennebunkport, Maine*

## THE CAPTAIN JEFFERDS INN

Pearl Street, Kennebunkport, Maine. Mailing address: P.O. Box 691, Kennebunkport, ME 04046. 207-967-2311. *Innkeepers:* Warren C. Fitzsimmons and Don Kelly. Open all year.

The Captain Jefferds Inn was built in 1804 as the home of sea captain William Jefferds, Jr. Captain Jefferds had eleven children, many of whom followed their father's vocation. With all that seafaring, it would stand to reason that the house would have at least one ghost, although none has been discovered so far. The innkeepers are still listening and hoping. Today the Captain Jefferds is a handsome inn with landscaped grounds, white picket fences, and even an antique shop in an adjoining barn. The inn's lawn adjoins the River Green, a small common. If you climb to the widow's walk on the river side of the inn, you can take in a splendid view of the river below.

Thanks to the innkeepers' expertise as professional collectors of antiques, the inn is filled with unusual pieces—folk art, quilts, and wicker. There is an air of country elegance throughout. Both a living room and a sun parlor have been comfortably furnished. Four of the guest rooms have working fireplaces, and all are papered with Laura Ashley prints; several have brass beds. Full country breakfasts and afternoon teas are served to guests.

*Accommodations:* 10 rooms, 6 with private bath. *Children:* Under twelve not permitted. *Driving Instructions:* In Kennebunkport, take Ocean Avenue. Turn left off Ocean at the "King's Wharf" sign to Pearl Street.

## THE CAPTAIN LORD MANSION

Pleasant Street, Kennebunkport, Maine. Mailing address: Box 527, Kennebunkport, ME 04046. 207-967-3141. *Innkeepers:* Beverly Davis and Richard Litchfield. Open all year.

The Captain Lord Mansion is one of the finest examples of nineteenth-century craftsmanship in current use as an inn in the State of Maine. Built in 1812 by a skilled crew of ships' carpenters idled by the British blockade of the harbor, the mansion is an impressive structure with multiple chimneys and a cupola large enough to hold a group of people. Captain Lord clearly could spend as much as he wished to perfect the details of his three-story house. The front door with its elaborate leaded-glass fanlight opens onto an unusual three-story unsupported elliptical staircase of strength and grace. The wide-board pine floors have been restored to their original warmth, and the walls of the mansion's common rooms and guest rooms have been covered with carefully selected reproduction wallpaper.

The entire mansion is carefully appointed with antiques. There are fifteen working fireplaces, eleven of which are in the guest rooms. The beds in the rooms are antiques and include a 10-foot-tall black walnut four-poster and a cannonball king-size bed. Plants, steamer trunks, handmade quilts, and old rugs add personal touches to the rooms.

The romantic qualities and serene atmosphere of this old home are certain to appeal to those who seek a quiet retreat. From the octagonal cupola, guests can enjoy the sunset, gaze at the stars, or watch the boats on the Kennebunk River. Flower gardens and chestnut and elm trees grace the inn's grounds. Guests are served country-style breakfasts around the big kitchen table. No other meals are served.

*Accommodations:* 16 rooms with bath. *Pets:* Not permitted. *Children:* Under twelve not permitted. *Driving Instructions:* Take exit 3 off Route I-95 and follow signs to Kennebunkport's Dock Square. At the square, turn right onto Ocean Avenue and go $\frac{3}{10}$ mile to Green Street. Take Green Street (left) uphill to Pleasant Street. The inn is on the corner.


## THE CHETWYND HOUSE

Chestnut Street, Kennebunkport, ME 04046. 207-967-2235. *Innkeeper:* Susan Knowles Chetwynd. Open all year (guests should be sure to check first).

The Chetwynd is a small guest house built in the mid-nineteenth century by Captain Seavey of Kennebunkport and recently redecorated. The blue-shuttered white clapboard house is in the heart of Kennebunkport just a few blocks from restaurants, art galleries, and craft shops on Dock Square. Across the street from the Chetwynd is the busy Kennebunk River, which empties into the ocean one-half mile away. There are two sandy beaches, and the rocks of the breakwater are a good place to sit and watch the parade of fishing boats and sailboats heading for the sea.

Inside, the Chetwynd House has been carefully decorated by innkeeper Susan Knowles Chetwynd. Wide pumpkin-pine boards glow with the patina of age. Victorian antiques mingle with comfortable upholstered furniture. The parlor is filled with books and is a relaxing spot to meet other guests after a day of exploring the village. A handsome staircase leads to the four guest rooms upstairs. Each bears Susan's touch: The Fern Room, for example, has wallpaper imprinted with small green ferns. The quilt on the bed picks up the fern color, and white wicker furniture provides contrast.

Every morning Susan serves breakfast in her breakfast room with its collection of blue and white china. It is a special meal with melon, strawberries, orange juice, and occasionally — if a guest fancies it —

oyster stew! Tea and coffee are available at Chetwynd House at any time.

*Accommodations:* 4 rooms, 1 with bath. *Pets:* Not permitted. *Children:* Permitted but not encouraged. *Driving Instructions:* From Dock Square take Ocean Avenue two blocks along the river toward the ocean and Chestnut Street.

## ENGLISH MEADOWS INN

Route 35 (RFD 1), Kennebunkport, ME 04046. 207-967-5766. *Innkeepers:* The Kellys. Open April through October.

English Meadows is a turreted Victorian farmhouse with an attached carriage house. Standing on a knoll, the inn is sandy beige with light green shutters, tangerine doors, and white trim. Within its main building are a huge living room, dining room, office, large country kitchen, and several second-floor guest rooms. English Meadows, run by antique-lovers who operate a small shop on the grounds, is filled with antique pieces and early art and prints.

The inn's dining room has a large eight-panel bow window with

views of nearby meadows (named after the Englishes, who first owned the property). In the morning, deer still come to feed within sight of the inn. The dining room houses Gene's collection of art-glass baskets and Staffordshire china. The upstairs guest rooms, decorated with old English hunting prints and other art, have brass and iron beds, hooked and rag rugs, and numerous antique pieces. Quite different in feeling are the rooms in the paneled carriage house. Remodeled in the 1940s, many of its rooms open off a large gathering room that has a fireplace and a collection of early wicker. Upstairs are two large rooms, with strawberry-patterned wall-to-wall carpeting, that share a connecting bath. All rooms in the inn and Carriage House contain sinks. Breakfast is a treat with something special everyday.

In addition to its antiques, decorative art, and architecture, an appealing feature of the English Meadows Inn is its location. Although within walking distance from the center of the village, it is far enough away from the bustle of this popular tourist spot to retain its country feeling. Available nearby are deep-sea fishing, white sandy beaches (a mile distant), walking tours of the village's historic streets bordered by sea captains' houses, and visits to the Brick Store Museum and to the Seashore Trolley Museum, the largest of its sort in the world.

*Accommodations:* 14 rooms. *Pets:* Not permitted. *Driving Instructions:* Take the Maine Turnpike (I-95) into Kennebunk and turn left onto Route 35. The inn is 5 miles down the road on the right.

## Kingfield, Maine

### THE WINTER'S INN

P.O. Box 44, Kingfield, ME 04947. 207-265-5421. *Innkeeper:* Michael Thom. Open all year; full restaurant facilities December 10 to April 15 and July 1 through November 1.

In the late nineteenth century, A. C. Winter and his friends the Stanley Brothers (inventors of the Stanley Steamer) returned from a day of hunting and, being at a loss for something to do, designed a house to be built on a hill overlooking the lovely little village of Kingfield. The result was Winter's mansion, a fine example of Georgian Colonial Revival architecture. An entrance of etched glass and oak welcomes guests to the Grand Salon, where a fire burns in one of the inn's three matched fireplaces. From here a large staircase ascends to a Palladian window on the landing and continues up to the curved maple bannister on the second floor. The mansion is furnished with antiques and period oil paintings and, in the second-floor guest quarters, big brass beds. The guest rooms on this floor are larger than those on the third floor. Guests are greeted by Balthazar the cat.

Off the Grand Salon are the dining rooms of the inn's restaurant, Le Papillon, serving *haute cuisine française* by candle- and firelight to guests and the public. These rooms overlook meadows.

The inn has tennis courts and a swimming pool for summer enjoyment. A seasonal ski shuttle is provided to nearby Sugarloaf.

*Accommodations:* 10 rooms, 7 with bath. *Pets:* Not permitted. *Driving Instructions:* Take Route 27 north from Farmington to Kingfield. Take a left on Depot Street to the intersection with School Street (at Tranten's General Store). Turn right up the hill to the inn.

## *Little Deer Isle, Maine*

### EGGEMOGGIN INN

Little Deer Isle, ME 04650. 207-348-2540. *Innkeeper:* Sophie Broadhead. Open May 30 through October 21.

If you have always thought of an island vacation off the coast of Maine, but have worried about the remoteness of many of this state's islands, a trip to Little Deer Isle may be in order. Now connected by bridge to the mainland, this tiny island has an abundance of unspoiled shoreline and peace and quiet.

You approach the Eggemoggin by a wooded road that finally gives way, at the inn's parking area, to an open shelf of rock protruding out into the sea. On this rocky ledge, with views of the water on three sides, stands the inn. Built as a private estate in 1906, it has retained many of its original antique furnishings, and many rooms have hand-hooked rugs. Above the porch, in the center of the house, is a broad balcony with access from either of the two front bedrooms. There are bedrooms on the third floor as well, and most are quite large and sunny. Breakfast is the only meal served here.

*Accommodations:* 9 rooms, 1 with bath. *Pets:* Not permitted. *Driving Instructions:* Take Route 1 to Bucksport. Go 5 miles north of Bucksport and turn on Route 15 toward Blue Hill. Follow Route 15 over the Deer Isle bridge to an information booth, and follow signs.

## NEWCASTLE INN

River Road, Newcastle, ME 04553. 207-563-5685. *Innkeepers:* Sandra and George Thomas. Open all year.

Newcastle Inn is a comfortable Maine inn of indeterminate vintage. The rooms throughout the inn are filled with antiques, folk art, and Victoriana, thanks to the antiquing prowess of the owner. Many of these pieces are for sale; so if something takes your fancy, ask about it. There are several intimate sitting rooms; but the favorite gathering spot seems to be the living room, where a fire burns nightly in the large hearth. The guest rooms are appealing with their varied antiques and wallpapers. A gourmet breakfast, the only meal served, is offered to guests in a room with vistas of a tidal river and the twin towns of Newcastle and Damariscotta. Rocky beaches are nearby, as is a particularly fine lighthouse.

*Accommodations:* 20 rooms, 11 with bath. *Driving Instructions:* Take River Road off Route 1 into Newcastle, 6 miles north of Wiscasset.

## CAPTAIN LORENZ PERKINS HOUSE

Route 1, North Main Street, P.O. Box 1249, Ogunquit, ME 03907. 207-646-7825. *Innkeepers:* Ron and Jean Mullenaux. Open March through November, other times by reservation.

Captain Perkins's house, more than a hundred years old when he and his family moved there in the late nineteenth century, remained in the Perkins family until the 1970s.

The house sits on almost 2 acres in the coastal village of Ogunquit. Guests stay in rooms named for the members of Captain Perkins's family. Antiques and country collectibles are set in rooms papered with floral prints. Some of the beds feature handmade quilts that match the colors of the walls and trim. The halls and stairs are covered with colorful wool rugs painstakingly braided many years ago by the Perkins women.

The popular spot with guests is the second-floor sitting room stocked with magazines and books about the area as well as with menus from local restuarants. Ron is the baker in the family, and his breads and coffee get rave reviews from guests, who eat family style around the dining room table.

In the adjoining carriage house, a 1920's converted garage, there are several antique-filled bedrooms and Jean's shop, "The Captain's Mistress," specializing in old glass, collectibles, and unique hand-crafted Maine gifts.

*Accommodations:* 12 rooms, 4 with private bath, plus 2 efficiencies. *Children:* Under three not permitted. *Driving Instructions:* Take exit 2 from Route 95. Follow Route 1 north to Ogunquit Village.

# OLD VILLAGE INN

30 Main Street, Ogunquit, ME 03907. 207-646-7088. *Innkeepers:* Alf B. Kristiansen and Frederick L. Thomas. Open all year.

When we first discovered the Old Village Inn one winter's evening several years ago, we were turned away at the door. The line of eagerly awaiting diners extended past the front porch, and there would be no more dinners available that evening. Such is the popularity of this inn in the center of a most popular southern Maine coastal village. The Old Village Inn was built as a hostelry in 1833 and has been improved and updated throughout the years, adding to the guests' comfort without detracting from its appeal. Upstairs are eight guest rooms, of which five are suites consisting of bedroom, sitting room, and bath.

One can dine at the Old Village in a diverse group of dining rooms. Views of the ocean can be enjoyed from the greenhouse dining room with its profusion of plants. The center dining room, known as the Keeping Room, has a beamed ceiling, richly stained panel walls, a fine collection of antique porcelain, and a framed copy of the 1947 *Saturday Evening Post* cover depicting the Old Village Inn. The Bird and Bottle room has damask walls and comfortable leather chairs. Recently the front porches that surround the inn's entrance were completely glassed in and now offer dinner guests a view of Main Street. The dining rooms serve brunch and dinner to both guests and the public. Entrées are about equally divided between seafood, poultry, and meat offerings including fish of the day, chicken Chablis, roast duckling, prime rib roast, and two cuts of steak. Lobster and scallops are featured when available.

The public parlors at the inn are spacious and decorated with period antiques. One has a fireplace and color television for the use of overnight guests; the other has a piano for those who enjoy playing. The Pub Room's bar was made from local oak. Glasses hang from racks behind the bar, and this room as well as the dining rooms feature art done by local artists.

*Accommodations:* 8 rooms, 5 with bath. *Pets:* By prior arrangement only. *Driving Instructions:* Take Route 1 into the center of Ogunquit Village.

## PERKINS COVE INN

Woodbury Lane, Ogunquit, Maine. Mailing address: Box 2336, Ogunquit, ME 03907. 207-646-2232. *Innkeepers:* Robert L. and Ann-Marie Johnson. Open mid-May to mid-October.

Perkins Cove Inn is a typical rambling waterfront Maine inn. From the porch that stretches almost the whole length of the freshly painted white clapboard building you can look out over a scenic cove. Ogunquit is a former fishing village in which fishing huts have been transformed over the years into galleries and boutiques to serve the vacationing summer people drawn to the area because of its quaintness, proximity to southern New England, and one of the finest beaches in southern Maine.

Guests at Perkins Cove return year after year for the warmth and companionship of the innkeepers and the other guests rather than for luxurious surroundings. The inn is immaculate and well maintained, and the large rooms are furnished simply in either maple or older assorted pieces. All but two of the rooms have ocean views, and a number have sitting areas. Four rooms have private outside entrances and porches. The main wraparound porch is a popular gathering spot where guests watch the boat traffic in and out of the cove.

The separate Letter Box Cottage at the inn is available for weekly rental. No meals are served at the inn, although coffee is available on the porch or in the office area. There are a number of fine restaurants across the bridge, on the cove.

*Accommodations:* 14 rooms, 11 with bath. *Pets:* Accepted only with advance arrangement. *Driving Instructions:* Take Route 1 to Ogunquit. Head south on Shore Road; bear right at the entrance to Perkins Cove. The next left is Woodbury Lane.

## HOMEPORT INN

Route 1, East Main Street, Searsport, ME 04974. 207-548-2259.
*Innkeepers:* Dr. and Mrs. F. George Johnson and Sally Wilson.
Open all year.

The Homeport Inn is a fine example of a wealthy sea captain's home.
The atmosphere, high-ceilinged rooms, and fine period antique furnishings from around the world are similar today to when wooden
clipper ships ruled the waves. The mansion, built in 1863, stands on a
hill just east of Searsport, offering glimpses of Penobscot Bay
through the shrubbery and shade trees. Scalloped picket fences
enclose the lawns and the circular drive. The interior, befitting a home
port of a world-traveling sailor, is filled with unusual antiques. The
Johnsons have been carefully restoring the house to its former glory
with the help of a young cabinetmaker, Phillip Nedza, who is truly a
master restorer. He constructed and installed a shell-shaped alcove,
now housing an Oriental vase, that looks as if it has always been there.
The paneled library is another fine example of his work. In many of

the rooms and halls, chandeliers hang from elaborate plaster ceiling medallions and Oriental rugs cover the floors. The front sitting room has a black marble fireplace, Oriental vases, palms, and brass chandelier and fireplace accessories. The dining room has another black marble hearth and a rounded cupboard displaying family antique china. Dr. Johnson's green thumb is evident in the profusion of greenery here. The plants are rivaled only by the number of grandfather clocks. There are so many clocks at the Homeport that virtually no one is able to keep up with all the winding required. One of the most inviting rooms is the Keeping Room with informal rag rugs, country pine cupboards, an old couch, and an iron stove to warm the room on winter days. The inn also has its own antique shop.

The four guest rooms upstairs share a modern hall bathroom. It is no small task picking a favorite room here. All of them have floor-to-ceiling windows; one has a working fireplace with an elaborately carved oak mantel; another room has a fine old desk. All feature unique antique bedsteads — two each in the front rooms — covered with puffs. Marble-top bureaus, fresh flowers in season, and green plants enhance each room. The Sun Porch is a pleasant spot to plan the day's adventures over a hot cup of coffee and some of the freshly baked muffins and breads. Or if you choose, you may breakfast in the formal dining room.

Homeport is just a short distance from the Penobscot Marine Museum. Also nearby is the town of Searsport, with its streets lined with antique shops. It is centrally located for visits to Bar Harbor, Acadia National Park, and picturesque Camden.

*Accommodations:* 8 rooms, 4 with private bath. *Pets:* Permitted in the kennels only. *Driving Instructions:* Follow Route 1 northeast from Searsport a short distance to the Homeport Inn on the right.

# THE BRANNON-BUNKER INN

Route 129, South Bristol, Maine. Mailing address: H.C.R. 64, Damariscotta, ME 04543. 207-563-5941. *Innkeepers:* Dave and Char Bunker. Open May through mid-October.

The Brannon-Bunker Inn, near the Damariscotta River, is on the edge of a meadow, complete with farm pond and resident white goose named White Cloud. Few guests can resist the temptation to go down to the pond and feed her bread and just watch her glide about. The inn consists of the Bunkers' 1820 Cape-style house connected to a big barn, once the site of a notorious dance hall in the Roaring Twenties. The barn now contains four guest rooms and a living room.

The Bunkers obviously adore collecting antiques, which they use throughout the inn. The guest rooms with their old-fashioned print wallpapers are decorated with marble-top bureaus; a sleigh bed is in one room, two old four-posters are in another. Rayo lamps, needlepoint chairs, and nautical prints in gilded frames in the sitting room all add charm. In addition to the rooms in the inn, there are several guest rooms and an apartment in the little barn just across the lawn. Guests are served a complimentary breakfast of fruits, juice, coffee, and homemade muffins and coffee cakes in the dining area. Setups are provided by Dave and Char in the living room at cocktail hour (guests bring their own liquor). Guests are welcome to use the kitchen and outdoor grill for cooking lobsters.

*Accommodations:* 6 guest rooms, 3 with bath, and 1 apartment suite. *Driving Instructions:* Take Route 1 through the town of Damariscotta to Route 129. Take Route 129 south about 5 miles.

## Southwest Harbor, Maine

### THE CLAREMONT

Southwest Harbor, ME 04679. 207-244-5036. *Innkeeper:* John Madiera, Jr. Open mid-June to mid-September.

When James Pease decided to put aside his career as captain of a sailing ship, he decided to remain by the sea and had a fine inn built on Mount Desert Island. The year was 1884, and the inn was the Claremont. Owned by only three owners in its century of existence, the Claremont remains today one of northern Maine's finest old inns. Located on Somes Sound, the only fjord on the Atlantic Coast, and listed in the National Register of Historic Places, the Claremont is a reminder of the late nineteenth century, when carriages would bring Bostonians from the steamer port at Southwest Harbor.

A new dining room was added in 1977, and now every table at the Claremont enjoys a view of Somes Sound. Among the kitchen's specialties are beef brioche, scallops en brochette, seafood crepes, tournedos, and boiled lobster. Public rooms at the Claremont include a large living room and a library, both furnished in a manner typical of 1900s resorts. The Claremont is a member of the National Croquet Association, and an annual croquet classic is held each summer on the lawn adjacent to the inn.

*Accommodations:* 22 rooms in the inn and 2 guest houses, most with private bath, plus 9 housekeeping cottages, some rustic and some modern. *Pets:* Not permitted. *Driving Instructions:* Take Route 3 to Mount Desert Island and Route 102 to Southwest Harbor. The inn is at the end of Clark Point Road. Moorings are available for people who come by boat.

*Tenants Harbor, Maine*

## THE EAST WIND

Tenants Harbor, ME 04860. 207-372-8800 or 372-8908. *Innkeepers:* Tim Watts and Ginnie Wheeler. Open all year.

In a corner of the peaceful fishing village of Tenants Harbor is the East Wind, built in 1890 and restored in 1975. The inn is on 350 feet of rocky coastline. Fishing draggers unload their daily catch on the dock just down the path, and guests enjoy watching the lobster boats.

The East Wind, built as a sail loft and ship chandler's operation, is a white-frame structure with a wraparound porch. The first floor contains a lobby-lounge and a spacious seaside dining room overlooking the coast and docks. Three meals are served daily to guests and the public. Dinners feature seafood including lobster, haddock, clams, scallops, and a shore dinner, with steaks and chicken for those who don't care for seafood. The sixteen guest rooms are furnished simply with antiques and wall-to-wall carpeting. Some have brass beds; two have private baths.

There are no traffic jams, no noise, no pollution, and no fast-food restaurants here. There is, instead, fresh sea air, four-season recreation, and congenial hosts.

*Accommodations:* 16 rooms, 2 with bath. *Children:* Under 12 not permitted. *Driving Instructions:* From U.S. 1, just east of Thomaston, take Route 131 south 9½ miles to Tenants Harbor; turn left at the post office and continue to the inn.

## The Forks, Maine

## CRAB APPLE ACRES

Route 201, The Forks, Maine. Mailing address: P.O., West Forks, ME 04985. 207-663-2218. *Innkeepers:* Chuck and Sharyn Peabody. Open all year.

Crab Apple Acres is an 1835 farmhouse overlooking the Kennebec River in a rather remote section of Somerset County. The inn offers seven guest rooms that share two baths. The farmhouse has many old-fashioned features, including the original fanlight over the door, a Dutch-oven fireplace, wide pumpkin-pine floorboards, original Christian-cross doors, and old hinges and thumb latches. The inn is popular with people seeking a peaceful retreat and with hunters, snowmobilers, and those on canoe trips. White-water rafting on the Kennebec River is the favorite sport here, and the Peabodys can steer guests to the best guides for an exciting run through the gorge.

Meals at Crab Apple are served family-style, mostly to guests, but the public is welcome by reservation. The Peabodys' home-style cooking often includes Chuck's French toast at breakfast and Sharyn's turkey, roast beef, and lasagna suppers.

*Accommodations:* 7 rooms, none with private bath. *Pets:* Not permitted. *Driving Instructions:* Take Route I-95 to the Skowhegan, Quebec, exit; then take Route 201 to the farmhouse in The Forks. Quebec City is about 140 miles north of here.

## OLDE ROWLEY INN

Route 35, North Waterford, ME 04267. 207-583-4143. *Innkeepers:* Michael and Debra Lennon and Peter and Pamela Leja. Open all year except one month in early spring.

The great appeal of the Olde Rowley Inn, built in 1790, is that it preserves, with few modifications, a roadside stagecoach inn much as it appeared in the early nineteenth century. A carriage house was added in 1825 to connect the barn to the inn. As soon as you enter the inn's keeping room, you are back in early America. Here are low exposed-beam ceilings, pumpkin-pine and hemlock floors, and a large open-hearth fireplace complete with bake oven and two warming cupboards above. A rocking chair, an old basket of firewood, and a high-backed bench are drawn up to the hearth.

Three dining rooms have about a dozen candlelit tables. One room has king's-pine wainscoting and rose and blue pineapple stenciled wallpaper. Another dining room, in the carriage house, has plaster walls and exposed-beam ceilings festooned with drying herbs and old baskets. The third dining room has a hand-stenciled mustard and red Christmas-candle pattern and is lit by copper wall lanterns. The Olde Rowley's menu includes starters like oysters bourguignon and deep-fried cheeses and entrées such as chicken Veronique, steak Diane, and shrimp amandine. Meals may be concluded with heaping portions of sherry trifle, walnut bourbon pie, fruit parfait, or brownie hot-fudge sundae.

Guest rooms, reached by climbing the narrow tight-winder staircase, all have period wallpapers and furniture. Some have four-posters and all have nice touches such as nightcaps, dried-flower arrangements, tin-lantern lighting, and reproductions of old children's book illustrations.

*Accommodations:* 5 rooms, 1 with private bath. *Pets:* Not permitted. *Driving Instructions:* Take Route 35 from Route 302 to North Waterford.

As you drive north through Wiscasset on Route 1 and you have left the central village, look to the right at the harbor and you will see one of the most eerie yet romantic sights of coastal Maine. There, at the shoreline, lie the remains of two grand old schooners. Gray, shadowy reminders of the glory of sailing days gone by, these majestic giants are now lying on their sides, slowly being reclaimed by the sea they once sailed.

Wiscasset is a much visited and photographed coastal village. There are many antique and craft shops here and several small, pleasant restaurants. Among the museums in the area are the *Lincoln County Fire Museum* with its collection of antique fire trucks, hearses, and carriages; the *Lincoln County Museum* and old *Lincoln County Jail;* the *Maine Art Gallery* with its collection of work by Maine artists, including art for sale; and, finally, the *Music Museum*, displaying a wide variety of old musical instruments.

## THE SQUIRE TARBOX INN

Westport Island, ME. Mailing address: RFD 2, Box 2160, Wiscasset, ME 04578. 207-882-7693. *Innkeepers:* Elsie White and Anne McInvale. Open Memorial Day through Columbus Day weekend.

The Squire Tarbox is a rare find in Maine — an old country inn in an incomparable setting. It is on a 10-mile-long island near Wiscasset, linked to the mainland by a bridge. Westport Island has one main road, Route 144, running the length of it. At the end of this road is an old house, part of it dating from 1793. The larger main building was added later. Today the property consists of a main house and a barn, with connecting smaller sections between. Through these the farmer and his family could walk from their house to the barn to do chores without having to go out into the bitter-cold winter weather.

The house was carefully restored some years ago, and it retains the original floors, carvings, moldings, fireplaces, wainscoting, and old glass windows so characteristic of a home of the early nineteenth century. This is not a large inn; the eight guest rooms are almost always occupied. Each summer, guests are drawn here by the crisp, clean Maine air. This is a place for people who love old things and do not require the organized activity of larger inns or resorts.

Everywhere at the Squire Tarbox, you will find pleasing details. It might be the Victorian marble-top tables in Miss Maude's Parlor, the antique chairs and tables in the dining rooms, any of the inn's eight fireplaces, or the wide pumpkin-pine floors. All quilts at the Squire Tarbox were made by innkeeper Elsie White's mother. The beams in the dining room were rescued from old sailing ships and repegged in place at the inn. The ground floor of the attached barn has been made into a sitting room with one wall that is all screen doors that open on warm days. Upstairs are two guest rooms.

Dinner is served every evening except Sunday, with a choice of two entrées, one of them a fish or shellfish. Lobster is not served at the inn; the innkeepers believe that lobster is best enjoyed "in the rough" at one of the places nearby specializing in boiled lobster. Entrées here include flounder, sole, haddock, or any of the native shellfish served in a variety of sauces. Each meal includes three vegetables, freshly picked that day from the inn's own garden, and unusual soups, such as apple soup or Portuguese tomato soup. Dessert might be a chocolate mint pie with whipped cream and almonds or an apple cake with whipped cream. Guests are served a complimentary breakfast.

*Accommodations:* 8 rooms, 2 with bath. *Pets:* Not permitted. *Driving Instructions:* Take Route 1 north from Bath. Turn right on Route 144, and follow it for 8 miles.

*Winter Harbor, Maine*

## HARBOR HILL

Grindstone Neck, Winter Harbor, ME 04693. 207-963-8872. *Innkeeper:* Mrs. Hugh Mackay. Open mid-June through Labor Day.

When we rounded the bend of the peaceful road leading out to Grindstone Neck one summer morning, we came upon a stone and shingle-turreted country-estate house that, to our delight, turned out to be Harbor Hill, the inn we had been seeking. This is an inn of great dignity, and the parlor is a perfect introduction to it. The grindstone in the name Grindstone Neck refers to ones cut from the many neighboring quarries and carried by schooner to mills up and down the coast a century ago. One such grindstone is set into the fireplace in the parlor.

Even the lobby entrance has its own fireplace, and to the left a broad staircase rises to the upstairs guest rooms. Light from a skylight filters down the staircase to the lobby below. Of the inn's seven bedrooms, one large one has a granite fireplace, wood paneling, and a bathroom with a marble-topped sink. The tower guest room has curved walls, a granite fireplace, and views of the grounds.

Downstairs, the inn's dining room has yet another large fireplace. An adjoining closed-in porch has soft blue-green wainscoting and five windows surrounded by more woodwork.

*Accommodations:* 7 rooms, including 3 single rooms. *Pets:* Not permitted. *Driving Instructions:* Take Route 1 to West Gouldsboro, then Route 186 south toward Winter Harbor. Watch for a road branching off to the right and follow the signs to Harbor Hill.

# Massachusetts

## THE BRAMBLE INN

Route 6A, Brewster, Massachusetts. *Mailing address:* P.O. Box 159, Brewster, MA 02631. 617-896-7644. *Innkeepers:* Karen L. Etsell and Elaine C. Brennan. Open May through October.

The Bramble Inn, in the heart of the Historic District of Cape Cod, is an old Cape house built in 1861, during the Civil War. Around 1890 the first telephone in Brewster was installed in the inn by W. W. Knowles and connected to what is now the Brewster General Store. The Bramble Inn has offered food and lodging to travelers for more than a quarter of a century.

The owners of the inn are artists, and they have created an extensive art gallery, using the walls of the public dining rooms. Works exhibited are by the owners and many local artists working in a variety of media. The Bramble Inn is within walking distance of the ocean, adjacent to tennis courts, and close to other Brewster attractions. Guests are housed in three little rooms in the main house and four renovated rooms in an equally appealing Greek Revivial house just two doors away. The dining room's menu offers several wines and beers, a choice of clam chowder or a soup of the day, and six entrées. For dessert there are Cape Cod Bramble and chocolate mint crepes. The public is welcome at both lunch and dinner.

*Accommodations:* 8 rooms, 3 with private bath. *Pets and children:* Not permitted. *Driving Instructions:* Take Route 6 toward Brewster to exit 10 (Route 124) and drive 4 miles to the dead end at Route 6A. Turn right; the inn is five buildings down on the left.

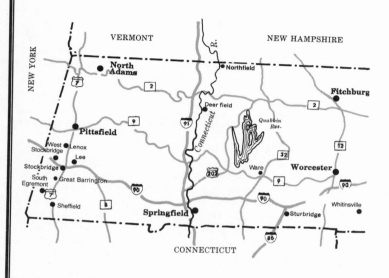

VERMONT

NEW HAMPSHIRE

NEW YORK

North Adams

Northfield

Fitchburg

Deerfield

Quabbin Res.

Pittsfield

West Stockbridge  Lenox

Lee

Stockbridge

South Egremont   Great Barrington

Sheffield

Ware

Worcester

Whitinsville

Springfield

Sturbridge

CONNECTICUT

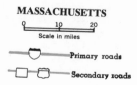

**MASSACHUSETTS**

0        10        20
Scale in miles

Primary roads

Secondary roads

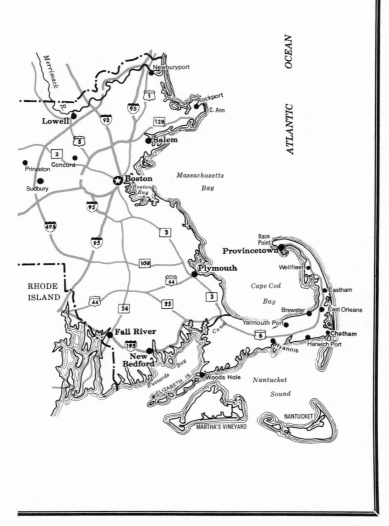

# INN OF THE GOLDEN OX

1360 Main Street, Brewster, Cape Cod, MA 02631. 617-896-3111.
*Innkeepers:* Charles and Ruth Evans. Open all year.

Overlooking Cape Cod Bay is the Inn of the Golden Ox. Originally the home of the First Universalist Church of Brewster, the building was constructed in 1828. The rooms all have the charm and quiet of an Old World inn, as does the restaurant. All rooms in the Golden Ox are furnished with antiques. The restaurant menu is made up exclusively of gourmet German dishes. A typical meal might begin with either shrimp and dill or marinated lentils as an appetizer followed by *Kassler Rippchen* (smoked loin pork chops), sauerbraten with potato dumpling, and red cabbage in red wine sauce, or a choice of one of six schnitzels (veal cutlet from milk-fed veal). Our favorite is Zigeuner schnitzel (made with piquant paprika, mushrooms, and sour cream). Old family recipes are used for the desserts — *Sacher Torte mit Schlag, Apfelküchen mit Schlag,* and creamy cheese cake. At the Golden Ox you'll enjoy good food and restful accommodations.

*Accommodations:* 4 rooms sharing 3 baths. *Pets:* Not permitted.
*Driving Instructions:* Take the Mid-Cape Highway (Route 6) to exit 9, go north to Route 6A, turn right on 6A.

## THE OLD MANSE INN

1861 Main Street, Brewster, MA 02631. 617-896-3149. *Innkeepers:* Sugar and Doug Manchester. Open all year.

The mansard roof on the Old Manse belies its age. The inn was built in the early nineteenth century by a Brewster sea captain. Later the roof was raised and a third floor was added, as well as a new mansard roof. As a result, rooms on the third floor actually have higher ceilings than the floor below. Slave quarters in the back of the house held coolie slaves brought back to Brewster by Captain Knowles during the China-trade era. During the Civil War the house was a link on the underground railroad, and during the 1940s church services were held in the sunroom. It was, in fact, the wife of the minister who first opened the Old Manse as an inn.

The Old Manse is decorated with antiques and hand-braided and Oriental rugs. Many of the rooms have fireplaces, although none of the guest room fireplaces is still in use. The beds have patchwork quilts. All guest rooms have curtained windows, old-fashioned print wallpapers, and fresh flowers or dried bouquets.

The Old Manse is a casual, homey place filled with games, books, and magazines for all to use. Continental breakfast (homemade bran, blueberry, or cranberry muffins) is served in the dining room. Dinners are by advance reservation only.

*Accommodations:* 10 rooms, 5 with bath. *Pets:* Not permitted. *Driving Instructions:* Take exit 9 off Route 6 to Dennis, then Route 134 north to Route 6A. Turn right on 6A and go 7½ miles to the inn.

# OLD SEA PINES INN

2553 Main Street, Brewster, MA 02631. 617-896-6114. *Innkeepers:* Stephen and Michele Rowan. Open mid-April through October.

How could anyone resist being fascinated by a place called the Sea Pines School of Charm and Personality for Young Women! Certainly the Rowans couldn't, and after much careful renovation they opened their inn in what was once a farmhouse dating from the mid-nineteenth century. From 1907 to the 1970s, the building served as Bickford Hall during the property's tenure as a finishing school.

The inn is on 3½ acres of wooded grounds within walking or biking distance of bayside beaches. Its large sunny rooms are furnished with pieces from the 1930s and 1940s, and its atmosphere is very much that of an old-fashioned summer home. Old wicker, mahogany, and maple furniture is set off nicely against period wallpapers and ruffled curtains. One wing has brass and iron beds, and two rooms have fireplaces. Guests may use a spacious living room with fireplace, and rockers are set out on the wraparound porch. Both are enjoyable spots for morning coffee and muffins.

*Accommodations:* 12 rooms, 8 with private bath. *Pets and Children:* Not permitted. *Driving Instructions:* Take exit 10 off Route 6. Turn right at the Brewster General Store. The inn is 1 mile down Main Street, on the left.

## Chatham, Massachusetts

### THE QUEEN ANNE INN

70 Queen Anne Road, Chatham, MA. Mailing address: Box 747, Chatham, MA 02633. 617-945-0394. *Innkeepers:* Nicole and Guenther Weinkopf. Open May 15 through December 30.

In the 1840s a young Methodist minister married Captain Howles's daughter. The best of all the wedding presents they received was a house built just for them. Their wedding present is still beautiful today, thanks to the painstaking restoration by innkeepers Nicole and Guenther Weinkopf. The Queen Anne Inn, as their home is now named, is a Victorian hotel with thirty guest rooms and suites and several public rooms, all decorated with many antiques of the period.

The Earl of Chatham, the inn's restaurant, is set up with bent-wood chairs, greenery, and formal table-settings lit by the many floor-to-ceiling windows and French doors that line the room's three walls. Fresh seafood from Cape Cod heads the list of offerings here, which include an array of Continental and New England dishes.

The guest rooms are individually decorated with period antiques and have a variety of bedsteads including a canopy or two. Though the rooms may appear to have come straight out of Miss Howles's time, they have been totally renovated and updated with modern bathrooms and telephones.

*Accommodations:* 35 rooms with private bath. *Driving Instructions:* On the Cape, take Route 6 east to exit 11, then Route 137 south. After 3 miles, turn left on Route 28 to Chatham. At the first traffic light turn right onto Queen Anne Road.

# TOWN HOUSE INN AND LODGE

11 Library Lane, Chatham, MA 02633. 617-945-2180. *Innkeepers:* Russell and Svea Peterson. Open all year.

In 1881, Captain Daniel Nickerson commissioned a fine new home to be built on the site of the old Captain Sears House on Library Street, on a knoll just above Main Street and the harbor. Public pressure was exerted against Nickerson's tearing down the original Sears dwelling, but his sturdy new Victorian proved to be a credit to its predecessor and the community. Captain Nickerson engaged in "anchor dragging" from his ship, *The Luther Eldredge*. Using a grappling hook, he salvaged scrap iron from wrecks in the harbor, and included in his spoils were a pair of cannons from a pirate ship downed in a gale in 1717.

The Town House Inn has been modernized over the years, and all of its guest rooms, including those in an adjacent lodge and cottage, have color television and refrigerators. Nevertheless, the building's high ceilings, original woodwork, and old-fashioned wallpapers capture the mood of the last century. Some of the carved molding and wood trim reveal harpoon and oar motifs. Some of the original walls recently exposed reveal hand-painted scrolling. Town House is a family-oriented inn with plenty of personal service and a warm, congenial atmosphere.

*Accommodations:* 21 rooms with private bath. *Pets:* Not permitted. *Driving Instructions:* From Route 6 take Route 137 south to Route 28; go east on Route 28 to the center of Chatham. Turn at the library onto Library Lane.

*Concord, Massachusetts*

## THE HAWTHORNE INN

462 Lexington Road, Concord, MA 01742. 617-369-5610. *Innkeepers:* Gregory Burch and Marilyn Mudry. Open March through December.

The Hawthorne Inn was built in 1870 across the street from a home once occupied by Nathaniel Hawthorne. The inn's grounds were once owned by Ralph Waldo Emerson and Bronson Alcott and then by Hawthorne himself. The famed New England writer planted a number of pines, two of which survive today on the old path to the mill brook beside the Hawthorne Inn.

The Hawthorne, originally a private home, was converted to a small inn in 1976 by Gregory Burch. The rooms have been carefully restored and decorated with antique furniture, handmade quilts, and some of the innkeeper's paintings and other art. Burch has inserted leaded-glass transoms over the doorways and has sanded and finished all the floors. The inn is presided over by a handsome striped cat, Ratface. The complimentary breakfasts include a selection of freshly baked breads and wildberry turnovers.

*Accommodations:* 6 rooms sharing hall baths. *Driving Instructions:* The inn is three-quarters of a mile east of the town center, on Lexington Road, across from the Nathaniel Hawthorne House.

## *East Orleans, Massachusetts*

### THE NAUSET HOUSE INN

P.O. Box 774, Beach Road, East Orleans, Cape Cod, MA 02643. 617-255-2195. *Innkeepers:* Diane and Al Johnson. Open April 1 through November 1.

The Nauset House, built around 1800, is an old Cape Cod farmhouse. This small country inn is furnished with antiques and family memorabilia, and on cooler evenings three fireplaces add their warmth to the atmosphere. There is an afternoon cocktail hour in the dining room, so that guests can get to know one another. The dining room is reminiscent of an old English pub, with a large fireplace and bar where the inn provides setups and ice for the guests (bring your own spirits). Breakfast is the only meal available—hearty country fare, served by the open hearth or out in the ornate Victorian greenhouse. The guest rooms are furnished with antiques, and one has its own fireplace. Nauset Beach can be seen from the inn across an unspoiled marsh. An early American antique shop is on the inn's property, as well as a new conservatory.

*Accommodations:* 14 rooms, 9 with bath. *Children:* Under twelve not permitted. *Driving Instructions:* Take Route 6 to exit 12; turn right and follow the signs to Nauset Beach. The inn is a quarter of a mile from the beach.

## SHIP'S KNEES INN

Beach Road, East Orleans, MA 02643. 617-255-1312. *Innkeepers:* Ken and Louise Pollard. Open all year.

The Ship's Knees is surrounded by landscaped lawns with a wide variety of trees and flowers. The original house belonged to an old sea captain and was built more than 150 years ago. It has recently been thoroughly restored and renovated, and a new section was added in 1970. Scenic Nauset Beach is only a short walk away. The doorways are lit by lanterns, and the house is decorated throughout with many antiques. Each guest room has its own special decor with large open beams, counterpanes on four-poster bedsteads, and colonial color schemes. Many of the rooms have ocean views. The favorite is the master suite, which has a working fireplace.

The Pollards have recently added Cove House to the inn complex. It overlooks Orleans Cove and has three guest rooms plus a one-bedroom apartment. Two housekeeping cottages on the grounds offer total seclusion. The Ship's Knees has its own swimming pool, and other sporting facilities are close by — golf, horseback riding, and ocean and bay swimming. To start the day, the Pollards provide a complimentary breakfast.

*Accommodations:* 23 rooms, 9 with bath. *Pets:* Not permitted. *Driving Instructions:* Take Route 6 exit 12 to the first stoplight, turn right, go two stoplights, turn right again. Follow the signs to Nauset Beach.

## Eastham, Massachusetts

### WHALEWALK INN

Box 169, Bridge Road, Eastham, MA 02642. 617-255-0617. *Innkeepers:* Ginny and Norm de la Chapelle. Open March through December.

Whalewalk, named for the widow's walk or "whalewalk" atop the inn, was built more than 150 years ago. Originally a whaling master's home, this example of Georgian architecture sits on more than 3 acres of fields and meadows on a quiet country road, a short distance from Orleans village, Cape Cod Bay, and the National Seashore.

Guest rooms at Whalewalk are available in the inn itself as well as in several cottages and a restored barn, which has several house-keeping and studio apartments. Both of the inn's two social rooms have fireplaces, and guests may bring their own spirits to the after-noon cocktail hours. A Continental buffet breakfast is included in the inn's room rates and is available at a small extra charge to guests staying in the apartments. Box lunches may be purchased, and candle-light dinners are served for a fixed price, with advance reservations.

*Accommodations:* 5 rooms, 2 with private bath, in the inn; 7 apartments in the barn and cottages. *Pets:* Not permitted. *Children:* Permitted in housekeeping units if over twelve. *Driving Instructions:* From the Orleans rotary, take the Rock Harbor exit and follow the arrow to Rock Harbor. Bridge Road is the first right past the Barn-stable County Courthouse.

## Great Barrington, Massachusetts

# WINDFLOWER INN

Route 23, South Egremont Road, Great Barrington, MA 01230. 413-528-2720. *Innkeepers:* Barbara and Gerald Liebert and Claudia and John Ryan. Open all year.

We were delighted to hear that our friends Gerry and Barbara Liebert of the Tulip Tree Inn had sold their popular Vermont inn and purchased what had been the Fairfield Inn in Great Barrington. This move to the south will give the Berkshires highly experienced innkeepers who will bring their special style of innkeeping to this attractive inn. Windflower is a Federal-style inn built in 1820, with one addition in the same style built about a century later. Some of the guest rooms have canopied beds. One guest room on the main floor has a stone fireplace that occupies most of one wall. With its own entrance from the terrace, this room is bound to be particularly popular for honeymooning couples. Just outside the door is the inn's swimming pool.

Windflower is the only inn we know of with a full-time mother-daughter chef team. Barbara and daughter Claudia will prepare two or three entrées every evening for their guests and a small number of diners from the public, who must make reservations in advance. A summer dining porch overlooks a small pond.

*Accommodations:* 12 rooms with bath. *Pets:* Not permitted. *Driving Instructions:* 3 miles west of Great Barrington on Route 23.

## *Harwich Port, Massachusetts*

### COUNTRY INN

86 Sisson Road, Harwich Port, MA 02646. 617-432-2769. *Innkeepers:* David and Kathleen Van Gelder. Open all year.

The Country Inn, with 6½ acres of farmland, is near the center of Cape Cod on the sound side. Built in 1773, the main building with its eleven fireplaces was once the summer home of the founders of the Jordan Marsh Company in Boston. Through the years several additions have been made to the inn, including three tennis courts and a swimming pool for guests. There are six guest rooms in the old inn, all with private bath. The fireplaces in the living room, tavern, and dining room are all put into use when the cool weather sets in. Those in the bedrooms are not used but do add to the decor. Dinner is served in the inn's dining room and features fresh seafood dishes, filet mignon, and chicken dishes. All meals include homemade breads and desserts. Favorites are the lemon and pumpkin breads and the Van Gelders' cinnamon ice cream on hot apple pie.

*Accommodations:* 6 rooms with bath. *Driving Instructions:* From exit 10 on Route 6 take Route 124 to Route 39 (Sisson Road). The inn is about a mile from Harwich center.

# DUNSCROFT INN

24 Pilgrim Road, Harwich Port, MA 02646. 617-432-0810.
*Innkeepers:* William and Maureen Houle. Open March through
December.

Dunscroft consists of two shingled buildings: the two-story gambrel-
roofed main inn and a smaller adjacent heated cottage. Built in 1930,
Dunscroft takes its name from the Scottish word for "home on the
dunes." Although the inn is not literally on the dunes, it is an easy
walk to the private beach 300 feet away. Dunscroft is also within
walking distance of the town, with its theaters and restaurants. The
inn retains its residential feeling with comfortable colonial and traditional furnishings and an abundance of plants and flowers. A television and piano are available to guests in the living room, where the
walls are lined with bookshelves and a fireplace is kept going.

The guest rooms are large and airy. In addition to the guest rooms,
the Houles have two efficiency apartments and a cottage for rent. A
Continental breakfast is served on the sun porch, which opens onto a
terrace for sunning. An annual Fourth of July picnic is held for
guests, and there are periodic fish-bakes during the season. There is a
spacious, shaded picnic area with tables, a shuffleboard court, and
horseshoes.

*Accommodations:* 6 rooms with private bath, 2 efficiencies, and 1
cottage. *Pets:* Not permitted. *Driving Instructions:* The inn is off
Route 28 in the center of Harwich Port.

## Hyannis, Massachusetts

### PARK SQUARE VILLAGE

156 Main Street, Hyannis, MA 02601. 617-775-5611. *Innkeeper:* Pete Johnson. Open all year.

Park Square Village comprises two old buildings and a number of newer structures constructed in a style in keeping with the early houses. Captain Sylvester Baxter House, built in 1855 by a retired sea captain, has the high-ceilinged rooms typical of the Italianate style. The other old home that is part of the Village is the 1710 House, one of the oldest in Hyannis. This typical Cape house is dormered and has both an apartment and two bedrooms that may be rented. A number of cottage efficiencies have been added recently, and a barn has been outfitted as a playroom. All are set back from the street among trees, flowers, granite curbs, and flagstone walks. Colonial lanterns enhance the atmosphere. Air conditioning and color television are available with most rentals. Although the inn does not offer food, Hyannis has so many fine restaurants that this omission causes no hardship.

*Accommodations:* 6 rooms, plus cottage efficiencies. *Pets:* Not permitted. *Driving Instructions:* Take Route 6 to Route 132.

# THE CANDLELIGHT INN

53 Walker Street, Lenox, MA 01240. 413-637-1555. *Innkeepers:* James and Lynne DeMayo. Open all year; the restaurant is closed Tuesdays except in July and August.

Any doubt that you have arrived at an inn that takes its cooking seriously will be dispelled just a few steps into the Candlelight Inn's large entryway. There you will be greeted not only by a chiming grandfather clock but also by a pastry cart laden with more than a half-dozen pies, cakes, and French pastries. Before dinner, many guests enjoy the conviviality of the well-stocked bar. For dining they may choose the front dining room with its original oil paintings, attractive wallpaper, and fire in the open hearth, or the side dining room with its deep red wallpapers, exposed beams, floral drapes, and china hutch. The extensive menu (two dozen entrées are offered) changes four times a year to allow chef-owner James DeMayo to choose meat, fish, and poultry that can be purchased fresh rather than frozen. House specialties include broiled Boston scrod, seafood casserole, chicken Kiev, sweetbreads in black butter, medallions of veal piccata, and filet mignon béarnaise. Service at the Candlelight is quite formal, with pewter place plates and sterling silver, as well as fresh table flowers. After dinner, guests frequently gather in the DeMayos' most recent addition, the downstairs piano lounge. In the summer the inn becomes alive with flowers. The dining room extends out into the patio where cutting beds border umbrella tables. Overflowing baskets of fuchsias line the porch. Upstairs, the seven large bedrooms have bright puffs on the beds and a blend of antique and traditional decor. Traditional wallpapers are the rule here.

*Accommodations:* 7 rooms with bath. *Pets:* Not permitted. *Driving Instructions:* Take the Massachusetts Turnpike to exit 2 (Lee) and Route 20 to Lenox. From New York, take the Taconic Parkway to Route 23, go east to Route 7, then north to Lenox.

## CORNELL HOUSE

197 Pittsfield Road, Lenox, MA 01240. 413-637-0562. *Innkeepers:* Allan Egly and Chuck Bowers. Open all year.

In 1980 Allan Egly and Chuck Bowers did what many people dream of doing: They quit their jobs and bought a country inn that needed repair. The new innkeepers closed the inn and labored seven days a week for five months before reopening it as Cornell House.

The inn was built in 1888, and the main building offers the most fully restored rooms with antique furnishings. The inn's carriage house, now called Hill House, also offers freshly redone rooms, but they are somewhat smaller and do not have antique furnishings. A number of the antique pieces in the Main House come from the innkeepers' families; for example, an appropriately stern portrait of Charity Cornell, Allan's great-great-grandmother, hangs in the front hall. A baby-grand piano graces the music room, and there is also a large living room and library. Continental breakfast including biscuits and muffins baked fresh every morning is served in the dining room. Behind the inn is the 400-acre Kennedy Park.

*Accommodations:* 16 rooms with shared baths. *Pets and children:* Not permitted. *Driving Instructions:* The inn is up a hill from the center of Lenox, just beyond the church and on the same side of the road.

## GARDEN GABLES INN

141 Main Street, Lenox, MA 01240. 413-637-0193. *Innkeeper:* Marie R. Veselik. Open all year.

This 190-year-old gabled inn was originally a private estate. Its last owner, Kate Carey, moved the house away from the road, added on, and built a 72-foot swimming pool—the first to be built in Lenox.

The inn is on the Main Street but it has a protected feeling because it is set back on 4 acres of lawns and shade trees. Mrs. Veselik is a great lover of animals, feeding the many birds that come most of the year; in autumn, deer occasionally come to eat fallen apples.

The older parts of the inn have some colonial antiques, while the newer extension is filled with turn-of-the-century antiques. Most of the guest rooms have private baths; others have running water and share hall bathrooms. The comfortable living room has a fireplace with a fire on cool evenings and a good supply of books and magazines as well as FM radio and television. Joining the inn is an interesting gift shop where guests are welcome to browse. Garden Gables accommodates only twenty guests at a time, enhancing its intimate feeling. The one meal served is breakfast, available only to guests, on an optional basis.

*Accommodations:* 10 rooms, 6 with private bath. *Pets:* Not permitted. *Driving Instructions:* The inn is on Main Street, facing Saint Ann's church.

## THE VILLAGE INN

16 Church Street, Lenox, MA 01240. 413-637-0020. *Innkeepers:* Clifford Rudisill and Ray Wilson. Open all year.

The Village Inn, built in 1771, is in the center of historic Lenox, a mile from Tanglewood. Its guest rooms are decorated in colonial fashion with country antique furnishings of the period. During the winter, open fireplaces add a glow of warmth to the lounges and dining room. A baby grand piano, available for guests and visiting musicians, graces the front reception room.

Below is the Village Tavern, where guests may enjoy cocktails, beer, and wine and light snacks in a room that has a hand-hewn bar and church pew seating. A breakfast and luncheon menu is offered daily in the inn's dining room. Dinner is served on Friday and Saturday evenings only. The dinner menu changes seasonally and includes beef, chicken, and fish offerings. Breakfast ranges from flapjacks and French toast to eggs Benedict; lunch includes homemade soups, quiche, and crepes. A traditional English afternoon tea is served daily.

*Accommodations:* 27 rooms and suites, 8 with private bath. *Pets:* Not permitted. *Driving Instructions:* Take Route 7 or Route 20 directly into Lenox.

## WALKER HOUSE

74 Walker Street, Lenox, MA 01240. 413-637-1271. *Innkeepers:* Richard and Peggy Houdek. Open all year.

One can look at some inns and tell at a glance that they are owned and run by people who truly love their work. The Walker House is one such place. Guests don't even need to go inside to get the message here. Immaculately cared-for grounds, a tidy, freshly painted home, and pots of flowers brimming with blooms set the mood.

The Federal-style inn was built in 1804, and a large back wing was added in 1906. One of Lenox's oldest buildings, it is set among beautiful pines and cedars. Each of the guest rooms is named for a different composer, in honor of nearby Tanglewood: Chopin, Mozart, Beethoven, and so on, are furnished with pieces appropriate to the period in which the room's namesake lived. There are canopied and brass beds and high oaken headboards. Four guests rooms have working fireplaces. The parlor and dining room, also cheered by fires in old fireplaces, are available to guests. The parlor has a grand piano, and there is usually a jigsaw puzzle in progress. Breakfasts are popular affairs where everyone eats together on the innkeeper's extensive collection of Depression glass, sharing plates of muffins, croissants, and fresh fruit. In the afternoons lemonade or hot tea and cookies are offered.

*Accommodations:* 6 rooms with private bath. *Pets and children:* Permitted with prior approval. *Driving Instructions:* From exit 2 (Lee) of the Massachusetts Turnpike, take Route 183, which becomes Walker Street, into Lenox.

## WHEATLEIGH

West Hawthorne, Box 824, Lenox, MA 01240. 413-637-0610. *Innkeepers:* Linfield and Susan Simon. Open all year.

In the heart of the Berkshires, in the midst of a lake, lawns, and gardens, stands Wheatleigh, a sprawling Italianate palazzo. Patios, porticoes, and terraces surround the chateau, which is on a 22-acre estate. The centerpiece is Wheatleigh, built in 1893 by industrialist H. H. Cook as a wedding present for his daughter, who married Count de Heredia. The multimillionaire New Yorker is reputed to have paid $1 million for the mansion. About 150 Italian artisans were said to have been imported to carve the mantels, ceilings, and walls. The public rooms include a Great Hall with original Tiffany windows and a winding staircase, as well as a library with a new bar. Some guest rooms have balconies with views of the lake and grounds; they are furnished with antique sofas and canopied beds, and have marble bathrooms. At this European-style small hotel the emphasis is on service and fine dining. Among the chef's specialties are homemade soups, prime beefsteak with mushrooms, poached salmon with dilled hollandaise sauce, veal cordon bleu, shrimp scampi, and pecan pie. Swimming and tennis are available on the grounds.

*Accommodations:* 18 rooms (13 in winter) with private bath. *Pets and children:* Not permitted. *Driving Instructions:* Starting in Stockbridge at the Red Lion Inn on Route 7, go up Prospect Hill Road, bearing left past the Stockbridge Bowl and Music Inn up the hill 5 miles.

## WHISTLER'S INN

5 Greenwood Street, Lenox, MA 01240. 413-637-0975. *Inn-keepers:* Joan and Richard Mears. Open May through October. Whistler's Inn is on 5 acres of woodland across from the "Church on the Hill," a Lenox landmark. The 1820 mansion was the home of James Whistler, nephew of the great American painter. Passing through the Dutch doors of the entrance, one finds an inn that preserves a bygone era. There are seven fireplaces throughout, an imposing dining room, a large library, and a music room. Two of the twelve guest rooms have working fireplaces, and all but two have private baths. Each has traditional furnishings in keeping with the building's heritage.

Fresh blueberry muffins, breads, and rolls, as well as juice and coffee or tea, constitute the Continental breakfasts included in the price of the room. The inn has a nice library of books that probably reflect the interests of innkeeper Richard C. Mears, author of the novel *Ebb of the River*. The Mearses recently added a restaurant and a gift shop, and they plan to add an art gallery.

*Accommodations:* 12 rooms, 10 with bath. *Pets:* Not permitted. *Driving Instructions:* Take Route 7 into Lenox.

## Martha's Vineyard, Massachusetts

### DAGGETT HOUSES

Edgartown, Martha's Vineyard, MA 02539. 617-627-4600. *Innkeeper:* Marguerite L. Miller. Open all year.

The Daggett Houses are a group of historic houses offering a variety of accommodations on the waterfront in Edgartown. The main house, called Daggett House I, was built in 1750, but it incorporates part of the old tavern run by John Daggett and dating back to the early 1660s. Its lawn slopes gently down to a sandy beach near a harbor. The old tavern room is now called the Old Chimney Room because of its fireplace of beehive construction. It has candlelight doors, a brass flintlock blunderbuss, Betty lamps, and a secret stairway. Breakfast is served in this room, often before an open fire. Accommodations are available in Daggett House I, as well as in the Garden Cottage near the water (a schoolhouse in the last century) and in Daggett House II—formerly Warren House, a whaling captain's home in the early nineteenth century.

*Accommodations:* 25 rooms (some in suites) in three houses, all with bath. *Pets:* Not permitted. *Driving Instructions:* From the center of Edgartown, turn left on North Water Street. Go three short blocks to the inn (across from the library).

## THE EDGARTOWN INN

North Water Street, Edgartown, Martha's Vineyard, MA 02539.
617-627-4794. *Innkeeper:* Catherine Scapecchi. Open April 1
through November 1.

The Edgartown Inn was originally an old whaling captain's home,
built in 1798 for Captain Thomas Worth. A few years later it began a
long career as a colonial inn. The Edgartown Inn has played host to
many notable guests through the years. Daniel Webster was at first
denied admittance because he was dark-skinned and thought to be an
Indian. He later returned as a guest, as did Nathaniel Hawthorne,
who came for a rest but stayed on to write *Twice-Told Tales*. John F.
Kennedy stayed here when he was a Massachusetts senator.

The inn is centrally located in the heart of Edgartown. Minutes
away by foot is the beach by the old lighthouse; for surf bathing, the
South Beach is a short ride by car or bike. Nearby are golf courses,
tennis, and fishing. The inn's front porch overlooks North Water
Street with its picket-fenced old captain's houses. The rooms at the
inn are much the same as they were in Captain Worth's time, but tiled
baths and many antiques have been added. Beyond the back patio
garden are the "Captain's Quarters," an old barn with guest rooms
without private baths for more modest rates. Country breakfasts
featuring homemade breads, muffins, and griddle cakes are served in
the paneled dining room and in the garden.

*Accommodations:* 12 rooms in the inn, 6 in Captain's Quarters.
*Pets:* Not permitted. *Driving Instructions:* Go to Woods Hole on
Cape Cod, then take the ferry to Martha's Vineyard.

## THE KELLEY HOUSE

Kelley Street, Edgartown, Martha's Vineyard, Massachusetts. Mailing address: Box 37, Edgartown, MA 02539. 617-627-4394. *Innkeeper:* John S. Moffet. Open all year.

The Kelley House was built as an inn in 1742 and is still going strong around 240 years later. The inn was completely renovated in 1973, and a new wing was added in keeping with the original house. The inn is quite large, with fifty-five guest rooms, and has an attractive colonial air about it both inside and out. The exterior of the Kelley House is painted white with black shutters and is set off by lawns, picket fences, and gardens. The public rooms, enhanced by fires in the inn's three fireplaces, are decorated with eighteenth- and nineteenth-century antiques. The guest rooms all have been redone and have color television, private baths, and telephones. The dining room serves breakfast, lunch, and dinner to guests and the public. Guests have tennis privileges at nearby courts and can swim in the inn's outdoor pool.

*Accommodations:* 55 rooms with private bath. *Pets:* Not permitted. *Driving Instructions:* From Woods Hole on Cape Cod take the ferry to Martha's Vineyard. The inn is in downtown Edgartown, two blocks north of Main Street on the corner of North Water.

## POINT WAY INN

Main Street, Edgartown, Massachusetts. Mailing address: Box 152, Edgartown, MA 02539. 617-627-8633. *Innkeepers:* Linda and Ben Smith. Open all year.

Ben and Linda Smith had just finished a 4,000-mile cruise when they moored their ketch in Edgartown harbor a few years ago. Soon after, they discovered and fell in love with the 150-year-old erstwhile sea captain's home that is now the Point Way Inn. After a winter of seemingly endless toil, the Smiths and their two daughters had created an inn with antique furnishings, ceiling fans, and working fireplaces in most rooms. (The Smiths provide plenty of wood for the fireplaces.) A recent addition to the inn is the living-room library with fireplace, bar, and refrigerator.

Continental breakfast is served in a sunny room complete with its own Franklin fireplace. Both American and English regulation croquet can be played on the spacious lawn, and afternoon lemonade is a warm-weather tradition. During the cooler months, afternoon tea takes the place of lemonade.

Like many East Coast resort areas, Martha's Vineyard is seeing much more year-around activity, and the Point Way Inn now remains open all year. Bicycles or mopeds are logical alternatives to automobiles here, just a short stroll from the center of town and the wharf area.

*Accommodations:* 12 rooms with private bath. *Driving Instructions:* The inn is at the corner of Main Street and Pease's Point Way.

## Nantucket Island, Massachusetts

### THE CARRIAGE HOUSE

4 Ray's Court, Nantucket Island, MA 02554. 617-228-0326. *Innkeepers:* Jeanne and Bill McHugh. Open all year.

The Carriage House was built in 1865 for the purpose that its name indicates. In the center of the Old Historic District, it is a nice example of early Victorian architecture now restored and transformed into an inn. Its location offers guests easy strolls to nearby restaurants, shops, and galleries. It has the added benefit of a quiet setting on a country-lane side street.

The interior of the guest house contains a cheerful and simple living room with a deacon's bench, Windsor rocker, floral-pattern area rug, and a profusion of potted plants and fresh and dried flowers. Outside there is an intimate patio bordered by hydrangeas and other flowering plants and shrubs, where a Continental breakfast is frequently served when the weather is good.

*Accommodations:* 7 rooms with private bath. *Pets:* Not permitted. *Children:* Under five not permitted. *Driving Instructions:* Take the Nantucket ferry from Woods Hole or Hyannis on Cape Cod.

## FOUR CHIMNEYS INN

38 Orange Street, Nantucket Island, MA 02554. 617-228-1912.
*Innkeepers:* Anthony and Betty Gaeta. Open May to December.
No fewer than 126 sea captains built their homes on this beautiful historic street in Nantucket. Four Chimneys, built in 1835 by Captain Frederick Gardner, is the largest of all.

The Gaetas have restored and decorated the lovely old house to the glory of the days when whaling ships and China clippers ruled the seas. The center hall takes guests into the past with its curving staircase, elegant wallpaper, and stately grandfather's clock. Betty Gaeta is an interior designer, and the decor of the inn is her tribute to the whaling days, Nantucket's golden era. The antique porcelains and Persian carpets are typical of the period. The double drawing room features twin fireplaces, a piano, and inviting sitting areas where guests can visit or enjoy a good book. The guest rooms are authentically furnished with antiques of the period, and most have fireplaces and four-poster or canopied beds and patchwork quilts. Many of the rooms have views of the harbor. A Continental breakfast and a cocktail hour are enjoyed by guests.

*Accommodations:* 11 rooms with private bath. *Pets and children:* Not permitted. *Driving Instructions:* Take the Nantucket ferry.

## FOUR SEASONS GUEST HOUSE

2 Chestnut Street, Nantucket, MA 02554. 617-228-1468. *Innkeeper:* Claire Cabral. Open all year.

In 1846 the town of Nantucket was virtually destroyed by a disastrous fire that swept the area. The Four Seasons Guest House was rebuilt shortly afterward and was later converted into a hostelry. It stands on a quiet side street in the heart of the Old Historic District. Old homes line the narrow, winding streets, and Nantucket's picturesque wharfs, museums, and restaurants are just a short way away. The guesthouse, furnished with a blend of antiques and family pieces, has eight guest rooms, four with their own baths. A ground-floor efficiency apartment with kitchenette opens onto a patio and the small backyard.

*Accommodations:* 8 rooms, 4 with bath. *Pets:* Not permitted. *Driving Instructions:* Take the Nantucket ferry from Woods Hole or Hyannis on Cape Cod.

## JARED COFFIN HOUSE

29 Broad Street, Nantucket, Massachusetts. Mailing address: Box J, Nantucket, MA 02554. 617-228-2400. *Innkeeper:* Philip Whitney Read. Open all year.

The Jared Coffin House recaptures the spirit and feeling of the days when Nantucket reigned as queen of the world's whaling ports. Built in 1845 by Jared Coffin, one of the island's most successful ship owners, the main house is a classic example of Greek Revival architecture. This house and later additions were restored in the 1960s to their

original style in both architecture and furnishings. The living room and library are furnished with Chippendale, Sheraton, and American Federal antiques.

Upstairs in the original house are nine restored guest rooms furnished with antiques and locally woven fabrics. The 1857 Eben Allen Wing has sixteen simply decorated rooms with antiques used wherever possible. The eighteenth-century Old House behind the wing has three bedrooms with canopied beds and examples of crewel embroidery. The Daniel Webster House across the patio was built in 1964. It has twelve spacious rooms furnished with a blend of contemporary and colonial reproductions. An 1821 Federal house directly across the street has six additional guest rooms with canopied beds.

Jared Coffin House offers a wide variety of dining for guests and the public. In summer, luncheons are served on the canopied patio. The main dining room, its tables set with American china and pistol-handled silverware, features New England and other American foods.

Holidays at the inn are special. There is an old-fashioned New England Thanksgiving. For the twelve days of Christmas the inn is decorated with holly, della robia garlands, and, on the front door, a cranberry wreath. At any time of the year the Jared Coffin House is a good place to spend a Nantucket vacation.

*Accommodations:* 46 rooms with private bath. *Driving Instructions:* Take the Nantucket ferry from Woods Hole or Hyannis on Cape Cod.

## MARTIN'S GUEST HOUSE

61 Centre Street, Nantucket, MA 02554. 617-228-0678. *Innkeepers:* Anne and Frank Berger. Open all year.

Nantucket Island, its homes, and its twisting streets have changed very little from the old whaling days. One seems to step off the ferry or plane and back into the nineteenth century. What better place to savor the atmosphere than in an old Nantucket home? Martin's Guest House fulfills the requirements. Built in 1805 with additions later in the nineteenth century, the house is on a brick-sidewalked street. There is a large lawn and pleasant side porch for relaxing. It is an easy walk to the beaches and downtown with its many shops and restaurants. Martin's has a large living room with a working fireplace. The Bergers offer a breakfast of juice, coffee, and home-baked breads and muffins. Reservations should be made six to eight weeks in advance.

*Accommodations:* 14 rooms. *Pets:* Not permitted. *Driving Instructions:* Take the Nantucket ferry from Hyannis or Woods Hole on Cape Cod.

## SHIPS INN

13 Fair Street, Nantucket, MA 02554. 617-228-0040. *Innkeepers:* Bar and John Krebs. Open Easter through Thanksgiving.

The Ships Inn was the home of whaling captain Obed Starbuck between voyages. He built the house in 1812 and many of the rooms are named for the ships he sailed. The furnishings in the inn today date back to Captain Starbuck's time, and the charm and atmosphere have changed little. The inn was also the birthplace of Lucretia Coffin Mott, one of the very first of the women abolitionists. Downstairs the living room and dining room are attractively decorated and, on chilly evenings, there are fires in the two fireplaces. The restaurant, The Captain's Table, features Nantucket's catch of the day, roast duckling, a daily chef's special, and marinated lamb chops. The Dory Bar is just that: a bar made from an old dory. Backgammon, cribbage, and darts are played here, entertaining islanders and tourists alike. The Ships Inn is a very friendly place.

*Accommodations:* 12 rooms, 10 with bath. *Pets:* Not permitted. *Driving Instructions:* Walk or bike; almost anyone at the ferry dock or the airport can direct you.

## WEST MOOR INN

Off Cliff Road, Nantucket Island, MA 02554. 617-228-0877. *Inn-keeper:* Nanci Walker. Open February through December.

The West Moor Inn, atop a windswept knoll, is one of the highest houses on the island and one of the few painted ones on an island filled with weathered-shingle homes. Built as a wedding present in 1917, the inn is a fine example of Federal architecture. The wide entry hall with front and rear entrances welcomes guests. There are spacious halls with seating areas, large living and dining rooms, both with working fireplaces, and a glass-enclosed dining area filled with plants. All guest rooms are furnished with antiques, have wide pine-board floors, and afford views of the moors and the sea. The inn has spacious grounds and a beach just 300 yards away. Nanci says pheasant, deer, grouse, and rabbits constantly parade across the lawn. Although the West Moor is secluded, Nantucket center is within a stroll. The inn's somewhat out-of-the-way location offers guests a respite from the more tourist-oriented parts of the island. A two-minute walk brings you to a neighboring riding stable and tennis club. Breakfast and lunch are served to guests at the inn; dinner will be served on special occasions. Liquor is not served but is permitted in the rooms.

*Accommodations:* 9 rooms, 6 with bath. *Pets:* Not permitted. *Children:* Under five not permitted. *Driving Instructions:* Take the Nantucket ferry from Woods Hole or Hyannis on Cape Cod.

## THE WOODBOX

29 Fair Street, Nantucket, MA 02554. 617-228-0587. *Innkeepers:*
The Tuteins. Open June through October.

Nantucket's oldest inn, The Woodbox was built in 1709 by a whaling
captain named Bunker. An adjoining house was built two years later,
and the houses were joined by cutting through the sides of both. This
lovely inn and its annex are both furnished with antiques of the
period. Besides double rooms there are suites here with one or two
bedrooms, a living room, and in some cases, working fireplaces.

The Woodbox's dining room has low-beamed ceilings, wide pine
boards everywhere, and tall ivory candles in polished brass candlesticks. Culinary specialties include fresh native seafood, duck à
l'orange, beef Wellington, fresh vegetables, homemade soups, and
hot popovers. Breakfasts include blueberry, peach, apple, or strawberry pancakes covered with hot maple syrup, as well as a variety of
omelets or eggs Benedict. Both breakfast and dinner are served to the
public.

*Accommodations:* 6 suites and 3 double rooms — each with private
bath. *Pets:* Not permitted. *Driving Instructions:* Take Main Street to
Orange Street; go two blocks on Orange to Plumb Lane and one
block on Plumb Lane to Fair Street.

*Newburyport, Massachusetts*

## MORRILL PLACE

209 High Street, Newburyport, MA 01950. 617-462-2808. *Innkeeper:* Rose Ann Hunter. Open all year.

A number of New England inns once belonged to sea captains. Morrill Place was owned by three. It is no surprise, therefore, to discover a widow's walk atop this three-story Federal home built by Captain William Hoyt in 1806. Thirty years later the house was purchased by Henry W. Kinsman, a junior law partner of Daniel Webster's, and in the years that followed, Webster was a frequent guest there. The name Morrill Place derives from the Morrill family, which made the house at the corner of High and Johnson Streets its home from 1897 until 1979, when it was purchased by Mrs. Hunter.

Ten of Morrill Place's twenty-two rooms are guest rooms where canopied brass-and-pineapple four-poster beds are the rule. The guest and public rooms are furnished with antiques, mostly of the Federal period, in keeping with the house. There are a formal front parlor and a library, as well as summer and winter porches that enjoy views of the inn's 2.5 acres of landscaped grounds. The inn's music room has both a square grand piano and a 1910 Steinway.

*Accommodations:* 10 rooms with shared bath, one with half bath.
*Driving Instructions:* Take I-95 to Route 113, and proceed eastward toward town. The inn is on the right, about 2 miles from the exit.

## NORTHFIELD COUNTRY HOUSE

School Street, Northfield, MA 01360. 413-498-2692. *Innkeepers:* Jan and Paul Gamache. Open all year except one week in January and the first two weeks in August.

Northfield Country House is an English manor house built in 1901 by a wealthy shipbuilding family from Boston. Drawn to the area by the evangelist Dwight Moody, the family fell in love with the Northfield countryside and built their eighteen-room home in a secluded spot. A long, tree-lined drive leads to the house with its rambling stone-columned porches.

Within, the inn has stucco walls trimmed with chestnut. Beams are exposed in several rooms, a wide, open staircase leads to a landing lighted by a large leaded-glass window. A fire usually burns in the living room fireplace, one of five in the house. Over the fireplace opening is: "Love Warms the Heart as Fire the Hearth."

Guest rooms are on the second floor, each decorated individually. Some have four-poster beds; others, brass or brass and iron bedsteads. Down comforters, antique furnishings, and herbal wreaths made by Jan contribute to the rooms' warmth. Jan, a former interior decorator, has used sheets effectively on several of the guest room walls. Three rooms have working fireplaces and velvet fireside chairs or love seats.

Every morning the Gamaches gather fresh eggs from their eighteen chickens out back, rising early so guests may awaken to the smell of freshly baking bread. Breakfasts include fresh fruit or juice, home-baked muffins, breads, or popovers, and a breakfast main dish such as quiche, Finnish pancakes, a sausage pancake wheel, or bacon and eggs. A special treat in the summer is fresh squash-flower fritters served with the Gamache's own maple syrup.

Northfield Country House is popular with groups, such as nature clubs, who sometimes book the entire inn. The Gamaches will prepare special dinners for groups, by advance reservation only.

*Accommodations:* 7 rooms with shared baths. *Pets:* Not permitted. *Driving Instructions:* Take exit 28A off I-91 and follow Route 10 north to Northfield Center. School Street is in the center of town, at the firehouse. The inn is 1½ miles down School Street, which becomes a wooded dirt road.

## *Princeton, Massachusetts*

## COUNTRY INN AT PRINCETON

30 Mountain Road, Princeton, MA 01541. 617-646-2030. *Innkeepers:* Don and Maxine Plumridge. Open all year, Wednesday through Sunday.

Don and Maxine Plumridge have left behind, respectively, careers in advertising and the fashion industry to create at the Country Inn at Princeton one of the region's most elegant classic French restaurants, set in formal Victorian trappings. Built in 1890, the twenty-three-room, gambrel-roofed Queen Anne mansion easily accommodates such an undertaking. Once the summer home of Worcester industrialist Charles G. Washburn, the mansion numbered among its prominent guests President Theodore Roosevelt.

The menu at the inn is slated to change several times each year. Among the chef's noted presentations are his cream of watercress soup, pheasant with port wine (as an appetizer), salmon fillet stuffed with mousse of scallops and watercress and served en croute, and roast lamb stuffed with chicken livers, ground veal, and pork. Six parlor suites continue the Victorian theme of the inn with antiques and reproductions, four-posters and high-backed beds.

*Accommodations:* 6 suites with private bath. *Pets and children:* Not permitted. *Driving Instructions:* Follow Route 31 from Holden to Princeton. In town, take Mountain Road up to the inn.

*Provincetown, Massachusetts*

## ASHETON HOUSE

3 Cook Street, Provincetown, MA 02657. 617-487-9966. *Inn-keepers:* Jim Bayard and Les Schaufler. Open all year.

Asheton House is actually two adjacent houses offering bed and breakfast to guests visiting Provincetown. One was a whaling captain's home built in 1840; the other is an early Cape house built about twenty-five years earlier. Both houses have been faithfully restored and reflect the gracious atmosphere of an earlier era. All rooms and the suite are appointed with American, French, English, and Oriental antiques from the owners' private collections, augmented by some contemporary pieces. Decorative touches reflect Les's twenty-five years as a professional interior designer.

The variety of rooms at Asheton House provides a wide range of choices. For example, a large bed-sitting room has French furnishings, a working fireplace, and a private bathroom and dressing room. Another room's campaign chests, Maharlika chairs, glass-topped wicker traveling trunk, and potted palm create a safari-like feeling. From still another room you can see the Pilgrim Monument as you lie in a large four-poster bed with complementing early-American furniture. From the inn's gardens and walks bordering the houses, you can watch the fishing boats rounding Long Point.

*Accommodations:* 6 rooms, 1 suite, 1 apartment. *Pets and children:* Not permitted. *Driving Instructions:* Drive on Route 6 to Provincetown; take the first Provincetown exit and go to the water. Turn right and follow Commercial Street to the corner of Cook.

## BRADFORD GARDENS INN

178 Bradford Street, Provincetown, MA 02657. 617-487-1616. *Innkeeper:* Jim Logan. Open April to Thanksgiving.

If you love the sea and a good country inn, you'll love Provincetown and Bradford Gardens. Built in 1820, Bradford Gardens is an informal country inn furnished with antiques and art work. In the old inn are eight individually decorated guest rooms, six with working fireplaces, overlooking the garden and, in the winter, the sea. There is the Jenny Lind Room with early spool furnishings and a fireplace, the Yesteryear Room with its brass bed and brass accents, and the Chimney Nook with garden and water views and a fireplace nook.

The Morning Room has a central fireplace and a bay window overlooking the garden. Here guests mingle and enjoy the inn's country breakfasts, the only meal served. No part of town is more than a mile from the inn, so a car is hardly needed. There are special parkland bicycle and walking trails and miles of beaches.

*Accommodations:* 8 rooms in the inn and 4 in other buildings — all with bath. *Pets:* Not permitted. *Driving Instructions:* Follow Route 6 to Provincetown.

## THE 1807 HOUSE

54 Commercial Street, Provincetown, MA 02657. 617-487-2173.
*Innkeepers:* Bob Hooper and David Murray. Open all year.

It may be more accurate to call this the 1783 House, because that is the year it was built. It was 1807 when the Cape-style house was floated from Long Point to its present location on higher ground. The 1807 House retains its original wide-board pine floors and has been decorated with designer fabrics and wallpapers. Antique furnishings include a four-poster in the Red Room and a Canadian pine armoire in the Master Suite. Other pine antiques and art by local artists grace the Hospitality Room. A brick patio underneath the oldest pear tree on Cape Cod has a bar with an ice machine, and a spiral staircase leads from the patio to the guest rooms above.

Continental breakfast is provided for guests renting inn rooms and includes home-baked blueberry muffins made with berries picked in the early summer on the hill behind the inn. Located in the quiet, historical West End of Provincetown, the 1807 House is within walking distance of the beach and downtown Provincetown.

*Accommodations:* 3 rooms with shared bath, plus 5 efficiency apartments. *Pets:* Not permitted. *Driving Instructions:* Take Route 6 to Provincetown. The inn is on Commercial Street (Provincetown's main street).

## LAND'S END INN

22 Commercial Street, Provincetown, MA 02657. 617-487-0706.
*Innkeeper:* David Schoolman. Open all year.

Land's End is a striking contrast to many New England inns we have written about over the years. In a number of ways this Art Nouveau summer "bungalow" is more reminiscent of inns we know in California. Land's End was built at the turn of the century by Charles Higgins, a Boston merchant. On a high dune overlooking Provincetown and all of Cape Cod Bay, the inn still houses part of Higgins's collection of Oriental wood carvings and stained glass. In fact, it is the inn's outstanding period glass—in both windows and in its hanging and table lamps—and its abundance of potted plants and flowers that distinguish it.

Throughout the inn, numerous Victorian pieces intermingle with a collection of more recent pieces including upholstered, bentwood, and caned chairs. Much of its original wainscoting has been retained, and the combination of the eclectic furniture and India-print spreads helps to create an atmosphere at once informal, artistic, and in keeping with the mood and style of the Art Nouveau period. No television or radio are in the rooms, but books abound. The house encourages quiet socializing or the enjoyment of the solitude of a spot away from the bustle of downtown Provincetown.

*Accommodations:* 15 rooms, 10 with private bath. *Pets and young children:* Not permitted. *Driving Instructions:* Take Route 6 or 6A to Commercial Street, following it almost to the end. Stop at the Land's End sign and walk up the hill to the inn.

# ROSE AND CROWN GUEST HOUSE

148 Commercial Street, Provincetown, MA 02657. 617-487-3332. *Innkeepers:* Preston Babbitt, Jr., and Thomas Nascembeni. Open all year.

The Rose and Crown is a classic Georgian "square rigger" built in the 1780s. Its orderly design was the model for many other homes in Provincetown. The guest house sits behind an ornate iron fence containing an unusually lush English garden. "Jane Elizabeth," a ship's figurehead, greets visitors from her post above the paneled front door.

During restoration wide floorboards were uncovered, and pegged posts and beams were exposed. Hooked rugs, patchwork quilts, and antique brass and silver accent pieces create a colonial atmosphere throughout the inn. Each guest room has its own special feature. Crown Room has exposed beams and Oriental rugs, while the brick fireplace wall in Rose Room displays a mysterious portrait of a girl holding a single rose. In addition to the rooms in the inn, the Rose and Crown has a cottage and an apartment, both with kitchen facilities. The inn is particularly appealing in the off season, when the pace slows and guests can relax in the living room and enjoy a breakfast of freshly baked breads and the Rose and Crown's special-flavored coffee.

*Accommodations:* 8 rooms, 3 with private bath, plus cottage and apartment. *Pets:* Not permitted. *Driving Instructions:* Take Route 6 (Mid-Cape Highway) to Provincetown.

## SOMERSET HOUSE

378 Commercial Street, Provincetown, MA 02657. 617-487-0383.
*Innkeeper:* Jon Gerrity. Open March to December.

The Somerset House is one of Provincetown's larger old homes, a black-shuttered yellow building behind a picket-fenced front garden facing the town beach a hundred feet away. The original house was built in 1850 by a successful ship chandler, Stephen Cook. An addition in 1890 doubled its size. Today the Somerset is a guest house offering twelve individually decorated guest rooms and two two-bedroom apartments. The furnishings throughout are an eclectic combination of antique and very modern enhanced by many plants, flowers, and original paintings and lithographs. Eleven of the guest rooms have tiled baths, and several rooms have water views of the harbor. The Somerset House serves no food, but the town has a great many unusual (and usual) restaurants, all within a short walking distance. The closest is three doors away.

*Accommodations:* 14 rooms, 11 with bath. *Pets:* Not permitted. *Driving Instructions:* Take Route 6 to Provincetown, east end exit. Follow Commercial Street (Provincetown's main street) along the water to Pearl Street.

## WHITE WIND INN

174 Commercial Street, Provincetown, MA 02657. 617-487-1526.
*Innkeeper:* Sandra Rich. Open all year.

The White Wind, a white Victorian mansion, was once the home of a prosperous shipbuilder. Built in the mid-nineteenth century, the inn is carpeted throughout, has high ceilings, chandeliers, and a blend of antiques and modern conveniences. There are twelve guest rooms, some with private sundecks. Directly opposite from a quiet stretch of beach, the inn is only a three-minute walk to the center of town with its myriad activities. Guests enjoy relaxing on the large shady front porch overlooking Main Street and the bay. In warm weather coffee is always available out here.

*Accommodations:* 12 rooms, 6 with bath. *Driving Instructions:* Take the Mid-Cape Highway to Provincetown. The inn is on the corner of Commercial and Winthrop Streets.

## Rockport, Massachusetts

### ADDISON CHOATE INN

49 Broadway, Rockport, MA 01966. 617-546-7543. *Innkeepers:* Margot and Brad Sweet. Open all year.

In 1851 this little house was the talk of Rockport. The first bathtub had arrived and was safely ensconced in the kitchen. Today there are seven baths, and although none is in the kitchen, all are most unusual with tiles and pewter faucets. The inn is decorated with collections of family antiques, such as ship models, old clocks, and quilts. Each guest room is furnished with antiques of a particular period or theme. The Sweets' enjoyment of innkeeping shows up in their attention to the decor and in the personal amenities they provide guests. Beds are turned down and surprises are left on pillows. There is even an ocean-racing yacht for sailing excursions. A large swimming pool set in the yard is surrounded by gardens and a profusion of tiger lilies, and rows of window boxes and hanging plants add splashes of color to the inn's white clapboarding. Guests are greeted each morning by the aroma of baking breakfast pastries, which are served in the dining room with its working beehive oven.

*Accommodations:* 7 rooms with private bath, plus efficiency cottage for two to four persons. *Pets and children:* Not permitted. *Driving Instructions:* The inn is in Rockport on Route 127.

## EDEN PINES INN

Eden Road, Rockport, MA 01966. 617-546-2505 or 617-443-2604.
*Innkeeper:* Inge Sullivan. Open mid-May through mid-November.
Eden Pines Inn, a gray-shingled building with black shutters, is on the rocky shore of this popular seacoast village. One can sit on its enclosed porch and watch lobstermen hauling their catches, fishermen at work, and larger ships going to and from European ports. In the distance is Thatcher's Island with its historic twin lighthouses. Also on the ocean side of the house is a spacious sundeck ablaze with red geraniums. Below it, water-smoothed rocks lead gently into the sea. On the street side a Romanesque-arched Palladian window overlooks the flower-bordered brick walk leading to the inn's entrance.

The guest rooms at Eden Pines are decorated in bright, fresh colors, and each has its own sitting area. All but one has an ocean view; two have private decks. A living room warmed by a fire in the fireplace contains the inn's television. A Continental breakfast served on the porch includes juices, coffee and tea, and a selection of Inge's Scandinavian pastries.

*Accommodations:* 8 rooms with private bath. *Pets and young children:* Not permitted. *Driving Instructions:* Take Route 128 north to the lights; turn left on Route 127 to downtown Rockport. Turn right on Mount Pleasant (Route 127A to Gloucester) and go a mile to Eden Road. Turn left on Eden and drive to the inn (on the ocean).

## THE INN ON COVE HILL

37 Mount Pleasant Street, Rockport, MA 01966. 617-546-2701. *Innkeepers:* John and Marjorie Pratt. Open late February through October.

The Inn on Cove Hill is a classic Federal-period home, New England in appearance with its white siding and black painted shutters. This is one of several Rockport mansions that were built with pirates' gold by the sons of Joshua Norwood, who had watched the pirates bury their loot. A perfectly pieced granite walkway leads up to one of the finest doorways in Rockport. Many of the architectural and decorative features of the house have been carefully preserved or restored, such as its Christian doors bearing their original hand-forged hinges, its wainscoting, wide pumpkin-pine floors, dentil molding, a ceramic-tile Vaughn fireplace, and the striking spiral staircase in the main entrance hall. The staircase was built with thirteen steps, a common tribute to the original colonies.

Complete restoration of the guest rooms is continuing. Guests are offered Colonial and Victorian settings with a combination of antique and reproduction furniture. There are such personal touches as hand-made pincushions for emergency mending, handmade afghans and quilts for winter comfort, and vases of marguerite daisies in summer or pumpkins in autumn.

The public areas in the inn include a third-floor porch with a panoramic view of the harbor, where whales can be sighted during their migrations. The living room for guests is furnished with a blend of new and antique furniture handed down through generations of the Pratt family. Among the treasures are a cherry-wood Winthrop desk and a Windsor chair built by a family ancestor 150 years ago. The walls are decorated with original oils and watercolors, a reminder that Rockport is an artists' colony.

Breakfast at the inn, often served outdoors on umbrella tables, features blueberry, cranberry, pumpkin, or blackberry muffins and fresh coffee and juice. Winter guests frequently enjoy breakfast in bed, and all year you can awake to the smell of freshly baking muffins.

*Accommodations:* 10 rooms, 7 with private bath. *Pets:* Not permitted. *Children:* Under 10 not permitted. *Driving Instructions:* Take Route 127 to Rockport; once in town, take Route 127A to the center; then turn right with Route 127A and continue on it two blocks to the inn on the left.

## OLD FARM INN

291 Granite Street, Rockport, Massachusetts. Mailing address: Box 590, Rockport, MA 01966. 617-546-3237. *Innkeepers:* The Balzarini family. Open early spring through late fall.

The Old Farm Inn is between Halibut Point and Folly Cove on the northernmost tip of Cape Ann. The date of the farmhouse is estimated to be 1799, but a house has been on the site since 1705. In the early 1900s, Antone Balzarini, an immigrant from Italy, rented the farm and raised dairy cows and twelve children there. The family later moved down the road. In 1964, one of Antone's sons, John, and his family bought the old place. The Balzarinis restored the farmhouse and furnished it with antiques, including the much used big black iron stove. They added on a dining room overlooking a meadow where ponies graze and a glassed-in terrace dining room. Another dining room has beamed ceilings, open hearths, and floor-to-ceiling windows. The Old Farm Inn specializes in fresh locally caught seafood. For dessert there is Indian pudding baked in the iron stove, and Uncle Charlie's rum bread pudding. Rockport is a dry town, so bring your own spirits and the restaurant will provide setups.

Guests can enjoy the inn's 5 acres of lawns and meadows, with towering trees and abundant flowers, or hike to the sea through the state park behind the inn. The guest rooms are in the building that was originally the farm's barn.

*Accommodations:* 6 rooms, 4 with private bath. *Pets:* Not permitted. *Driving Instructions:* Take Route 128 to Gloucester, then follow signs to Rockport. Turn left at Railroad Avenue and follow the sign to Pigeon Cove (about 2 miles).

## ROCKY SHORES INN AND COTTAGES

Eden Road, Rockport, MA 01966. 617-546-2823. *Innkeepers:* Gunter and Renate Kostka. Open April to October.

Rocky Shores is a substantial building with seven fireplaces, a wide staircase, and handsome detailing on its interior woodwork. The Kostkas furnished the inn with a number of antiques and added touches of greenery here and there to give it a homey feeling. In warm weather the inn's broad porch is a natural gathering place for guests. In any season the sun parlor and large living room are popular spots. Rocky Shores overlooks the twin lights of Thatcher Island. All the guest rooms have television. The larger rooms have ocean views. Rocky Shores also has a dozen two- and three-bedroom cottages with complete housekeeping facilities. A full breakfast, the only meal served at Rocky Shores, is included in the room rate for rooms in the inn.

*Accommodations:* 10 rooms in the inn, 8 with bath; 12 housekeeping cottages. *Pets:* Not permitted. *Driving Instructions:* Take Route 127 to Rockport. Turn right onto Route 127A, and go one mile to Eden Road. Turn left on Eden Road, and go ½ mile along the ocean to the inn.

## SEACREST MANOR

131 Marmion Way, Rockport, MA 01966. 617-546-2211. *Innkeepers:* Leighton Saville and Dwight MacCormack, Jr. Open all year except January.

The Seacrest Manor, built as a luxurious private home in the early 1900s, stands on a scenic rocky outcropping of rugged Cape Anne. An easterly wing and sunny deck were added in the 1960s; from here, guests enjoy outstanding panoramic views of the sea, Straitsmouth Island, and the historic twin lighthouses of Thatcher's Island. One can even see the far-off Mount Agamenticus, nearly 40 miles away in Maine. The Manor resembles an English bed-and-breakfast place with its leather club chairs at fireside in the library, afternoon teas in the sunny living room, and large breakfasts in the breakfast room overlooking the old-fashioned gardens dotting the 2 acres of lawns and woodland. On cool days there is a fire in the breakfast-room hearth. Breakfast is included in the room rate, with special choices each morning: one day it might be blueberry buttermilk pancakes; another day, corn fritters or French toast. There is always a choice of seasonal fruit, beverages, eggs, bacon, and spiced Irish oatmeal.

The eight guest rooms are furnished with a comfortable blend of antiques and traditional contemporary furnishings. They are carpeted and decorated in a simple, unpretentious manner. Four have private baths; the others share adjoining bathrooms. In the evenings guests find their beds turned down and mints on the bedside table. Shoes left outside the door will be polished mysteriously in the night and will be waiting outside next to the morning paper. These are just a few of the amenities found at the Seacrest Manor.

*Accommodations:* 8 rooms, 4 with bath. *Pets:* Not permitted. *Children:* Under 16 not permitted. *Driving Instructions:* The inn is up the hill (Mount Pleasant Street) from the center of town. Marmion Way is the second left after the Den Mar nursing home.

## THE SEAFARER

86 Marmion Way, Rockport, MA 01966. 617-546-6248. *Innkeepers:* Gerald and Mary Pepin. Open April 15 through October 31.

Marmion Way is a horseshoe-shaped road that hugs the coast overlooking the cove near Rockport. Primarily a residential street, it also serves several of the inns we describe in the Rockport area. The Seafarer, an 1893 gambrel-roofed inn, has been in continuous operation since 1900. Originally part of a large inn and cottage complex called the Straitsmouth Inn, the Seafarer stands at the edge of Gap Cove, overlooking Straitsmouth Island. An old-fashioned porch with deck chairs takes full advantage of the ocean view and breezes.

The inn's airy guest rooms display original oil paintings of the area done by local artists. Doors to the rooms bear brass Lloyds of London certification plates with names like Captain's Quarter, Chart House, or First Mate's Quarters instead of numbers. Every room has an ocean view. Two rooms on the third floor, with breakfast nooks and efficiency kitchenettes, have the finest views but are rented on a weekly basis and are appropriate only for guests planning longer stays.

The inn's living room has a fireplace that is used on cool evenings. Soft music blends with the gentle sound of the fog horn and seagulls over the water. Throughout the inn the Pepins have utilized many pieces of authentic and reproduction ship paraphernalia, including ships' lamps, paintings, pieces of brass, and teak in the nautical motif. This is a quiet inn where the land merges gently with the sea and its

shore and water activities. Other than a Continental breakfast no
meals are served.

*Accommodations:* 8 rooms, most with bath. *Pets:* Not permitted.
*Children:* Inquire about bringing as most guests are adults. *Driving
Instructions:* Take Route 127 into Rockport. At the traffic light, turn
right and follow Route 127A one mile to Marmion Way. Turn left and
proceed to the inn.

## SEAWARD INN

Marmion Way, Rockport, MA 01966. 617-546-6792. *Innkeepers:*
Roger and Anne Cameron. Open mid-May to mid-October.
The Seaward is a group of several cottages and a central inn set on
land surrounded by lilacs, roses, high-bush blueberries, and stone
walls overlooking the rocky shore stretching out from Marmion Way.
Each of the six cottages — including The Breakers, whose nine rooms
belie the term "cottage" — are perched on granite outcroppings and
surrounded by small gardens and lichen-covered ledges. The
Breakers, a popular choice, is directly above the surf on orangey-pink
granite ledges. From its windows guests can enjoy views across the
water of Sandy Bay to the village of Rockport.

The main inn has a glass-enclosed terrace that runs across the
front of the building. This is a pleasant spot from which to watch the

changing light on the ocean, join other guests in conversation, or put together an intricate jigsaw puzzle. Anne Cameron has decorated the inn's rooms in colonial style ranging from homespun to elegant simplicity. Guests may choose to take their meals in the long main dining room with its ocean view or in the smaller room that looks out on the lilac bushes where goldfinches at the feeder frequently entertain guests. Each evening guests have a choice of two entrées. Specialties include fresh seafood, salads made from vegetables grown in the Camerons' gardens, and freshly baked rolls and breads. Guests arriving on Saturday can enjoy their weekly boiled lobster dinner. Mrs. Cameron has been supervising the kitchen since 1945 and recently compiled a collection of her recipes, published as the *Cook's Book from the Kitchen of Seaward Inn*.

Roger Cameron has created a sanctuary where rhododendrons are in full bloom in June. Many of the plantings in the sanctuary are gifts from grateful guests over the years. On the property is a swimming pool that the Camerons developed from a small duck pond.

*Accommodations:* 33 rooms with private bath. *Pets:* Not permitted. *Driving Instructions:* From the center of Rockport, go ¾ mile east on Route 127A and then north ½ mile on Marmion Way.

## Salem, Massachusetts

**COACH HOUSE**

284 Lafayette Street, Salem, MA 01970. 617-744-4092. *Innkeeper:* Patricia Kessler. Open all year.

The Coach House was built by Captain E. Augustus Emmerton, who was a central figure in the development of the Far East trade in Salem. Emmerton, born in 1827, followed the footsteps of his father, who had owned and sailed numerous cargo ships. The junior Emmerton became master of the barque *Sophronia* and other ships that sailed to Far Eastern ports bringing back treasures to Americans thirsty for the newly discovered Oriental arts. Many of these items were built into the Coach House, adding to its Victorian atmosphere.

Detailing within the inn is in keeping with the sea captain's era. There are seven marble fireplaces and rooms with French hand-screened wallpapers, Oriental rugs, stencil-painted furniture, and period antiques. In many ways the interior is reminiscent of a series of Victorian stage sets. Each room is simply furnished, in some cases with four-poster beds topped with pineapple finials.

*Accommodations:* 15 rooms, suites, and efficiency apartments, 11 with bath. *Driving Instructions:* From Boston, take Route 1A to Salem State College (junction of Routes 114 and 1A). Turn left onto Lafayette Street. The Coach House is two blocks north on the left.

*Sheffield, Massachusetts*

## IVANHOE COUNTRY HOUSE

Route 41, Sheffield, MA 01257. 413-229-2143. *Innkeepers:* Carole and Dick Maghery. Open all year.

The Ivanhoe Country House, built in 1800, is alongside the Appalachian Trail at the foot of one of the Berkshire Mountains. Actually this peaceful country inn is in the heart of the famed mountain chain, with its combination of excellent hiking and cross-country ski trails. Ski areas and Lenox's Tanglewood Music Festival are quite nearby.

The inn is a comfortable, quiet retreat furnished with antiques. Guests enjoy lounging by the fireside in the Chestnut Room. Here the Magherys offer a library, games, table tennis, and television. A special Continental breakfast including homemade blueberry muffins magically appears by each guest-room door in the morning. The inn has nine guest rooms, three with kitchenettes. The 25 acres of grounds provide cross-country skiing and sledding in winter and a swimming pool and hiking in summer.

*Accommodations:* 9 rooms with private bath. *Driving Instructions:* The inn is 3½ miles south of Route 23, on Route 41.

# STAGECOACH HILL INN

Route 41, Sheffield, MA 01257. 413-229-8585. *Innkeepers:* Ann and John Pedretti. Open all year; restaurant closed Wednesdays. The Stagecoach Hill Inn is a handsome brick building constructed in the early 1800s as a stagecoach stop. Its public rooms are reminiscent of an old English inn. The dining room has red walls with lanterns, chintz curtains, portraits of the royal family, and old English hunting prints. The pub, which predates the rest of the inn, is a dark paneled room with a blazing fire in season. In keeping with the pub atmosphere, English beer is on tap. Dining at the inn features food prepared by John and Ann, both fine cooks. The menu features fresh seafood, veal dishes, and steaks. Roast beef with Yorkshire pudding is available on Saturday evenings. Also popular are the traditional steak and kidney or steak and mushroom pies, as well as New England oyster pie.

Accommodations are currently offered in a large cottage, known as "the poorhouse," behind the inn. The name was derived from a less cheerful use of the building many years ago. Accommodations are also available in a series of chalets on the property.

Butternut Basin and the Catamount Ski Area are just a few minutes away, and mountain climbing and cross-country skiing start at the doorstep. In the summer Tanglewood and Jacob's Pillow are an easy drive away.

*Accommodations:* 12 rooms, 10 with bath. *Pets:* Not permitted. *Driving Instructions:* Take the Massachusetts Turnpike to the Lee exit, Route 7 to Great Barrington, then Route 41 South for 10 miles.

## *South Egremont, Massachusetts*

### THE 1780 EGREMONT INN

Old Sheffield Road, South Egremont, MA 01258. 413-528-2111.
Open all year; restaurant closed Mondays.

The Egremont is an old stagecoach inn built beside the Albany–
Boston Post Road in 1780. The inn's grounds slope down to a brook
just down the road from the site of Shay's Rebellion, a famous tax-
payers' revolt in 1786–87. The oak-beamed living room–lobby was
once the inn's stables, reflecting a day when housing the horses was as
important as housing the people they served. Fires burn in the curving
brick hearth that once served the blacksmith's forge.

Over the next hundred years the inn was greatly enlarged, incorporating guest rooms with private baths, porches, and a combined dining room and tavern. Here, before a central exposed-brick hearth, diners can sit on antique benches and enjoy apertifs. Another popular spot for sipping a drink while waiting for a table is the parlor, with its Oriental rugs on polished pine floors, formal nineteenth-century antiques, and chintz-upholstered antique furniture. Beyond this room is the living room–lobby, where decorator fabrics brighten the old woods in its beams and in the antique desks, the high-backed benches, and the paneled door doing service as the coffee table in front of the fireplace. Out on an enclosed porch is a formal dining room with blue trim and white walls and curtains. The tables are set with stemware, white napery, and arrangements of millinery flowers in antique containers.

The two upper floors house the inn's guests in individually decorated, old-fashioned–looking rooms with antique beds and bureaus and floral-print wallpapers. Our room contained a Victorian bedroom set, its scrolly woodwork painted with sprays of flowers. The bath stood on old-fashioned claw feet. Other rooms feature high bedsteads of walnut or oak as well as other Victorian antiques. A grandfather clock stands sentry by the ground-floor landing.

Guests and the public are served three meals a day. The dinner menu features French cuisine, simply presented. We began with grilled cheese wrapped in pastry. The fresh trout was served in a butter sauce along with julienned carrots, zucchini, and turnips, cooked until barely tender and served with the same sauce. Other offerings were roast duck with cranberry sauce, veal with champagne sauce, fresh lemon sole with beurre meunière, and rack of lamb.

The Egremont has a swimming pool and tennis courts on its grounds. Tanglewood and the year-round offerings of the Berkshires are within an easy drive.

*Accommodations:* 21 rooms with private bath. *Pets:* Not permitted. *Driving Instructions:* Go 100 yards east of the center of South Egremont and turn onto Old Sheffield Road. The Egremont Inn is within sight of the village.

## WEATHERVANE INN

Route 23, South Egremont, Massachusetts. Mailing address: P.O. Box 388, South Egremont, MA 01258. 413-528-9580. *Innkeepers:* Anne and Vincent Murphy. Open all year.

The Weathervane Inn comprises three buildings, all dating from the first third of the nineteenth century. The main inn is a typical sprawling New England building that has seen several additions. It houses the inn's "fireside room" with its bar, a comfortable living room, and the dining room with its southern exposure. On weekends, the dining room offers a small but elegant menu for lunch and dinner. Sunday brunch has become a favorite event for both guests and friends.

Six guest rooms are within the main inn, and two larger apartments are in the Coach House. The inn's barn, dating from 1820, has a massive stone fireplace and is the home of the Robbie Burns Pub, where Dixieland and Bluegrass music is played in the summer months and an après ski menu is offered during the winter season. The Weathervane Inn is surrounded by 10 acres of lawns and woods, and the grounds include a swimming pool and places to play volleyball, badminton, and croquet.

*Accommodations:* 8 rooms, 6 with private bath. *Pets:* Not permitted. *Driving Instructions:* Take Route 23 west from Great Barrington about 3 miles.

*South Lee, Massachusetts*

## MERRELL TAVERN INN

Route 102, Main Street, South Lee, MA 01260. 413-243-1794. *Innkeepers:* Charles and Faith Reynolds. Open all year except December 24 and 25.

General Joseph Whiton built this fine brick structure in 1794. The historic structure was purchased by its current owners from the Society for the Preservation of New England Antiquities with a historic convenant to preserve the building.

Merrell Tavern is on the Housatonic River, and a pathway leads down to the river's edge from the inn. Beartown Mountain is directly in back, and gardens have been established among the old stone foundations of barns and livery stables that once graced the property.

Within, there are working fireplaces in three guest rooms and the old tavern room, which is used for breakfast and as a public sitting room in cooler weather. It remains virtually unchanged from the days when William Merrell wined and dined drovers and their passengers there. Lighted by candlebeam sconces and chandeliers, it has what is believed to be the only remaining complete circular colonial bar in America. Five guest rooms have canopy beds, and two have four-posters. Most furnishings are in the Hepplewhite and Sheraton styles and are set off by authentic paint colors of the period.

*Accommodations:* 7 rooms, 5 with private bath. *Pets:* Not permitted. *Driving Instructions:* From the Lee exit off the Massachusetts Turnpike, take Route 102 about 3 miles to the inn.

## Stockbridge, Massachusetts

**THE RED LION INN**

Main Street, Route 102, Stockbridge, MA 01262. 413-298-5545.
*Innkeeper:* Betsy M. Holtzinger. Open all year.

The Red Lion is the grande dame of old Colonial inns. First built in 1773 as a small tavern and stagecoach stop for vehicles serving the Albany, Hartford, and Boston runs, the inn was greatly enlarged in 1862. Although the Red Lion has had several owners, it was owned from the Civil War until the early 1960s by members of the Treadway family. Over the years, various modernizations have been accomplished without disturbing the basic charm of this long-term resident of the Berkshires.

The inn has an extensive collection of antiques that grace its public rooms and greatly add to the feeling of the past. The tavern is paneled in old wood with the warm patina of age. There is a feeling of grandeur in both the dining room and the parlors with their Oriental rugs and grand pianos. In its long history the inn has been host to five presidents of the United States.

Meals are served to the public. Dinner at the Red Lion features twenty or so entrées, including such specialties as entrecote with herb butter, veal à la Oscar, stuffed pork chop, three different lobster dishes, or scallops in mushroom and wine sauce. There are also a modest list of appetizers and a good selection of desserts.

*Accommodations:* 103 rooms, about half with bath. *Pets:* Permitted for a daily fee. *Driving Instructions:* Take exit 2 on the Massachusetts Turnpike to Lee. Follow Route 102 to Stockbridge.

## *Sturbridge, Massachusetts*

The town is most famous for *Old Sturbridge Village*, a re-created town of the 1790–1840 period. As they do the work of early New Englanders, costumed personnel talk with tourists. In addition to the actual working farm village, there are craft work, exhibit galleries, a visitors' center, and shops selling the craft products and period merchandise. *Wells State Park*, off Routes 20 and 49, offers swimming, boating, horseback riding, cross-country skiing, and other recreational activities.

### THE COLONEL EBENEZER CRAFTS INN

Fiske Hill, Sturbridge, Massachusetts. Mailing address: c/o Publick House, Sturbridge, MA 01566. 617-347-3313. *Innkeepers:* Patricia and Henri Bibeau. Open all year.

At the top of Fiske Hill, with its vistas of the surrounding hills, stands the Colonel Ebenezer Crafts Inn. The restored farmhouse was built in 1786 by Mr. Fiske, a local craftsman-builder (the hill was named in honor of his grandfather). The Bibeaus are justifiably proud of the house and gladly show interested visitors around its rooms furnished with a blend of colonial antiques and reproductions. The Cottage Suite, furnished by the Sturbridge Yankee Workshop, is attached to the inn by an arched breezeway. The Ebenezer Crafts is named in honor of the Revolutionary War officer who founded the Publick House (below), and the flavor of the inn's beginnings is well preserved.

In the morning there are complimentary juice, coffee or tea, and freshly baked muffins. At teatime, candies, cookies, fresh fruits, and tea are set out for guests. Other meals are available a mile or so down the hill at the "mother" inn, the popular Publick House where guests at the Ebenezer Crafts should check in. The small swimming pool on the inn's grounds is a treat for summer visitors.

*Accommodations:* 10 rooms with bath. *Driving Instructions:* From Hartford, take I-84/I-86 east to exit 3, bear right and then left along the service road to the back entrance of the Publick House. From Albany or Boston, take the Massachusetts Turnpike to exit 9. The Publick House is on the Common at Sturbridge on Route 131. Stop at the main desk to register and ask for directions.


## PUBLICK HOUSE

On the Common, Sturbridge, MA 01566. 617-347-3313. *Innkeeper:* Buddy Adler. Open all year.

The Publick House was built two hundred years ago to serve coach travelers on the colonial Post Road. The tavern and barn were constructed by Colonel Ebenezer Crafts, an officer who drilled his cavalry troops on the Common during the Revolutionary War. The inn, completely restored and expanded in 1937, is listed on the National Registry of Historic Places. An enormously popular place, then and now, the Publick House offers twenty-one guest rooms, each with the furniture and decor of the colonial period. Some have beamed ceilings and wide plank flooring, and all have modern bathrooms and air conditioning. The Penthouse Suite has large rooms for either two couples or a family. The fan windows in both rooms afford views of the Common and the inn's grounds.

Visitors to Old Sturbridge have a choice of two other accommodations offered by the Publick House. Both the Colonel Ebenezer Crafts Inn (which see) and the Chamberlain House have the atmosphere of yesteryear that adds continuity to the village experience. The Chamberlain House quite near the Publick House has been fully renovated and restored and is also on the National Registry of Historic Places. It is decorated more formally than the other inns. The rooms (suites really) are furnished with queen-sized beds, wing chairs with quilted upholstery, wall-to-wall carpeting, and modern baths. Each has its own patio overlooking the pasture where sheep graze only a few feet from the door. No meals are served here, but the Publick House is just a few steps away.

There five dining rooms and two cocktail lounges that serve the many tourists who come to the historic inn and Old Sturbridge Village are furnished with antiques and reproductions of the period. Three of the eight fireplaces in the public rooms are in use. Visitors may choose from a large menu including roast beef with onion popovers, roast Cornish game hen with wild rice stuffing, and baked lobster pie. For dessert there are deep-dish apple pie with chunks of Vermont cheddar cheese, mince pie, and Indian pudding with a scoop of vanilla ice cream.

Holidays and winter weekends are very special here. Guests are treated to horse-drawn sleigh rides through the village, with hot buttered rum and roasted chestnuts by a fire at the end of the ride. Wild-game dinners, including venison, mince pie, and apple pan dowdy, top off the day. Arrangements should be made well in advance for these weekends, especially those of Thanksgiving and the twelve days of Christmas. The winter weekends continue from January through March.

*Accommodations:* 21 rooms with bath in the Publick House; 4 suites and 1 room in the Chamberlain House. *Driving Instructions:* Take the Massachusetts Turnpike to exit 9 or Route I-86 to exit 3. The Publick House is on the Common on Route 131.

# Sudbury, Massachusetts

Sudbury was first settled in 1638 by a group of Englishmen and was primarily an agricultural village for many years. Today Sudbury is a suburban village about 20 miles west of Boston on the old Boston Post Road, now Route 20. Most famous as the home of Longfellow's Wayside Inn, the village boasts an enjoyable, picturesque *Wayside Country Store* with an old-fashioned nickelodeon. A short distance away in neighboring Southboro is one of our favorite country stores, the *Willow Brook Farm*, with its herd of buffalo and its store filled with old-fashioned and newer products, including a meat department that specializes in prime aged beef, buffalo meat, and a variety of game in season. This is an enjoyable stop for people of all ages. Neighboring Framingham is home of the *Garden in the Woods*, with its extensive collection of wildflowers. Historic Concord and Lexington are just 10 to 15 miles away.

## LONGFELLOW'S WAYSIDE INN

Wayside Inn Road (off Route 20), Sudbury, MA 01776. 617-443-8846. *Innkeeper:* Francis Koppeis. Open every day except Christmas.

The Wayside Inn is now a designated national historic landmark. To stay here is to stay at a great museum: It is the oldest inn in America. Originally the Red Horse Tavern, the name was changed following the publication of Longfellow's *Tales of a Wayside Inn*, which were based on his knowledge of the Red Horse. This inn was run by four generations of the Howe family for almost 200 years. It was purchased, along with 5,000 surrounding acres, in the 1920s by Henry Ford, who completely restored it and reproduced a water-powered gristmill that operates today grinding meal for the breads served at the inn. Ford later built a replica of a typical New England chapel nearby, and it is currently popular with members of every faith for weddings. In 1928, Ford purchased a one-room schoolhouse, which had been the real school of Mary and her little lamb in the early 1800s. He moved the school from its original site at Sterling, Massachusetts, to its present location near the inn.

Built in stages, starting in 1702, the inn is an extraordinary collec-

tion of exposed-timber rooms with original paneling and museum-quality antiques. There is no television or radio. The ten guest rooms, each different and special, have been modernized to add private baths. When you are here, it is hard to remember that the center of Boston is only forty minutes away. The rural quality is made possible by the tract of surrounding land that Ford purchased to protect the inn. For the day visitor, the common rooms of the inn are open for inspection daily, although there is a very small fee to help support the museum. Shortly before his death, Ford deeded the entire property to the Wayside Inn Corporation.

The Wayside Inn dining room is one of the most popular eating places in this area. House specialties include roast duckling, stuffed fillet of sole with lobster sauce, and deep-dish apple pie. A reminder: the New England fall foliage season (late September through October) brings a deluge of travelers. Those wishing country-inn rooms should make reservations well in advance!

*Accommodations:* 10 rooms with bath. *Pets:* Not permitted. *Driving Instructions:* Take the Massachusetts Turnpike to Route 495, go north to Route 20 East, then 8 miles to the Wayside Inn (1 mile after the turn at the Wayside Country Store). From the east, take Route 128 North to exit 49 and go 11 miles west on Route 20.

# THE WILDWOOD INN

121 Church Street, Ware, MA 01082. 413-967-7798. *Innkeepers:* Margaret and Geoffrey Lobenstine. Open all year.

Wildwood is a rambling Victorian inn with a classic wraparound porch and grand carriage house. It is on a maple-lined residential street on 2 acres of grounds surrounded by stone walls. On the property are maples, apple trees, birches, black raspberries, and a stand of firs. There is a brook with a swimming hole. In the forested park behind the inn, a river winds. A canoe is provided for guests' use.

Inside Wildwood the Lobenstines have created a warm and inviting inn, where Margaret and Geoff and their twin daughters, Heather and Lori, work together to make guests feel at home. The rooms contain pine antiques, braided rugs, and such special pieces as a spinning wheel in one corner, a collection of classic New England cradles, a cobbler's-bench coffee table, and an old carpenter's chest filled with games. Some pieces have been in the family longer than a century.

The inn's five guest rooms are decorated to show off the Lobenstines' collection of handmade afghans and old patchwork quilts. Each room has its own unique piece — an old washing-machine wringer as a luggage rack, a queen-size four-poster bed, an oak armoire, a wicker cradle at the foot of a bed. In the morning Margaret's homemade bread baking creates tantalizing aromas. A Continental breakfast is included in the room rates, with some extras available at nominal additional charges. Margaret tries to make things that people don't often have at home, such as soufflé-type puff pancakes, Norwegian noodle pudding, or gingerbread and cornmeal surprise. Breads are served with her homemade peach butter, and popovers are often available with morning coffee, tea, and juice. This is the kind of inn where guests frequently feel at home enough to sit before the fire in their flannel nightgowns enjoying the warmth of the hearth.

*Accommodations:* 5 rooms sharing 3 hall baths. *Pets:* Not permitted, but there is a heated kennel in town. *Driving Instructions:* Take Route 32 from exit 8 of the Massachusetts Turnpike into Ware. Take Main Street (Route 9) to Church Street (at the traffic light by the fountain opposite South Street). Turn on Church and drive to the inn, ¾ mile up the road on your right.

*Wellfleet, Massachusetts*

## THE HOLDEN INN

Commercial Street, Wellfleet, Massachusetts. Mailing address: P.O. Box 816, Wellfleet, MA 02667. 617-349-3450. *Innkeepers:* Letitia and William Fricker. Open late June through Labor Day.

Like many inns on the Cape, the Holden is actually three buildings on one piece of property. The main inn was built in 1840 as a sea captain's house. The building has wide-board pumpkin-pine floors and is furnished with antiques and wicker furniture. Behind the main house is the larger building known as the Lodge, which has both a view of the bay and a large screened porch. The remaining rooms are in the white clapboard cottage next door. Although the inn serves no meals, there are many fine restaurants nearby. The Holden is a five-minute walk from one of the largest Cape Cod marinas. The area abounds with good fishing spots. Guests who prefer to spend time on the ocean rather than the bay can take any of the meandering back roads 4 miles across this narrow part of the Cape to the oceanside.

Wellfleet is one of the headquarters of the Cape Cod National Seashore and a wonderful spot for bird-watchers and hikers.

*Accommodations:* 24 rooms, 6 with bath. *Pets:* Not permitted. *Children:* Under ten not permitted. *Driving Instructions:* Take a left (west) off Route 6 at the sign reading Wellfleet Center and a left at the sign to The Pier; continue on this road to the inn on the right.

## West Harwich, Massachusetts

### THE LION'S HEAD

186 Belmont Road, West Harwich, Cape Cod, Massachusetts. Mailing address: Box 444, West Harwich, MA 02671. 617-432-7766. *Innkeepers:* Kathleen Hendren and Linda Silvius. Open April 1 through October 31.

The Lion's Head is a Cape Cod guest house. It was built early in the nineteenth century as a Cape half-house and has been enlarged over the years. The old house, once the home of sea captain Thomas Snow, has the original "captain's stairs," with very high risers. The entire house has recently been restored and redecorated with many antique and traditional pieces. A hearty breakfast is included in the room charge. Home-baked breads and muffins are a specialty. In the late afternoon, complimentary wine is served in the living room, where chess and backgammon are available to guests. On the grounds are two cottages available for weekly rental.

*Accommodations:* 4 rooms, 2 with private bath, in the inn, plus 2 cottages. *Pets:* Not permitted. *Children under twelve years:* Permitted in cottages only. *Smokers:* Not preferred. *Driving Instructions:* The inn is half a block from Route 28 in West Harwich.

## West Stockbridge, Massachusetts

## WILLIAMSVILLE INN

Route 41, West Stockbridge, MA 01266. 413-274-6580. *Inn-keepers:* David and Suzan Saxon. Open all year except the first three weeks in November and three weeks after Easter.

The Williamsville Inn is near the base of a 2,000-foot mountain. Christopher French built the old farmhouse in the eighteenth century. He had lived 100 yards away on the Williams River, but the neighboring Indians were so noisy he was forced to move his family up the hill. Later, Mr. French deeded all but the front room, a room over it, and the cellar beneath to his son. He retained possession of his section of the house until his death. The Christopher French Room is now a favorite guest room. It is hard to pick one room over another here at the Williamsville. All are decorated with period antiques, their many angled walls covered with floral-print papers, their wide-board floors covered with antique braided rugs.

The inn is a clapboard house surrounded by 10 acres of lawns and shade trees. There is a swimming pool and tennis courts for guests' enjoyment. The inn has eight working fireplaces, two in guest rooms. The Christopher French Room has one, along with an antique four-poster bed with long curtains tied back at each of the posts. Upstairs guest rooms contain interesting antiques and nooks and crannies.

Rooms in the barn have Victorian furnishings including marble-topped bureaus and walnut bedsteads. The attic bedrooms are more rustic with very wide floorboards, exposed beams and roof under-pinnings, and skylights.

The parlor is the perfect spot for getting into the colonial mood of the inn. Here one can curl up on the camelback settee and enjoy a before-dinner drink, chat with other guests or the snaggle-toothed cat, Socks, or just listen to the fire in the hearth. There are three intimate formally set dining rooms just beyond the parlor. One, the library, is decorated with richly designed wallpapers, lots of books, and a working fireplace. The other two rooms are equally pleasant, with a large fieldstone fireplace dominating the scene. Windows look out on the lawns, and the tables are set with white linens, blue Wedgwood, and, always, fresh flowers. Guests are served breakfast in the sunny back room with its bright-blue flowered tablecloths.

Everything here is made from scratch. The extensive menu offers interesting dishes prepared with a French emphasis. A dinner might begin with a rough country pâté; salmon mousse with sauce verte; or crepe au jambon. Some of the feature entrées when we were there included roast duckling with Grand Marnier sauce; seafood au gratin; and a breast of chicken stuffed with artichokes, mushrooms, and Gruyère cheese. The steaks served here bring guests back time after time, as do the fresh popovers and lemon bread. Be sure to save room for dessert — fudge nut tortes, individual fruit tarts, or cheesecake Williamsville topped with fresh fruit.

The inn, its two innkeepers, and the food are all highly thought of. A recent *Wall Street Journal* article proclaimed the inn to be "enchanting," the "service cheerful and professional," and the restaurant "perfect."

*Accommodations:* 8 rooms in the inn; 4 in the converted barn and 2 cottages; all with private bath. *Pets:* Not permitted. *Driving Instructions:* The inn is on Route 41, 4 miles south of West Stockbridge.

## *Whitinsville, Massachusetts*

### THE VICTORIAN

583 Linwood Avenue, Whitinsville, MA 01588. 617-234-2500. *Innkeeper:* Martha Flint. Open all year.

The Victorian is an old dowager of an inn presiding over a 50-acre woodland estate. Built in 1871 by a wealthy mill owner, this mansion has been impeccably restored and maintained by the innkeeper.

Today the inn houses one of New England's finest restaurants, whose popularity is enhanced by the Victorian setting. The inn is striking in appearance with its dark walnut and mahogany woodwork set off by the wallpapers and draperies of the period. From the finely etched glass doors to the turn-of-the-century furnishings the total effect is one of formal elegance. The guest rooms are all spacious, in keeping with the period. The master bedroom, with its dressing room, is probably the most coveted. One of the guest rooms has a working fireplace, and most have king-size beds.

Meals are served in the inn's well-stocked library and drawing room. The menu features an interesting collection of Continental dishes. Appetizers might include a crab Veronique, blinis with caviar and sour cream, a country pâté, and a crepe du jour. A recent sampling of entrées included scallopini al pesto, a poached salmon Nantua, and several fresh seafood dishes. You might even dine on a classic pheasant dish if you make prior arrangements. The Victorian is a mansion where one can dine, relax, and sleep in a bygone era.

*Accommodations:* 8 rooms, 6 with bath. *Driving Instructions:* Take 122 south from Worcester and turn right at Linwood Avenue.

## Yarmouth Port, Massachusetts

### COLONIAL HOUSE INN

277 Main Street, Yarmouth Port, MA 02675. 617-362-4348. *Innkeeper:* Malcolm J. Perna. Open all year.

In the 1730s the Josiah Ryder Family built a hip-roofed colonial home on the Old King's Highway on Cape Cod. It was later sold to Captain Joseph Eldridge, and for the next hundred years the Eldridges added on here and there. One addition was floated over from Nantucket in 1820, and in the 1860s a third floor complete with mansard roof and Doric portico transformed the house into a stylish Victorian.

Today, as a Cape Cod inn, the Colonial House sits on 3 acres of land with extensive gardens and a small pond and fountain. The guest rooms, named for former owners, are furnished with antiques and reproduction pieces. Three dining rooms, each with a working fireplace, offer New England fare emphasizing fresh local seafood. The three rooms have distinct personalities. Oak Room features tiger- and golden-oak tables; the more formal Colonial Room has hand-stenciled walls; and the Common Room is a glassed-in veranda overlooking the gardens and town green. The inn is open seven days a week for lunch, dinner, and Sunday brunch.

*Accommodations:* 12 rooms with private bath. *Pets:* Not permitted. *Driving Instructions:* The inn is on Route 6A.

## OLD YARMOUTH INN

223 Main Street, Yarmouth Port, MA 02675. 617-362-3191. *Innkeeper:* Shane E. Peros. Open all year.

The Old Yarmouth Inn has the distinction of being the oldest inn on Cape Cod. Built in 1696, the inn has grown over the years, and guests are now given overnight accommodations in the Old Yarmouth Manor, a separate building dating from 1780. The Manor was built in the late-Georgian style. Its decor varies from room to room and includes French Provincial and early-American styles. Each room has wall-to-wall carpeting, television, and a private bath.

The Old Yarmouth serves both lunch and dinner to guests and the public from April through October. On the dinner menu are a broad range of seafood items including seafood casserole, lobster pie, and scrod with lobster sauce. Among other offerings are chicken cordon bleu, roast duckling, and several steak and beef dishes.

*Accommodations:* 12 rooms with private bath. *Pets:* Not permitted. *Driving Instructions:* The inn is on Route 6A in the village.

## THE VILLAGE INN

92 Main Street, Yarmouth Port, Massachusetts. Mailing address: Box 1, Yarmouth Port, MA 02675. 617-362-3182. *Innkeepers:* Mac and Esther Hickey. Open all year.

The Village Inn is a small, family-operated inn housed within what was once the private home of a locally renowned sea captain. In the Yarmouth Port Historic District, the inn has ten guest rooms, of which six have private baths and the other four are really family suites that share baths. There are two comfortable lounges, a spacious porch, and more than an acre of landscaped grounds.

Mac and Esther Hickey have made the Village Inn one of the finest on the Cape by their attentive service to their guests and with their comfortable rooms. We have been privileged to read many of the letters sent by their overnight guests heaping praise on them for their helpfulness and warmth. Here is an inn where you can expect more than to be shown to your room. Many are the times that the Hickeys have gotten an absentminded guest a tube of toothpaste or an extra toothbrush, lent an author a typewriter, or obtained last-minute reservations at a crowded summer theater or a popular restaurant. No meals are served at the inn, except for the unusually generous breakfast cooked "as you like it" every morning, but many nearby restaurants are highly regarded.

*Accommodations:* 10 rooms, 6 with bath. *Driving Instructions:* The inn is on Route 6A.

# New Hampshire

---

**DAVID'S INN**

Bennington Square, Bennington, New Hampshire. Mailing address: Box 35, Bennington, NH 03442. 603-588-2458. *Innkeeper:* David H. Glynn. Open April 1 through November 30.

First let's establish that David's Inn is in Bennington, *New Hampshire.* Although Bennington, Vermont, is a lovely spot, it would be a shame to drive all the way to southwestern Vermont only to miss a chance to stay, or at least eat, at David's.

The town of Bennington, once known as Hancock Factory, was originally part of the town of Hancock. The inn was built in 1788 by a family named Burtt. As was so frequently the fashion in the northeast, the house was moved from its original site, once in 1838 and again in 1928. So ingenious were early New England house movers that they even managed to float houses across lakes and pull them on logs up the sides of mountains. Nothing so adventurous was required to move David's, but this is the only inn we know of that has occupied three different sites.

The Cape Cod–style house has been fully restored to its post-colonial design, retaining much of its original plaster, all its original beams, and its wide-board floor. Many of these floorboards, according to David, were once known as "illegal boards" because they were wider

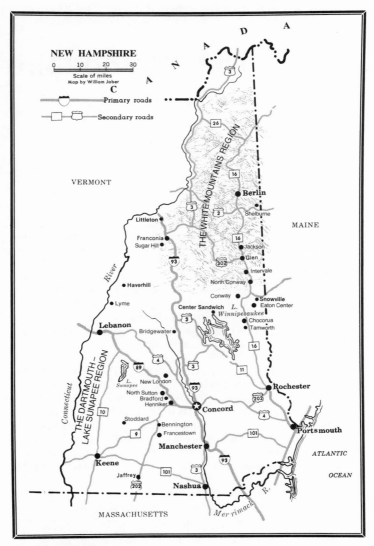

NEW HAMPSHIRE

0 10 20 30
Scale of miles
Map by William Jaber

Primary roads

Secondary roads

CANADA

VERMONT

MAINE

THE WHITE MOUNTAINS REGION

Littleton

Franconia
Sugar Hill

Haverhill

Lyme

Lebanon

Bridgewater

Center Sandwich

Berlin

Shelburne

Jackson

Glen

Intervale

North Conway

Conway

Snowville

Eaton Center

L. Winnipesaukee

Chocorua

Tamworth

Connecticut River

THE DARTMOUTH–
LAKE SUNAPEE REGION

L. Sunapee

New London

North Sutton
Bradford
Henniker

Stoddard

Bennington

Francestown

Concord

Rochester

Portsmouth

Manchester

Keene

Jaffrey

Nashua

ATLANTIC

OCEAN

Merrimack R.

MASSACHUSETTS

than 12 inches and were, by decree, supposed to be reserved for the use of the king of England. One of the most noteworthy aspects of the meticulous restoration at the inn is the use of traditional New England stenciling. When restoration was started, a set of stenciled walls attributed to Moses Eaton was discovered. These were duplicated throughout the inn.

David's grandmother once ran a boardinghouse in what is now his inn, so the tradition of innkeeping in his family is deeply rooted. A native of the area, David specializes in fine New England–style cooking. For him this means taking regional foods and presenting them in both traditional and inventive fashion. Thus you might choose from country chicken pie, salmon pie with egg sauce, pan-fried New Hampshire brook trout, Maine lobster pie with crumb crust, or broiled Cape scallops from among the dozen or more entrées of the day. Accompanying each meal is an assortment of condiments prepared at the inn. Among the specialties are five-bean salad, fresh cranberry relish, and pickled pumpkin. Many of these preserves and relishes as well as selected antiques may be purchased by guests at the inn.

David's has a small living room with a fireplace and two very attractive upstairs bedrooms, each with private bath. The inn is furnished throughout with early period furniture. The grounds are lovingly cared for, as is the house.

*Accommodations:* 2 rooms with bath. *Pets:* Not permitted. *Driving Instructions:* Take Route 123 to Hancock and Route 137 into Bennington.

## *Bradford, New Hampshire*

## THE BRADFORD INN

Main Street, Bradford, NH 03221. 603-938-5309. *Innkeepers:* Tom and Woody Best. Open all year.

There has been an inn at the Bradford's Main Street location for two hundred years, although the Bradford Inn dates from the early 1890s. The Bests bought the old Bradford Hotel in 1976 and have been gradually remaking it into a true country inn, with twelve guest rooms. The rooms are simply but comfortably furnished, and three of them have private baths. The inn itself is decorated with antiques and Woody and Tom's memorabilia, collected over the years. The sitting room and lounge fireplaces burn on chilly days.

The Bests describe their inn as a "place for rustic romantics who relish the casual luxury of sleeping in country comfort, dining on home-cooked specialties, and reaping the daily rewards of New England life." Tom's meals often include roast beef, stuffed flank steak, and broiled scallops. Pickles, relishes, preserves, breads, muffins, and desserts are made from scratch in the inn's kitchen. Dinner and breakfast are available to the public also, but reservations are necessary for dinner. Liquor is served in the lounge.

*Accommodations:* 12 rooms and 2 suites; 7 with bath. *Pets:* Not permitted. *Driving Instructions:* Take Route I-89, exit 9, then 103 to Bradford. The inn is near the junction of Routes 114 and 103.

# THE PASQUANEY INN

Newfound Lake, Bridgewater, New Hampshire. Mailing address: Star Route #1, Box 1066, Bridgewater, NH 03222. 603-744-2712. *Innkeepers:* Marge and Roy Zimmer. Open all year except April and most of November.

The Pasquaney has been welcoming guests on this spot since 1840. The inn retains the flavor of a turn-of-the-century lakeside resort with its many antiques, comfortable couches and lounge chairs, and relaxing pace. The dining and living rooms have fireplaces. The piano is tuned up for anyone wishing to try his hand at entertaining the rest of the guests. The main attraction is still Newfound Lake, reputed to have the clearest water in New England. The inn has more than 600 feet of lakefront and 6 acres of gardens and lawns. There are many lawn games available and on rainy days or in the evenings the recreation barn affords space for square dances, basketball, and table tennis. And the lake is there for swimming and boating as well as fishing, another popular pastime in season. In winter there is cross-country skiing, as well as downhill skiing nearby.

The inn serves hearty country breakfasts and dinners. Homemade soups include cream of broccoli, New England clam chowder, and sometimes even dill-pickle soup. A variety of special dieters', vegetarians', and children's meals are available. The rooms have views of the lake and the sunset over the surrounding mountains.

*Accommodations:* 28 rooms, 10 with private bath, in summer; 18 rooms, 10 with private bath, off season. *Pets:* Not permitted. *Driving Instructions:* From I-93 North, exit 23, follow Route 104 west to Bristol. Then go north 5½ miles on Route 3A.

## Center Sandwich, New Hampshire

## THE CORNER HOUSE INN

Routes 109 and 113, Box 204, Center Sandwich, NH 03227. 603-284-6219. *Innkeepers:* Don Brown and Jane Kroeger. Open all year.

Corner House Inn has continuously served travelers for more than one hundred years. It is in the center of a tranquil, unspoiled New England town in the White Mountains, on the shore of Squam Lake, the setting for the movie *On Golden Pond*. Don Brown and Jane Kroeger recently took on the task of renovating the downstairs rooms and barn, transforming them into appealing dining rooms complete with tie-back organdy curtains, painted wide-board floors, and old-fashioned print wallpapers. The inn is decorated throughout with country antiques and many examples of local crafts and art.

Center Sandwich is the home of the original shop for The League of New Hampshire Craftsmen (1925), and the town remains highly committed to the encouragement of local craftspersons and artists. The inn reflects this commitment through its use of handmade quilts, appliqués, and artwork. Guests stay in rooms with ruffled curtains, plants, the colorful quilts, and antique furnishings. Tiny-floral-print wallpapers decorate the guest-room walls, and seasonal fresh flowers add a personal touch.

*Accommodations:* 4 rooms, 1 with private bath. *Driving Instructions:* Take exit 24 off I-93. Follow Route 25 to Moultonboro, then Route 109 north to Center Sandwich.

## Chocorua, New Hampshire

## STAFFORD'S-IN-THE-FIELD

Route 113, Chocorua, NH 03817. 603-323-7766. *Innkeepers:* Ramona and Fred Stafford. Open all year

At the end of a country lane is Stafford's-in-the-Field overlooking fields, forests, and a brook. Built about 1778, the Federal-style house had several additions made between 1880 and 1905. Stafford's is one of the most handsomely redecorated inns in New Hampshire; each of its guest rooms is special. An attic bedroom, for example, has exposed barnboard and the original hand-hammered nails as well as a brass bed and a hooked rug.

Downstairs the Stafford's collection of antiques is visible everywhere. There are sitting rooms, a library, and a large dining room. In the last, bold blue-and-gold wallpaper extends up to the original tin ceiling. Tables are set with gold-checkered cloths and pressed-oak chairs. Here guests eat family-style.

To work off these meals, guests can square-dance in the Stafford's barn, swim in the old swimming hole in summer, or hike the long, winding road that leads to Lake Chocorua, with its view of Mount Chocorua. In the winter there is cross-country skiing on the property or at other, nearby touring centers.

*Accommodations:* 8 rooms, 2 with bath. *Pets:* Not permitted. *Children:* Welcome in summer only. *Driving Instructions:* The inn is on Route 113, a mile west of the intersection of routes 113 and 16.

## Conway, New Hampshire

# THE DARBY FIELD INN

Bald Hill, Conway, New Hampshire 03818. 603-447-2181. *Innkeepers:* H. Marc and Maria Donaldson. Open all year except April and early November.

A thousand feet above Mount Washington's valley is the Darby Field Inn. On top of Bald Hill in the White Mountains, the inn commands an outstanding view of the famous mountain and the surrounding peaks and valley. The inn was named for Darby Field, the first white man to climb Mount Washington.

Each of the guest rooms is decorated in country style, with quilts, four-posters, and a mixture of antique and newer furniture. Downstairs, guests have the use of the living room, with its stone fireplace.

The pub and the dining room at the Darby Field are open to the public in the evenings but only to guests for breakfast. The dining room has a view of Mount Washington; its candlelight dinners, presented with an almost Japanese simplicity and best described as "country gourmet," feature the freshest meats and vegetables.

In summer guests can swim in the inn's pool, and in winter they can ski at least 10 miles of trails that lead from the inn.

*Accommodations:* 11 rooms, 9 with private bath. *Pets and children:* Permitted if "civilized." *Driving Instructions:* Off Route 16, a half mile south of Conway, turn onto Bald Hill Road. Turn right 1 mile up the road, at the sign of the Darby Field Inn. Follow this road a mile.

# PALMER HOUSE

Route 153, Eaton Center, NH 03832. 603-447-2120. *Innkeepers:* Frank and Mary Gospodarek. Open all year.

The Palmer House is a two-and-a-half-story balustraded country inn just south of Conway, New Hampshire. The inn is named for Nathaniel Palmer, who built it overlooking Crystal Lake in 1884 as his home. Soon after its completion, Palmer began to take in summer lodgers, and it has been known as the Palmer House ever since. The Palmer House is noted for its family-style country-casual New England atmosphere. Except for a plethora of modern paneling, the inn is furnished much as it was a century ago, with lots of marble-topped dressers, wicker and oak furniture as well as a Victorian high-back, and iron and brass beds and braided rugs.

An attached New England–style barn has been remodeled to serve as the lounge and dining room. The latter has received local acclaim for such home-smoked delicacies as its game hen, turkey, ham, and locally caught trout. A single entrée is prepared each evening and might be veal Zuricher Art, roast pork with applesauce, chicken cacciatore, turkey with oyster stuffing, or beef Stroganoff. All soups and desserts are made from scratch at the inn. The Palmer House is noted for its country breakfasts — bacon or sausage and blueberry pancakes with real maple syrup or eggs and toast.

A deer head presides sedately over the granite fireplace in the guest lounge with its piano, dartboard, and abundance of overstuffed furniture. This is a popular gathering spot in the winter for the many skiers who use Palmer House as a base. Nearest ski areas to the inn are the family-oriented King Pine and the big four — Cranmore, Wildcat, Attitash, and Black Mountain. White Mountain ski areas are within an easy drive. Several cross-country skiing trails depart right from the door of the inn. In the summer, guests may use the sandy beach at Crystal Lake, which also offers sailing and fishing for pickerel and brook trout. Clay tennis courts and riding stables are nearby. The Kancamagus National Forest Highway affords an outstanding scenic drive and access to dozens of national-forest hiking trails.

*Accommodations:* 4 rooms with shared bath, 1 family room with bath, and a dormitory sleeping area. *Driving Instructions:* The inn is 6 miles south of Conway on Route 153 (at Crystal Lake).

*Francestown, New Hampshire*

## THE INN AT CROTCHED MOUNTAIN

Mountain Road, Francestown, NH 03043. 603-588-6840. *Innkeepers:* Rose and John Perry. Open Memorial Day weekend through October 31 and Thanksgiving to the end of skiing.

Originally built as a farmhouse by James Wilson in 1822, the inn served as a stopping point on the underground railway — slaves were hidden in a secret tunnel that connected the cellar to the Boston Post Road. During its first century, the inn was used as both a farm and a boardinghouse. Purchased by Sidney Winslow in 1929, the property was named "Hob and Nob Farm" and became one of New England's most renowned farms, with prize-winning sheep, champion horses, Angora goats, and numerous other farm animals. In the mid-1930s, a tragic fire destroyed most of the farm. The Winslows rebuilt it in its present state. John and Rose Perry purchased the property in 1976.

The ivy-covered inn sits on the northern side of Crotched Mountain with a 40-mile view of the Piscataquog Valley. The inn is a relaxing place with fireplaces including working ones in four of the guest rooms. Dinner and breakfast are available to guests and public alike. The inn offers guests two clay tennis courts, a mountainside pool, and the Winslow Tavern with a fireplace for chilly evenings. Nearby there are fishing in mountain streams and ponds, hiking and mountain-climbing, three golf courses, and, of course, skiing.

*Accommodations:* 14 rooms, 5 with bath. *Driving Instructions:* In Francestown, turn off Route 47 onto Mountain Road for a mile.

# THE HORSE AND HOUND INN

Franconia, NH 03580. 603-823-5501. *Innkeepers:* Sybil and Bob Carey. Open Christmas through the end of skiing and Memorial Day to late October.

This secluded White Mountain inn is a little off the beaten track, on the side of a quiet road under Cannon Mountain. The core of the inn, the dining room, was originally a farmhouse, built in the early nineteenth century. The balance of the inn was built just after World War II. An entryway leads to the inn's living room, which is dominated by its fireplace, a puzzle table, sofa and chairs, and a Steinway grand piano. The adjoining bar, paneled in thick New Hampshire pine, was originally the library of the house and has the feeling of an intimate English pub. It looks out onto the inn's gardens. There is no noisy TV or game room, and few children come here.

The two dining rooms are noted for their food. The larger one, which occupies the original farmhouse, and its smaller counterpart are uncrowded, setting a relaxed tone. Tables are set with white linens and tall white dinner candles. Every evening the dinner menu includes a half-dozen starters and ten or so entrées that reflect a variety of Continental cooking traditions. Inventiveness is the cornerstone here, with such appetizers as pâté of duck liver, sausage, and brandy and garlic; mussels poached in cream and lemon; and spinach crepe with warm horseradish mayonnaise. These might be followed by beefsteak Diane, duckling au poivre, chicken with mustard and sauce diable, or saltimbocca. The wine list includes four house and sixty vintage labels. Recorded chamber music is played throughout dinner, and after dessert Bob Carey often plays old-time torch songs on the piano.

The Horse and Hound is clearly well suited for lovers. Guests who come in winter will appreciate the inn's closeness to the Cannon Mountain ski area.

*Accommodations:* 7 rooms with private bath. *Pets:* Not permitted. *Children:* Permitted, but facilities are not well suited for them. *Driving Instructions:* From Franconia Village, take Route 18 south toward Franconia Notch. The inn is halfway up the 3-mile-long hill. From Route 93, take Route 18 a mile and a half south of the turnoff.

## SUGAR HILL INN

Route 117, Franconia, NH 03580. 603-823-5621. *Innkeepers:* Lois and Karl Taylor. Open all year except between the end of the fall foliage season and Christmas week and between the end of skiing and mid-May.

At Sugar Hill the distinctive mark is that of Lois Taylor's skill and enthusiasm for early-American decorative art. She has executed stenciled walls, colorful designs on velvet, and gold-leaf trays that appear throughout the rooms. There are stenciled Hitchcock chairs—an American furniture tradition for more than a century—and country tin accent-pieces in the dining room. Complementing these works of art are many antique pieces, such as old brass and spool-beds, Queen Anne living room furniture, and more than a dozen Oriental rugs. In the Pub Lounge a player piano adds a jaunty flair. Wood stoves here and in the living room burn most of the night and on frosty mornings.

Dinners in this converted 1748 farmhouse are served country-style, with a different menu every day. You get to know your waitress by name when she tells you the particular dishes that Lois has prepared that day. A typical meal might start with a shrimp mousse, proceed to veal Smetana or chicken breast stuffed with crabmeat, and end with apple strudel, raisin squares with brandy sauce, or blueberry pie. After dinner, relax on the front porch. If it is still light your view will include fields sloping toward Cannon and Lafayette mountains.

*Accommodations:* 15 rooms, 9 with private bath. *Pets:* Permitted only in the separate motel unit. *Children:* Under six not permitted. *Driving Instructions:* The inn is on Route 117, about half a mile west of Route 18.

*Glen, New Hampshire*

## BERNERHOF INN

Route 302, Glen, NH 03838. 603-383-4414. *Innkeepers:* Ted and Sharon Wroblewski. Open Christmas to April 15 and Memorial Day to mid-November.

The Bernerhof Inn was built in the early 1890s by a local businessman to serve travelers on their way to the Mount Washington Hotel. Since then it has been in continuous service as a hostelry, and even today a trail to the peak of Mount Washington originates at the inn.

The inn is furnished with a number of antiques; an intimate dining room and the oak-paneled Zumstien Room (the lounge) contain Swiss and other European artifacts. The innkeepers recently installed a Pianocordor reproducing piano system in their front parlor.

Dinner at the inn is distinctly European, with such specialties as delice de Gruyère, escargots bourguignon, and Wiener schnitzel.

Upstairs, the nine guest rooms vary from those with simple country furnishings and 1940s furniture to the recently completed sitting-room suite with private bath. The Tower Room has its bed tucked under the eaves in the building's turret. Floral striped wallpaper and a small stained-glass window complete the decor of this popular room.

*Accommodations:* 9 rooms, 1 with private bath. *Pets:* Not permitted. *Driving Instructions:* The inn is 6 miles north of North Conway (1 mile north of the intersection of Routes 302 and 16).

*Haverhill, New Hampshire*

## HAVERHILL INN

Dartmouth College Highway, Box 95, Haverhill, NH 03765. 603-989-5961. *Innkeepers:* Stephen Campbell and Katherine DeBoer. Open all year.

The Haverhill Inn, built as a private residence, is a fine example of classic New England Federal architecture. Set on a rise amid towering sugar maples, the house looks across lawns and an old granite-post-and-board fence to the oxbow bends of the Connecticut River and beyond to the Vermont mountains.

The building was the home of Arthur Carleton, a wealthy eccentric whose impending birth in 1810 had forced a hurried completion to the construction of his future home. Local speculation has it that the two iron rings set into the ceiling of the study held a swing where Arthur sat during the Civil War, gun in his lap, protecting himself and the family fortune. Successfully, it is presumed.

One enters a world of fires in open hearths, New England country antiques, and the aroma of freshly baked breads and pastries. The Haverhill Inn breakfast would do any New England farm wife proud.

All rooms at Haverhill Inn, including the guest rooms, have antique furniture and working fireplaces. Afternoon tea is served in the parlor downstairs, or guests may help themselves to a glass of sherry from the desk in the front hall and bring it to the hearth.

*Accommodations:* 4 rooms with private bath. *Pets and Children:* Not permitted. *Driving Instructions:* The inn is on Route 10, just north of the Common.

Henniker, founded in 1768, is a small New England village with a population of about 2,200. It is the home of New England College, a private liberal arts school. The town is situated along the Contoocook River, with many lakes and ponds nearby. An old covered bridge crosses the river in Henniker. The town has many antique shops, and numerous auctions are held throughout the summer and fall.

## COLBY HILL INN

West Main Street, Henniker, NH 03242. 603-428-3281. *Innkeepers:* The Glover family. Open all year.

Colby Hill Inn is a white country house built around 1800. Once a working farm, with 5 acres remaining, the many barns, sheds, and old stone walls offer a glimpse of the farm life of a hundred years ago. The inn has ten spacious guest rooms comfortably furnished with antiques; eight have private baths. Looking out the many-paned windows, one is treated to open vistas of the surrounding hills and mountains. Guests can waken to the smell of freshly baked bread coming from the farm kitchen. The Glovers' menu features traditional New England fare using locally produced ingredients when available, including vegetables fresh from the farm garden. The inn serves breakfast to guests only but is open to the public for dinner. Homemade soups and desserts are specialties of the house. There is a selection of wines, spirits, and lagers available with dinner. Colby Hill Inn also has a lounge for its guests.

Year-round and seasonal activities abound here, from canoeing and fly fishing in the many ponds and lakes in summer to white-water canoeing and ice fishing in other seasons. And, of course, there is skiing — downhill at nearby areas plus 10 miles of local cross-country trails.

*Accommodations:* 10 rooms, 8 with private bath. *Pets:* Not permitted. *Children:* Welcome if over six years. *Driving Instructions:* Take the Henniker-Bradford exit off routes 9 and 202. Take Route 114 south to the town center. Turn right on Main Street about half a mile to The Oaks. The inn is on the right, just off West Main.

## Intervale, New Hampshire

### HOLIDAY INN

Route 16A, Intervale, NH 03845. 603-356-9772. *Innkeepers:* Lois and Bob Gregory. Open May 30 through fall foliage (late October) and December 26 through the skiing season (late March).

The Holiday Inn — no relation to the big chain — has been in continuous operation since the 1800s. Situated in the heart of Mount Washington Valley, with spacious grounds, mountain views, and a heated swimming pool, this small inn is a comfortable place on 50 acres. A meandering stream runs through the inn's property. The woodland behind the inn offers 8 miles of hiking and cross-country skiing trails. Inside, the welcoming atmosphere of the Holiday Inn is immediately evident in the parlor-living room. A fireplace glowed when we were there, and several guests had gathered for before-dinner drinks (bring your own bottle) and a chance for some get-acquainted conversation. Dinner is served in the inn's dining room at tables set with white cloths. A different entrée is served each evening, with fillet of sole, beef stroganoff, roast beef, and chicken Parisienne indicative of the range of offerings.

Upstairs, the rooms are furnished in the style of an old New Hampshire home, with flowered wallpaper, spindle beds, and white curtains. One of our favorites has pale blue flowered wallpaper, organdy tiebacks, a blue rug, and white spreads. The room has pine antique furniture including even an antique towel-rack. The room's washstand comes with a bowl and pitcher set. On the third floor a bedroom has been tucked under the eaves of the inn's mansard roof. There is also a separate stone cottage that was once the law office of Marion W. Cottle, one of the area's first woman lawyers. The cottage has two guest rooms, one with a stone fireplace. The Holiday Inn has something for everyone: swimming and canoeing in the summer, skating on the inn's lighted rink and cross-country skiing from the front door in winter.

*Accommodations:* 10 rooms with bath. *Pets:* Not permitted. *Driving Instructions:* Take Route 16 out from the north end of North Conway; go 1½ miles to Route 16A, toward Intervale.

## THE NEW ENGLAND INN

Intervale, NH 03845. 603-356-5541. *Innkeepers:* Linda and Joe Johnston. Open all year.

The New England Inn matured slowly over 170 years. It began its life as the Bloodgood Farm, taking in road-weary travelers en route from Boston to Montreal. It provided them with a good bed, substantial meals, and a place for their horses. By the mid-1800s, the travelers were replaced at the farm by artists and other summer visitors. The White Mountain School of Art developed nearby, and even today the inn has paintings swapped for room and board. It has been modernized over the years, and most of the farm buildings have been converted into additional residences, but the modernization is not intrusive within the buildings. The farm grounds now offer a number of sports facilities, including several excellent clay tennis courts (most of the big name tennis pros who play at the Volvo Tennis Tournament practice here during that week) and swimming and wading pools. The inn has a complete Cross Country Learning Center with EPSTI certified skiing instructors.

As soon as you enter the New England Inn you know you are in a place rich in history. The lobby area was once the inn's country kitchen and the original fireplace with its black kettle-hook is still there today. A springer spaniel was curled up on the braided rug before the hearth as we checked in. The inn's living room has traditionally low ceilings (built to conserve fireplace warmth). Family

antiques including an old desk, an elaborately carved cupboard, and several family portraits set the tone of this room. Several staircases lead to the upstairs guest rooms, indicating how the house has grown in fits and starts over the years. Our large bedroom had a painted Victorian country bureau, a now unused fireplace, and its own bath.

In addition to the main building at the New England Inn there are five duplex cottages, four single cottages, the meeting house (a building in traditional style across the street offering lodging and small conference facilities), a motel unit, and the sports facilities. All cottages have working fireplaces, with one daily wood delivery included in the room rate.

The inn serves a full country breakfast and offers complete dinners in Anna Martin's Restaurant, which occupies the ground-floor portion of one wing of the main building. Breakfasts include baked apples, eggs, and blueberry pancakes. Dinners begin with such appetizers as pumpkin bisque, escargots, or hearts of palm and feature gourmet selections such as chicken Elizabeth, which combines boneless chicken with Alaskan king crabmeat, wrapped in puff pastry and topped with hollandaise sauce. Desserts include hot apple pie and lemon pie. The dining room is closed in April.

*Accommodations:* 50 rooms in several buildings, all with private bath. *Pets:* Permitted in cottages only. *Driving Instructions:* The inn is on Route 16A, 3½ miles north of North Conway.

## Jackson, New Hampshire

# DANA PLACE INN

20 Pinkham Notch Road, Jackson, NH 03846. 603-383-6822. *Innkeepers:* Betty and Malcolm Jennings. Open late May to late October and mid-December to mid-April.

Before a backdrop of the White Mountains and Mount Washington, alongside the clear Ellis River, is the 1890 farmhouse-turned-inn, Dana Place. It is surrounded by 300 acres of orchards, gardens, meadows, and deep woods that adjoin the White Mountain National Forest. The Ellis River Trail, well known among Nordic skiers, offers ideal trekking from Jackson Village 5 miles along the river to the Dana Place Inn's door. In summer the natural swimming hole formed at the base of a small waterfall is the hands-down favorite spot with visitors.

The inn's interior has been renovated and updated. Some parts have been modernized, and others retain the old-fashioned air of a country farmhouse. Two dining rooms are quite contemporary, with picture-window walls looking out at Mount Washington in the distance. The third dining room, the original one, has deep blue flowered wallpapers and decorative touches contrasting with the bright white of the working fireplace's mantel. The menu features a wide selection of Continental dishes.

The Dana Place Inn has a friendly atmosphere enhanced by sunny rooms. The sitting room has a cathedral ceiling and a large airtight wood-burning stove. The guest rooms are papered with old-fashioned flower prints and furnished with farmhouse antiques. Downstairs is a piano bar with a performer on weekends.

*Accommodations:* 14 rooms, 6 with bath. *Pets:* Not permitted. *Driving Instructions:* Take Route 16 north from Jackson.

## Jaffrey, New Hampshire

### MONADNOCK INN

Main Street, Jaffrey Center, New Hampshire. Mailing address: Box 167, Jaffrey Center, NH 03454. 603-532-7001. *Innkeepers:* The Roberts family. Open all year.

The Monadnock was built in the early nineteenth century; in the 1870s, Mrs. Sarah Lawrence began taking in summer visitors. She named the placed "Fairview" and later "The Monadnock." The Monadnock has changed hands many times since then but has been operating as an inn ever since (with a short rest in the early 1900s). The Roberts family took charge several years ago, and now the inn contains a comfortable mixture of early American, colonial, and Victorian furniture, a large living room with a fireplace, and an old-fashioned lounge and bar warmed in winter by a wood stove. Lunch and dinner are served to the public and guests; breakfasts are Continental-style, for guests only. Featured in *Gourmet* magazine, the inn's dining room offers delicacies that include oysters baked with Parmesan cheese, saltimbocca, gratin of scallops, sautéed pork in mustard sauce, and steak Diane. These and many other dishes are complemented by a good selection of wines.

*Accommodations:* 13 rooms, 7 with bath. *Pets:* Not permitted. *Driving Instructions:* Take Route 124 to Jaffrey Center. The inn is on Main Street.

## BEAL HOUSE INN

Main Street, Littleton, NH 03561. 603-444-2661. *Innkeepers:* Doug and Brenda Clickenger. Open all year.

Beal House Inn was built in 1833 as a farmhouse at the edge of the tiny town of Littleton. In traditional New England fashion, the house was connected to the barn by a carriage house. Today the inn sits on 4½ acres of land; its carriage house and main building house romantic, antique-filled guest rooms, while the barn, an antique shop, overflows with country antiques. Most of the antiques and decorative pieces in the inn are for sale.

The Clickengers scoured New England for just the right country inn before settling on Beal House. That they love their new profession is evident in their warm welcome and their attention to guests' comfort, and in the relaxed visiting-a-friend-in-the-country atmosphere. Fireside breakfasts are special occasions where the harvest table is set with candles and Blue Willow china on a soft antique red cloth. One might find waffles topped with local maple syrup or hot popovers and scrambled eggs served in antique Hens-on-Nests china.

*Accommodations:* 14 rooms, 9 with private bath. *Pets:* Inquire first. *Driving Instructions:* From I-93 take exit 42 and drive to the intersection of Routes 18 and 302 (Main Street).

## EDENCROFT MANOR

RFD 1, Route 135, Littleton, NH 03561. 603-444-6776. *Innkeepers:* Barry and Ellie Bliss and Bill and Laurie Walsh. Open all year except two weeks in early spring.

Edencroft Manor is a large white country inn with a view of the White Mountains to the east. Built as a farmhouse in the 1890s, it was greatly enlarged in the years following the Depression. The estate became known for its lavish parties and elaborate gardens. As an inn, it now features candlelit dining rooms offering fireside meals where everything, from the basket of warm breads to the rich tortes and trifles, is made from scratch in the inn's kitchens. Specialties of the house are veal and duck dishes and prime ribs. Guests and the public may choose to enjoy desserts, coffee, and after-dinner drinks in the living room by the fireplace. The common room has an extensive library for guests, and there is even a children's corner. Baroque and other classi-

cal music plays softly in the background, or one can crank up the old Victrola for a livelier session.

The guest rooms are decorated with antiques and new, firm beds. The wallpapers and thick handmade comforters add bright touches to the decor.

*Accommodations:* 6 rooms, 4 with private bath. *Driving Instructions:* At the end of I-93 in Littleton, turn right onto Route 18. Drive 0.2 mile and turn right on Route 135.

## 1895 HOUSE COUNTRY INN

74 Pleasant Street, Littleton, NH 03561. 603-444-5200. *Innkeeper:* Susanne Watkins. Open all year.

1895 House is a perfectly preserved Victorian building that retains its impressive front door with inset beveled glass. The oaken woodwork inside glows with the patina of age. There are oaken wall panels, smooth oaken floors, and an oaken staircase rising three stories. Through tall sliding wooden doors one enters a parlor where guests relax in Victorian spendor on Queen Anne chairs or a Chippendale camelback sofa. The bay windows offer views of the town and surrounding White Mountains. Another set of doors leads to the dining room with its carved oak mantel with the head of Old Man Winter in bas-relief. Breakfast is served here, and the hands-down favorite with

houseguests is Susanne's zucchini bread slathered with cinnamon butter and raspberry jam. Soft strains of classical music provide a soothing background.

Guest rooms are also a celebration of Victorian oak brightened by Oriental or colorful braided rugs and Susanne's hand-made quilts and tie-back curtains. A guest who takes a particular fancy to a bed or a piece of art should Susanne know; most of the antiques and artwork are for sale.

*Accommodations:* 6 rooms, 2 with private bath. *Pets:* Not permitted. *Driving Instructions:* Take I-93 to exit 41, continue across the bridge to the traffic light, then turn west on Main Street and take the first street on the right (Pleasant Street).

## Lyme, New Hampshire

## LYME INN

Lyme, New Hampshire. Mailing address: P.O. Box 68, Lyme, NH
03768. 603-795-2222. *Innkeepers:* Fred and Judy Siemons. Open
all year except the three weeks following Thanksgiving and three
weeks in late spring.

When the Lyme Inn first opened in 1809, it was known as the Grant
Hotel. Over the years it saw service as an inn, a tavern, and a grange
hall and gradually fell into disrepair before being saved and restored
by its three previous owners. The result is an on-the-common inn
whose face and interior show the love bestowed on it by skillful
restorers. The job of transforming it into an exceptional place to stay
was done with such care that even the fire escape — which often mars
the beauty of other inns — has been hidden behind a columned
portico.

One enters the inn through double doors that open onto a full-
length glassed-in porch, which retains its original painted pressed-tin
ceiling. In summer the porch is cool and inviting with bright yellow

cushions on its wicker furniture. In winter a collection of sleds replaces the wicker. Rooms at the Lyme Inn are decorated individually. Each bed is of particular interest, be it a hand-painted Victorian highback, a scrolly iron one, or one with a canopy. Each of the fifteen rooms has wallpapers ranging from floral patterns and pinstripes to traditional colonial prints. Accessory furnishings and antique prints complement the period of the room established by the bed. Most of the pieces of furniture and the prints are for sale.

The inn has three dining rooms. The decorative theme of one is based on early samplers; the second has old Currier and Ives prints; and the third contains the inn's map collection. In the small tavern is a collection of early hand-tools. The dinner menu's diverse offerings include hasenpfeffer, filet au poivre, Wiener schnitzel, Cape scallops, and loin lamb chops among many others. Dinners (not served on Tuesdays) may start with escargots, quiche, smoked salmon, or rumaki (chicken livers wrapped in bacon). For those who prefer lighter supper-style meals, there are veal Marengo and seafood crepes. Breakfast is served to guests only; lunch is not available.

The area surrounding the inn offers year-round activities such as Alpine and cross-country skiing, canoeing, tennis, and fishing. At Dartmouth College, 10 miles away, there is theater and other entertainment.

*Accommodations:* 15 rooms, 10 with private bath. *Pets:* Not permitted. *Children:* Not permitted. *Driving Instructions:* The inn is 10 miles north of Hanover on Route 10.

## HIDE-AWAY LODGE

New London, NH 03257. 603-526-4861. *Innkeepers:* Lilli and Wolfgang Heinberg. Open mid-May through October.

Hide-away Lodge is one of those places that make you think "I shouldn't really be sharing this." It is literally hidden away down an unpaved country lane just past Little Lake Sunapee. The lodge is not a romantic old-fashioned inn, nor is it historic. It was built in the 1930s as a summer retreat for poet-author Grace Litchfield and retains the flavor of a private home that just happens to have five intimate dining rooms. These rooms and the food served in them is what all the fuss is about. Wolfgang and Lilli Heinberg, the innkeepers, run a restaurant that has achieved national acclaim.

The dining rooms are decorated with old-fashioned oak furniture, Oregon fir–paneled walls, and simple country pieces. The tables are set more formally with starched tablecloths and soft napkins arranged with polished silver and attractive glassware. The menu features an array of unusual and original dishes created from fresh seasonal fish, game, vegetables, and berries. Dinner begins with cocktails out on the porch and proceeds to a selection of at least six appetizers, including poached egg in tarragon aspic with lemon mayonnaise, peach halves filled with mousse of ham, or Danish fruit soup. From a menu of perhaps ten or eleven entrées, one might select a grilled lamb steak with rosemary, veal cutlet "archduke," or terrine of sole and salmon with oil sauce, accompanied by a wine.

Overnight guests are welcome to relax on the wide sun porches or settle down next to a fire in the living room's granite fireplace. The inviting rooms are paneled throughout with Oregon fir. There are four comfortable guest rooms on the second floor and four more in an adjoining guest house. Each has a private bath. The lodge is set on landscaped grounds with trees, lawns, and a mountain brook complete with a fieldstone bridge. The beach on Little Lake Sunapee is just a short walk down the lane. The lake has a rowboat and sailboat.

*Accommodations:* 8 rooms with private bath. *Driving Instructions:* The inn is 2 miles from New London. Take Main Street out past Colby-Sawyer College. Main Street becomes Little Sunapee Road. Follow signs on the unpaved road past the lake to the inn.

## NEW LONDON INN

Main Street, New London, NH 03257. 603-526-2791. *Innkeepers:* Clara and George Adame. Open all year.

The New London Inn is a classic old New England inn with two stories of wide verandas overlooking the main street of this serene New Hampshire town. The white clapboard structure, built in 1792, is furnished throughout with antiques spanning the years.

The inn has twenty-four guest rooms, each furnished in its own special style with four-posters, period wallpapers, and other appealing country-Colonial items. Many guests return year after year, trying out different rooms each time. Working fireplaces are in the lobby and the sitting room, which has a wall of books and groupings of floral-upholstered chairs and couches with reading lamps.

The New London Inn has two dining rooms. The main one offers a menu of seafoods and steaks with house specialties of roast duckling with fresh peach glaze, shrimp scampi flamed in anisette, and veal with fresh mushrooms and shallots. Nelson's Tavern serves from a moderately priced menu in a casual atmosphere. The inn is near Colby College and the town's many antique and craft shops.

*Accommodations:* 24 rooms with bath. *Pets:* Not permitted. *Driving Instructions:* Take I-93 to I-89, exit 11. The inn is in the village.

## PLEASANT LAKE INN

North Pleasant Street, New London, New Hampshire. Mailing address: Box 1030, New London, NH 03257. 603-526-6271. *Innkeepers:* The Jaggard family. Open all year.

On the shores of Pleasant Lake, this inn was originally built as a farmhouse. Although the earliest parts of the inn date from 1770, its main portions were constructed in 1868. In the days when the property was a farm, the countryside surrounding the lake was shared by the farmers with the Penobscot Indians, with whom the families had friendly relations. The conversion to an inn was done by a Civil War veteran who operated it first as a summer and fall inn.

All but one of the guest rooms share several baths (no more than two rooms to any bath), and much of the inn is furnished with country antiques. The Jaggards (two brothers and their families) go out of their way to have each guest feel as if he is visiting the Jaggard home. Days start with a large country breakfast, and many guests join the family for late afternoon tea. Dinners may be selected from a menu that offers such daily specials as chicken Pleasant Lake and shrimp au Rolf.

*Accommodations:* 13 rooms, 1 with private bath. *Pets:* Not permitted. *Driving Instructions:* Take Route 11 to New London, turn onto North Pleasant Street at the Shell Station, and go 1½ miles to the bottom of the hill at the lake.

## North Conway, New Hampshire

### CRANMORE INN

Kearsage Street, North Conway, NH 03860. 603-356-5502. *Innkeepers:* Norm and Mary Jane Provost. Open Memorial Day weekend through October and December 26 through March.

During the golden age of railroading, up to twenty-six trains daily brought passengers to North Conway from most major cities in the Northeast. At that time, the Cranmore was one of five inns on Kearsage Street. Today the Cranmore is the only one that has survived. When the Cranmore was built in 1863, it was known as the Echo House. Over the years the building has been renovated and modernized, but what remains is a homey, old-fashioned place. An additional appeal in this day of limited and costly gasoline is the inn's location within walking distance of the center of North Conway. Guests can take public transportation to the inn and have a totally car-free vacation.

Typical of many Victorian mountain inns, the living room is particularly spacious. A wood stove was recently installed in the fireplace in this room. Across the hall is a smaller sitting room with its original tin ceiling. It is here that the inn's only television set resides. Beyond are a game room and the inn's two sunny dining rooms, both of which have braided rugs on their floors and tables bearing a name card for every guest. In the mornings the inn serves a full country breakfast. At night there is a single sitting where guests and, occasionally, old friends and neighbors are served traditional New England suppers. One entrée is available each day, such as roast lamb, turkey or beef, or a boiled beef and cabbage dinner.

Some of the 25 guest rooms at the Cranmore are in a relatively new wing. Many of the rooms have nice wallpapers, and most have simple but comfortable furniture. The hall has a modest slope to it, showing how the building has quietly settled over the century. All of this adds up to a happy and unpretentious place likely to appeal to those who come to this mountain village for its surrounding natural beauty rather than to find urban sophistication in the country.

*Accommodations:* 25 rooms, about half with private bath. *Pets:* Not permitted. *Driving Instructions:* Take Route 16 to North Conway. Turn east on Kearsage Street, and drive one block to the inn on the left.

## CRANMORE MOUNTAIN LODGE

Kearsage Road, North Conway, New Hampshire. Mailing address: Box 1194, North Conway, NH 03860. 603-356-2044. *Innkeepers:* Bob and Dawn Brauel. Open all year.

Bob and Dawn Brauel, the inn's youthful innkeepers, have come to innkeeping as a retreat from the more hectic lifestyle of earlier careers as a certified public accountant and a social worker, respectively. Their contentment in their new profession is evident in their enthusiasm for their work.

Cranmore Mountain Lodge was built in several sections, the earliest of which dates from the mid-nineteenth century. First a farmhouse, the early building was converted into an inn in the late nineteenth century by the addition of an octagonal wing. Later additions have included a main dining room, added in the 1930s, and tennis courts, swimming pool, basketball court, and an outdoor Jacuzzi. At one time, the lodge was run by Babe Ruth's daughter. The Babe was a frequent guest, using the inn as his hunting and fishing retreat. His room was furnished with oaken twin beds, and it continues to be the favorite room of many guests.

The guest rooms have various bed arrangements that can accommodate small or large families. There are also dorm facilities

with bunk bedding in the old barn. These are used most frequently for larger groups of skiers during the winter months. The main floor of the inn has a sitting room with fireplace, a television and game room, and a dining room serving home-cooked single-entrée meals (to guests only). The inn has an alpine ski shop.

*Accommodations:* 11 rooms in the inn and 4 dorm rooms, all with shared bath. *Pets:* Not permitted. *Driving Instructions:* Take Route 16 to North Conway. At the traffic light turn east on Kearsage Street, which dead-ends as Kearsage Road. The lodge is 1 mile to the north.

## NERELEDGE INN

River Road, North Conway, NH 03860. 603-356-2831. *Innkeepers:* The Edwards and Von Zamft families. Open all year except April. The Nereledge Inn, built in 1787, has two parlors (one with a fireplace) and a dining room that serves both guests and the public. The White Mountain furnishings are unpretentious. Most guest rooms have maple furniture with knobby spreads. A typical room has a brass headboard, a Victorian pine bureau, a pine nightstand, and a rush-seated chair. The attractively wallpapered hall bath retains the original claw-footed tub with a shower.

The dining room has a panoramic view of the Saco River, Intervale, and White Horse and Cathedral ledges. The inn is known locally

for its hearty breakfasts, which include home-fried potatoes and hot apple pie. The evening meal features European and American home-style cooking. Meats, chicken, and fish are prepared to order, and daily specials are likely to include Greek, English, or Yankee delicacies.

*Accommodations:* 10 rooms with 3 shared baths. *Pets:* Not permitted. *Driving Instructions:* The inn is 300 feet from Route 16 on River Road in North Conway.

## STONEHURST MANOR

Route 16, North Conway, New Hampshire. Mailing address: P.O. Box 1037, North Conway, NH 03860. 603-356-3113. *Innkeeper:* Peter Rattay. Open all year.

Stonehurst Manor is a turn-of-the-century mansion that looks as if it should have a thatched roof and be in the English countryside. One part of the ground floor is built of fieldstones, accounting for its name. Once the home of the Bigelow Carpet family, it now contains guest rooms and a dining room serving both guests and the public.

The manor's interior has turned spiral columns, baronial-size fireplaces with detailed mantelpieces, and intricate stained glass in many windows and doors. The lounge has thick pile rugs, seats built into the arched-top windows, and modern rattan furniture whose bent-wood curves echo the curves of the window tops. The main dining room's round tables are covered with print fabrics topped with white linen and are surrounded by high arch-back wicker chairs.

There is additional dining on the sunny glassed-in porch where hanging plants thrive. Evening menu selections include about eighteen entrées, stressing veal, seafood, and steaks. Before dinner, cocktails are served in the Manor library by the fire.

The most appealing rooms are within the Manor itself, although there are an additional ten rooms in a motel unit. Here, as in the rest of the inn, the innkeepers have used rattan and wicker as the basic furnishings with plush wall-to-wall carpeting and print wallpapers the rule. The inn is set back from the highway on 30 acres of pine trees. On the grounds are a large swimming pool and a clay tennis court.

*Accommodations:* 25 rooms, most with private bath. *Driving Instructions:* Go on Route 16 for a mile north of North Conway to the inn.

## WILDFLOWERS GUEST HOUSE

North Main Street, North Conway, NH 03860. 603-356-2224. *Innkeeper:* Eileen Davies. Open all year except occasional off-season weeks; call first.

Wildflowers is a cottage that was built about a hundred years ago under the direction of the respected Boston architect Stephen C. Earle, who broke with local tradition by facing the house away from the main street. Thus the building takes full advantage of both morning and afternoon sunlight. The intriguing exterior has both board-and-batten and cedar shingling and a porch.

When Eileen Davies bought the building in 1978 it needed a total renovation. She stripped endless layers of paint off the beaded door and window trim, steamed off tired old wallpapers, and then set out to create a decor that would carry out the theme suggested by the inn's name. Eileen clearly had fun selecting the papers for the six guest rooms and the dining room on the first floor. Each is printed with a different flower or grain. A corner bedroom (a favorite of hers and ours) has bold poppy and miniature-flower patterns on a black background. Furnishings in the rooms are an eclectic blend of antique pieces and "vintage yard sale" items. The living room is heated by a wood stove.

*Accommodations:* 6 rooms with shared bath. *Pets:* Not permitted. *Driving Instructions:* The guest house is on Route 16, north of the village of North Conway.

## North Sutton, New Hampshire

### FOLLANSBEE INN

North Sutton, NH 03260. 603-927-4221. *Innkeepers:* Larry, Wendy, and Joan Wadman. Open all year except parts of November and April.

Like so many New Hampshire inns, the Follansbee has grown over the years to accommodate an increasing number of overnight guests. The lake-front inn was originally a two-story farmhouse built in the early nineteenth century, and two stories were added in 1928–30. The result is an imposing structure with full lounge and dining facilities. The innkeepers shed earlier careers in the states of Delaware and New Jersey and came to the inn filled with enthusiasm for their new family venture. The inn is popular with cross-country skiers because trails lead right to its door.

The talented young chef prepares a wide variety of dishes, the best known being the "drunken bird" and "pig Bee." Dinner is not served on Monday.

*Accommodations:* 23 rooms, 11 with private bath. *Pets:* Not permitted. *Driving Instructions:* The inn is 4 miles south of New London on Route 114, behind a white church.

## *Portsmouth, New Hampshire*

### INN AT CHRISTIAN SHORE

335 Maplewood Avenue, Portsmouth, New Hampshire. Mailing address: P.O. Box 1474, Portsmouth, NH 03801. 603-431-6770. *Innkeepers:* Charles Litchfield, Louis Sochia, and Thomas Towey. Open all year

Portsmouth, a shipbuilding and fishing community settled in the early seventeenth century, was originally named Strawberry Banke. It had its heyday around 1800, a period that saw the construction of many Federal homes, including the building now known as the Inn at Christian Shore — a name derived from the Christian Shore area.

The guest rooms are furnished in keeping with the period, with a few concessions to guests' comfort, such as wall-to-wall carpeting, air conditioning, and color television in the rooms.

Downstairs, a comfortable sitting room is furnished with period and reproduction Federal furniture. The walls are papered with a bold floral print, and a fireplace is faced by wing chairs and a Sheraton settee. The breakfast room is reminiscent of an early tavern room, with its long center table surrounded by eight bow-back Windsor chairs. Several smaller tables are located around the room's periphery, and a large fireplace dominates this low-ceilinged exposed-beam room. Breakfast includes a variety of traditional foods.

*Accommodations:* 5 rooms, 2 with bath. *Driving Instructions:* Take exit 5 from I-95. At the traffic circle take Route 1 north. Exit by Lum's restaurant. The inn is the sixth house on the left when you are headed downtown.

## THE INN AT STRAWBERRY BANKE

314 Court Street, Portsmouth, NH 03801. 603-436-7242. *Innkeepers:* Mark and Kerrianne Constant. Open all year.

This little bed-and-breakfast inn was built in 1800 for Captain Holbrook. The antiques in its rooms are typical of those made during Portsmouth's early days as a prosperous seaport town. The inn is ideally located just around the corner from the waterfront and Strawberry Banke, Portsmouth's historic restoration. After a day of exploring Strawberry Banke's living museums and the narrow winding streets of this beautiful old seaport with its tiny shops and dockside restaurants, it would seem appropriate to preserve the atmosphere of yesteryear by staying in a house of the same vintage. Complimentary sherry is served in the inn's sitting room, and strawberry sweets (of course) are set out on pillows in the guest rooms. Light breakfasts of fresh fruits, juices, and bread and muffins start the day. Innkeepers Mark and Kerrianne provide bicycles for sightseeing tours and will gladly steer guests to area restaurants, art galleries, and the city's many antique shops.

*Accommodations:* 4 rooms with shared bath. *Pets:* Not permitted.

## PHILBROOK FARM INN

North Road, Shelburne, NH 03581. 603-466-3831. *Innkeepers:*
Nancy Philbrook and Constance P. Leger. Open May 1 to October
31 and December 26 to March 31.

The Philbrook Farm Inn is a typical New Hampshire building that,
like so many others, has expanded gradually over the generations.
The first section was built in 1934, and the Philbrook family has lived
here since 1861. The Philbrooks have always been proud of their
relaxed atmosphere: an inn "filled with peace, quiet and contentment
in a world turned upside down." The Philbrook survives as the only
inn in an area that used to abound with inns. Some guests are now the
fourth and fifth generation from their families to visit Philbrook
Farm.

The inn is furnished with family antiques and with paintings done
by guests, old maps of the area, and Currier and Ives prints. There are
several fireplaces, including ones in the two living rooms and the dining room with its knotty pine paneling. The playroom has table
tennis, a pool table, and a collection of old farm tools and kitchen
things, as well as its own fireplace. Meals are served family-style from
a menu that changes daily. Much of the food served in the summer
months is raised in the inn's garden. Meals generally include a homemade soup followed by a roast meat or poultry, vegetables, potato,
and dessert. On Saturday nights there is a New England baked bean
supper, and Sunday morning breakfast traditionally consists of fish-
balls and corn bread.

The nineteen guest rooms are in the inn's main building and the
Lodge, the Little House, Undercliff, the Casino, and Birch Cliff.
Most of the last are rented by families or larger groups.

*Accommodations:* 19 rooms, 7 with bath. *Pets:* Permitted in
summer cottages only. *Driving Instructions:* The inn is 1½ miles off
Route 2. Look for the direction sign, turn, cross the railroad tracks
and bridge, then turn right at the crossroads and drive for ½ mile.

*Snowville, New Hampshire*

## SNOWVILLAGE LODGE

Foss Mountain Road, Snowville, NH 03849. 603-447-2818. *Innkeepers:* Pat and Ginger Blymer. Open all year.

For many years Pat and Ginger Blymer had careers in filmmaking, he as a lighting designer and she as a hair stylist. In 1977 they realized they longed for a place in the mountains where they could have animals and welcome people as guests coming to relax and renew themselves, just as the Blymers would do. They left Los Angeles and toured New England searching for the country inn of their dreams, and when they drove up the mountain road from Snowville, New Hampshire, they found Snowvillage Lodge, a 1916 summer estate house large enough for themselves and their three daughters.

Today the lodge overflows with dogs, cats, and even a pet pig, who lives in "Gracie's Mansion." Fourteen guest rooms decorated in country New England style are in the main house, over the Swiss chalet–style dining room, and in the Barn. On the inn's covered porch one can sit and view fields, woods, and the White Mountains.

Meals at the Snowvillage Lodge are special occasions. Tables are laid with linen tablecloths and napkins and crystal glasses. From the kitchen come carefully prepared dishes such as veal piccata, chicken Veronique, roast beef with Yorkshire pudding, or coq au vin.

*Accommodations:* 14 rooms with private bath. *Driving Instructions:* From Conway take Route 153 for 5 miles south to the Snowville Road. In Snowville, take Foss Mountain Road to the inn.

## PITCHER MOUNTAIN INN

Stoddard, NH 03464. 603-446-7000. *Innkeepers:* Bill and Dawn Matthews. Open Wednesday through Sunday all year except March to mid-April and three weeks in November.

Stoddard is one of those little New England towns full of historic old homes and laced with country roads and ancient stone walls and fences. Pitcher Mountain Inn is in one such colonial-style building, constructed as a private farmhouse in 1830.

In 1978, Bill and Dawn Matthews were casting about for an appropriate setting for their restaurant when they discovered the old place. They redid it, adding their own antiques and old-fashioned touches. Given the building's rather austere exterior surrounded by terraces and stone walls, visitors are pleasantly surprised by the warmth of the interior. The main dining room, with its open hearth, dark wood paneling, and exposed-beam ceiling, offers views of the large formal garden enclosed by a serpentine stone wall. Here flowers bloom in profusion, with flowery sedums as well as kitchen herbs, edible flowers, and bright perennials. Bill and Dawn use the blooms to enhance many of their dishes. A purple chive flower might float in a homemade soup, or a yellow day lily could spark up a pâté. Among their much acclaimed dishes are chicken Normandy (Gruyère cheese, white wine, and cognac with chicken breasts and chopped apples); swordfish steak with hollandaise sauce; scallops Provençal; or a light calamari (squid) salad. Dawn's specialties are the rich pastries brought out on trays for diners' selection. Brunch is served on Sunday, and lunch is offered from July through the fall foliage season.

The three guest rooms here are small with antique beds and shared bathrooms. All, in keeping with the age of the house, are cool in winter — and the better for sleeping, we say!

*Accommodations:* 3 rooms sharing baths. *Pets and children:* Not permitted. *Driving Instructions:* Take Route 9 east from Keene or west from Hillsboro to Route 123N. The inn is 2 miles in on Route 123 in Stoddard.

## Sugar Hill, New Hampshire

Sugar Hill is quite near all the attractions of the White Mountains region. The town has several antique and gift shops, including The Sugar Hill Sampler, Colonial Cottage Antiques, Harman's Country Store, the Hildrex Maple Sugar Farm, and Miss Lynn and Miss Monahan's, and there are many antique shops in the surrounding countryside. There are country auctions by the dozen in the warm months—several each week. Golf and cross-country skiing are available at the *Sunset Hill House*. Sugar Hill Historic Museum is in the town.

### THE HOMESTEAD

Sugar Hill, NH 03585. 603-823-5564. *Innkeeper:* Esther T. Serafini. Open Memorial Day to November 1, Thanksgiving weekend, and Christmas through April 15.

The Homestead has been in Esther Serafini's family since the Teffts, her grandparents, first opened the old farmhouse to guests in 1880. The original house was built, using hand-hewn beams, in 1802 by Sugar Hill's first settler. Many of the handmade antiques at the Homestead today were brought here in ox-drawn carts by the settlers.

Mrs. Serafini's grandparents enlarged the farmhouse to its present size in 1898. In 1917, the inn's property was expanded again with the addition of the Chalet, built entirely of stones gathered in the surrounding meadows and logs hauled here in horse-drawn sleds.

The Homestead offers seventeen guest rooms—ten in the inn and seven in the other three buildings on the property. The Family Cottage and the Early Family Home are both small farmhouses containing rooms with private baths. They have porches and verandas with views of rolling meadows and the White Mountains. The Chalet can be rented as a unit. It has a 44-foot living room with a cathedral ceiling and an unusual brick-and-fieldstone fireplace. From the balcony porch one can see three mountain ranges. The Chalet also has a kitchen, a dining room, and two bedrooms. It is decorated with antiques, and handmade threshing equipment is displayed on its walls.

All the rooms in the inn are filled with antiques and family memorabilia. The inn has two floors for occupancy, each with five guest rooms and two hall bathrooms. Mrs. Serafini points out that although the rooms are full of antique dressers, lamps, and beds, the mattresses are definitely *not* antique. There are many up-to-date comforts here that in no way detract from the character of the old inn.

Downstairs, the hand-hewn ceiling beams are exposed to view, and there is an entrance hall, a reading room, a Victorian parlor with a fireplace, and the pine-paneled dining room. The cupboards in the dining room are filled with Mrs. Serafini's extensive glass and china collection. Dinners are hearty and a real New England farm treat. Everything is homemade, from the relishes and conserves to the pies, parfaits, and sauces, and there are no steam tables. Breakfasts are the kind grandmother would make. The public may eat here for dinner but only with a reservation. Gentlemen must wear jackets.

*Accommodations:* 17 rooms, 7 with bath. *Pets and children:* Not encouraged. *Driving Instructions:* Sugar Hill is off I-93 (exit 38 coming north or exit 39 coming south).

## Tamworth, New Hampshire

### TAMWORTH INN

Main Street, Tamworth, NH 03886. 603-323-7721. *Innkeepers:*
Larry and Kelly Hubbell. Open all year except late fall.

The Tamworth was first constructed in 1830, with additions made
from 1870 through 1900; it has been an inn since 1888. It has a pub
room with entertainment on weekends. The pub and the living room
both have working fireplaces and many antiques. The Tamworth has
its own pool, and there is excellent trout fishing in the stream behind
the inn. This is a fine base for using the many cross-country skiing
trails nearby. A summer stock theater is in the nearby town.

The inn's menu features a variety of items ranging from seafood
through teriyaki to barbecued ribs. In summer, guests may have
luncheon and cocktails on the outdoor patio.

*Accommodations:* 21 rooms, 10 with private bath. *Pets:* Not permitted. *Driving Instructions:* Take Route I-93 to exit 23, Route 104
East to Route 3, Route 3 a short distance to Route 25, then drive
northeast to Whittier and Route 113, which runs north to Tamworth.

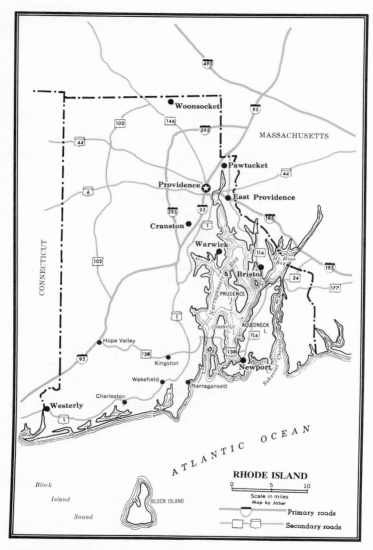

# Rhode Island

## *Block Island, Rhode Island*

### HOTEL MANISSES

Spring Street, Block Island, RI 02807. 401-466-2836 or 466-2421. *Innkeepers:* Joan and Justin Abrams. Open Easter through January 1.

The Manisses, the showplace of Block Island when it opened in 1872, has entered its second century with a flourish — restored, renovated, and refurnished in Victorian splendor. The Abramses spared no effort getting the Manisses ready to receive guests once again. Its guest rooms are decorated with authentic Victorian hotel furnishings against the period wallpapers. With a bow to the comforts of the 1980s, the rooms have private baths; some even have Jacuzzis. The parlors glow with light from splendid stained-glass windows. Old-fashioned flower gardens can be seen from the windows here. High tea with sweets and savories is served in the afternoons at the hotel, where the Victorian atmosphere is enhanced by the authentic costumes worn by the staff. Included in the room rates are a mini-buffet breakfast, and wine and hors d'oeuvres at cocktail hour.

*Accommodations:* 18 rooms with private bath. *Pets:* Not permitted. *Driving Instructions:* Block Island may be reached by ferry from Point Judith, Rhode Island, or New London, Connecticut.

### Newport, Rhode Island

## ADMIRAL BENBOW INN

93 Pelham Street, Newport, RI 02840. 401-846-4256. *Innkeeper:* Jane McKenna. Open all year.

The Admiral Benbow, in the Historic Hill section of Newport, was built in 1855 by Augustus Littlefield, a mariner, and has been an inn ever since. Its freshly painted exterior is noteworthy for its tall, wide Romanesque windows. In restoring the Admiral Benbow, authentic Victorian colors and wallpapers were chosen. Following guidelines for historic preservation, the inn's exterior lines were not changed, but a number of private baths were tucked into guest rooms. All guest rooms have brass beds, except room 9, which has a canopied four-poster. All are furnished with a mixture of period reproduction pieces and antiques. Room 12, on the third floor, has its own deck and commands a fine view of the harbor.

In the morning a continental breakfast is served that includes hot muffins and pastries, English jams, and beverages. The breakfast area is open all day, with hot coffee and tea available for guests. The inn offers off-street parking and is within walking distance of Bellevue Avenue and the bustling wharf area.

*Accommodations:* 15 rooms with private bath. *Pets:* Not permitted. *Children:* Cots, cribs, and special facilities not available. *Driving Instructions:* The inn is one block from Bellevue Avenue and two blocks from the wharf.

## INN AT CASTLE HILL

Ocean Drive, Newport, RI 02840. 401-849-3800. *Innkeeper:* Paul McEnroe. Open all year for rooms with Continental breakfast. The dining room has a reduced schedule in spring and fall and is closed from January until just before Easter. Inquire first.

In 1874, Alexander Agassiz, son of the naturalist Louis Agassiz, built a fine summer home that would serve as a base for his studies in marine biology. The Woods Hole Marine Biological Laboratory eventually assumed the function of the Agassiz laboratory, and the property was later purchased by the O'Connell family, who still own it today. During World War II a local real estate agent persuaded Mr. O'Connell to rent rooms to young naval officers who could not find lodgings in crowded Newport. From that time the building's operation as an inn developed gradually. A public restaurant was added in 1950, and a separate shingled building added six rooms a few years later. In the mid-1970s the inn was leased to Paul McEnroe, who redecorated all the rooms extensively. The result is one of the most attractive inns in New England.

The guest rooms, as well as the public rooms, have a refined country atmosphere. The flavor varies from print wallpapers and white wicker to the warmth of polished wood paneling. Besides the main inn, there are nineteen beach cottages, each with its own kitchen, which are rented by the week in the summer season. The shingled Harbour House, with more guest rooms, has been done in floral prints. Its porch is at the top of the cliff. A stairway leads down to a secluded bathing cove the family likes to call "Grace Kelly Beach." The stairs were built when the actress was a guest at the inn, to provide more privacy for her here than at the hotel's large sandy beach.

The dining rooms of the inn, among the area's finest, offer a wide

sampling of Continental fare augmented by a selection of local seafood. Service is formal and luxurious — appropriate to the Newport setting. Among the offerings are crabmeat baked in puff pastry, sautéed trout with caviar, veal française, rack of lamb, breast of duck sautéed with peppercorns, and Grand Marnier soufflé.

*Accommodations:* 10 rooms in the inn, 7 with bath. Rooms also in Harbour House and 19 cottages. *Pets:* Not permitted. *Driving Instructions:* From downtown Newport, follow all signs to Ocean Drive.

# QUEEN ANNE INN

16 Clarke Street, Newport, RI 02840. 401-846-5676. *Innkeeper:* Peg McCabe. Open all year.

The Queen Anne Inn is a pretty Victorian town house in the heart of Newport's most historic district. The location is ideal for walking tours of the city; the inn is surrounded by tiny old Colonial houses and is just a short walk from the restored wharf area, with its many boutiques, antique shops, and waterfront restaurants. Built in 1890, the Queen Anne has a cheerful elegance, from its rose-and-pink Victorian exterior, through its oaken door with delicate flowers etched in its glass panes, to the bouquets of fresh flowers everywhere. When we were there, flowers adorned the staircase landings and were even placed on the washstands in the immaculate hall bathrooms. Innkeeper Peg McCabe has obviously had fun restoring and decorating her inn. The hardwood floors glisten with polish, and fresh floral wallpapers brighten the rooms and halls. The guest rooms are furnished with antiques and some newer pieces. Several rooms have large bay windows; one has heavy Victorian furnishings including a large armoire. Another has a quilt-topped four-poster.

Mornings find guests plotting the day's adventures in the parlor, where Peg puts out baskets of breads and sweet biscuits accompanied by pots of jam and butter, as well as coffee and tea, on the antique sideboard. Across the hall is a nook lit by a gem of a stained-glass window all lacy with pinks, blues, and greens. The Queen Anne has another bonus — off-street parking, quite a boon in this town of narrow side streets.

*Accommodations:* 12 rooms with 6 shared baths. *Pets:* Not permitted. *Driving Instructions:* Take the ramp from the Newport Bridge. Turn right on Farewell Street to Thames Street. Drive to Washington Square and Touro Street. Turn left on Touro, and take the first right onto Clarke Street.

## SHELTER HARBOR INN

Post Road, Shelter Harbor, Westerly, RI 02891. 401-322-8883. *Innkeepers:* Jim and Debbye Dey. Open all year.

Shelter Harbor Inn is set well back from the road, fronted by a large, grassy field. The inn was built as a farmhouse in the early nineteenth century and was converted to an inn in 1911. In 1978, innkeeper Jim Dey completed the conversion of the farm's barn into the inn annex with ten double rooms with baths, a large living room, and a redwood deck overlooking a secluded wooded area. The eight guest rooms in the old farmhouse are decorated with print wallpapers and old-fashioned country furnishings appropriate to the setting. Guests may use the inn's library.

The fields around the inn are filled with wild roses and blueberry and Juneberry bushes. Guests may use the inn's Sailfish and its private sandy beach, a short drive away.

Meals are served in the dining room, with its exposed beams, and in the sun parlor. The restaurant is open to the public for breakfast and dinner, which features traditional New England fare, including such specialties as finnan haddie, Rhode Island's ubiquitous johnny-cake, and stuffed flounder.

*Accommodations:* 18 rooms with private bath. *Driving Instructions:* The inn is 5 miles east of Westerly, on Route 1.

# Vermont

## ARLINGTON INN

Arlington, VT 05250, 802-375-6532. *Innkeeper:* Ron Brunk. Open all year, except first three weeks of November.

If you haven't been to the Arlington Inn in a few years, you are in for a real treat. This stately 1848 mansion has been renovated from stem to stern. Its long rows of columns and black shutters were given fresh coats of paint, and the interior woodwork was stripped and refinished to show off the no-expense-spared craftsmanship of the trim, stairways, wainscoting, and doors. The foyer sets the Victorian mood with potted plants, Oriental rugs, period antiques of walnut and mahoganies, and dark woodwork everywhere, even on the ceiling. The thirteen guest rooms are individually decorated in an authentic manner with heavy, dark carved wooden bedroom pieces set off by wallpapers of deep colors with miniature floral prints.

The dining rooms and the Deming Tavern downstairs—very popular spots with tourists, guests, and townsfolk—also feature Victorian pieces. The walls, decorated with Norman Rockwell prints, and the tables, attractively set with fresh linens and candles, blend to create a casually gracious feeling. Dinners feature a number of hot and cold appetizers, such as oysters Rockefeller, fettucine a' la Panna, or smoked salmon. Soups include cucumber and red onion or

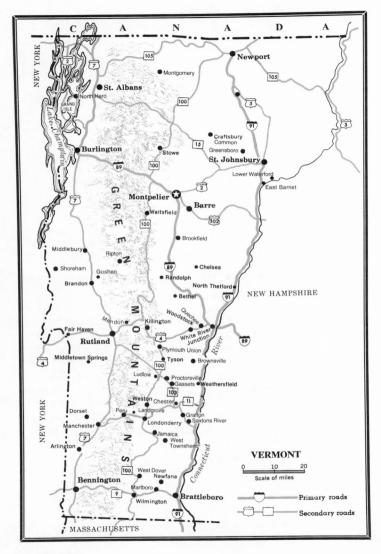

gazpacho, and among the salads are mushrooms and spinach or the Middle Eastern tabulee. Entrées are primarily steaks and chops from the grill, several fresh seafoods, and usually a vegetarian dish or two.

Guests enjoy exploring the inn, its well-maintained grounds, and even the ancient graveyard across the street. The front porch contains two of the largest rocking chairs we have ever seen. Guests who love the supernatural will be happy to learn that the Arlington has its own resident ghost, a fellow named Sylvester Deming. We've been assured that he is not troublesome and happens to be quite fond of children. Sylvester was the father of Martin Deming, "scion of a rich local family," who built the Arlington in 1848 for his family. Dad was so upset by the mansion's cost ($4,800) and ostentation that he tried unsuccessfully to destroy it. Sylvester died just after its completion, but his somewhat disgruntled spirit remains. He appears now and then and does nothing more than float about.

*Accommodations:* 13 rooms with bath. *Pets:* Permitted only in the cottage units on the property. *Driving Instructions:* The inn is on Route 7 in Arlington.

## WEST MOUNTAIN INN

Arlington, Vermont 05250. 802-375-6516. *Innkeepers:* Wes and Mary Ann Carlson. Open all year.

The West Mountain Inn, on a hill with spectacular views of the Battenkill River and the Green Mountains, is surrounded by 150 acres of woodland, meadow, and a spring-fed pond. It was originally a smaller farmhouse built in the late nineteenth century. During the 1920s, an affluent Texas couple enlarged the building for their summer home. They peaked the roof to form seven gables, built the spacious barn for their horses, and planted more than fifty species of evergreens, which along with maples, tower above the inn today. One of the barns is now a stoneware potter's studio.

On the main floor are the living area, plant room, lounge, and dining room. Meals are served by candlelight before an open hearth and feature New England country cuisine. After dinner, guests often gather to play backgammon or Scrabble, sing songs around the piano, or curl up with books.

The bedrooms upstairs are individually decorated with authentic antiques, Colonial-style furniture, and homemade quilts. A bowl of fresh fruit is placed in each room. The African violet in each room is a gift from the innkeepers and may be taken home.

There are miles of wooded trails for hiking and quiet country roads for cycling. The Battenkill provides fly-fishing, swimming, and canoeing. In winter the estate offers wilderness cross-country skiing, as well as tobogganing and snowshoeing.

*Accommodations:* 12 rooms, 5 with private bath. *Pets:* Not permitted. *Driving Instructions:* The inn is ½ mile west of Arlington on Route 313.

*Bethel, Vermont*

## GREENHURST INN

Bethel, VT 05032. 803-234-9747. *Innkeepers:* Lyle and Barbara Wolf. Open all year.

Greenhurst is a turreted, many-gabled mansion built in 1891 as a private summer home for a wealthy Philadelphia family. Much of its original elegance remains, including chandeliers hanging from high ceilings and eight fireplaces, four of which are in guest rooms. Each has Italian tilework around the hearth and beveled mirrors.

The inn, on 5 landscaped acres on the White River, is surrounded by old lilacs and hydrangeas. After a day of antiquing or seasonal recreation (the inn is quite near six major ski areas and Silver Lake), it is a pleasure to curl up by the fire with a good book from the Wolfs' library of more than three thousand volumes or join in songs after dinner around the piano. Continental breakfast is included in the room rates, and the Wolfs offer special evening meals for house-guests, who are welcome to help with the menu planning.

*Accommodations:* 9 rooms, 2 with private bath. *Driving Instructions:* Take Route 12 for ½ mile south from Bethel.

## CHURCHILL HOUSE INN

Route 73 East, Brandon, Vermont. Mailing address: RFD 3, Brandon, VT 05733. 802-247-3300. *Innkeepers:* Michael and Marion Shonstrom. Open all year except April 1 through May 15 and November 1 through December 15.

The Churchill House is a three-story farmhouse built in 1871 by the Churchill family from local lumber. Mike and Marion Shonstrom have furnished the house with a large collection of antiques supplemented by a few contemporary furnishings. There are high bedsteads of maple, oak, and cast iron; commodes; and blanket chests.

Food here is the product of the hard work of Marion, who loves provincial cooking, be it Vermont style or with a Continental flare.

The inn has several special package plans that will appeal to travelers in every season. It offers in the spring, early summer, and fall a special series of fly-fishing programs. Because the inn is on the Neshobe River and has easy access to local beaver ponds, lakes, and other rivers, it has become a gathering place for fly fishermen. Local guides are available for interested guests. The inn offers canoe rentals and a shuttle service for canoers on Otter Creek. Bicyclists will enjoy the variety of bicycle tours organized by this inn, which include evening stops at several inns. Also popular is a similar "hike inn to inn" program.

The Churchill House Inn maintains a complete ski-touring center with 22 miles of cross-country trails, as well as a ski shop with rentals, instruction, and guided tours available.

*Accommodations:* 8 rooms, 6 with private bath. *Driving Instructions:* Take Route 7 to Brandon, then Route 73 east to the inn.

## Brookfield, Vermont

### GREEN TRAILS COUNTRY INN

By the Floating Bridge, Brookfield, VT 05036. 802-276-3412. *Innkeeper:* Joyce Butler. Open all year except April.

The Green Trails Country Inn is in an 1840 farmhouse with a recently opened lodge adjacent to it. Green Trails is in the historic Vermont village of Brookfield near a floating bridge that dates from 1820. Guest rooms here are furnished with a combination of Victorian and early-American antiques. Many winter guests use the inn as a base for enjoying the cross-country skiing trails that originate there, as well as the downhill areas in central Vermont. Summer visitors may swim and fish in Sunset Lake, relax at the private beach owned by the inn, and also enjoy hiking. The Fork Shop Restaurant, which is open to the public, is decorated with antique forks, rakes, and tools, and there is a working player piano in the lounge.

*Accommodations:* 10 rooms in the inn, plus 5 in the lodge. *Pets:* Not permitted. *Driving Instructions:* Bearing right at the fork on Route 66, follow Route 14 north for 6 miles to East Brookfield, then follow the sign to Floating Bridge and Green Trails (2 miles up to the Brookfield State Highway from Route 14).

## THE INN AT MT. ASCUTNEY

Brook Road, Brownsville, VT 05037. 802-484-7725. *Innkeepers:* Eric and Margaret Rothchild. Open all year except April and November.

This 180-year-old farmhouse-turned-inn looks out from the top of its own mountain across the valley to Mount Ascutney and its ski area. The scenic vistas are outstanding at any time of the year, and in winter the ski slopes are lit up at night, creating a light show. The living room takes full advantage of this with a picture window offering the best of two worlds on chilly days — excellent views and a fire in the fireplace.

In the original section of the house there is a dining room with wide pumpkin-pine floorboards and harvest tables. A sitting area just off this room also has a fire in the hearth. The old farm kitchen has been transformed into a private dining room filled with English antiques. The inn's new kitchen has become part of the decor of the public dining room. Here one can watch Margaret prepare her dishes. We watched her assembling a Chocolate Ascutney, a house specialty and not to be missed. Margaret, a graduate of the Cordon Bleu school, is an accomplished chef, offering a Continental menu that might include shrimp Florentine, Persian lamb, or sole stuffed with salmon mousse. Eric has a fine selection of wines to complement the meals. Breakfasts are served to guests only. The morning room has a wraparound view, and where the windows end, colorful wallpapers begin.

Guest rooms at the inn have their own special personalities. One features sloping eaves, exposed beams, and rose prints and trim; another has lovely quilts, and another room, bright calicos. The country pond on the property is well stocked with trout, and guests enjoy swimming there in summer and skating in winter. The mountain affords excellent hiking and, with the winter snows, cross-country and downhill skiing.

*Accommodations:* 8 rooms. *Driving Instructions:* Take Route 44 to Brownsville. From Brownsville, take Brook Road to the inn.

## Chelsea, Vermont

### SHIRE INN

Main Street, P.O. Box 82, Chelsea, VT 05038. 802-685-3031. *Innkeeper:* Fred Sisser. Open all year.

Shire Inn is a striking brick Federal home built in 1832 and surrounded by 36 acres of peaceful Vermont land in a village of 600 people. The first branch of the White River flows through the property, which has its own private fishing bridge. The forest and back fields are ideal for cross-country skiing and hiking. One is immediately taken with the inn's "sunburst" doorway set back behind a tidy picket fence.

Inside, the original woodwork and old brass hardware are still in place after a century and a half. Wide spruce floorboards are set off by Oriental carpets. Throughout, the rooms are furnished with period antiques, many a legacy from earlier owners. A writing desk still stands in the hall, where it has been since 1866, and a spiral staircase leads to the guest rooms above. Four bedrooms have working fireplaces; two have four-poster beds; and one room has a canopied bed built in 1826 for one of Fred Sisser's ancestors. For houseguests, Fred provides breakfasts and dinners that stress regional produce.

*Accommodations:* 6 rooms, 3 with private bath. *Pets:* Not permitted. *Driving Instructions:* Take Route 110 to the center of Chelsea.

## CRANBERRY INN

Route 11, Chester, VT 05143. 802-875-2525. *Innkeepers:* Barbara and Michael Yusko. Open all year.

The Cranberry Inn is a New England colonial farmhouse set behind stately pines. Built in 1810, it is one of Chester's oldest brick homes. The front porch overlooks the fields across the road and houses a collection of creaky rocking chairs and an old-fashioned porch swing. The farmhouse is attached to the big red barn by an addition that contains the entrance hall and desk under an extremely low beamed ceiling. Upstairs the wing contains one of Barbara Yusko's favorite bedrooms with nooks and crannies and a dormer flanked by rough exposed logs, bark and all. The room is papered with a deep blue calico print providing a backdrop for the exposed woods and brass bed. The ten guest rooms retain the period look with antique furnishings, exposed beams, rolling wide-plank pumpkin-pine floors, and low ceilings. Many of the beds are sturdy pine four-posters or brass and iron. Four of the rooms have fireplaces that are not used for safety's sake but certainly add to the romance of the country inn, as do the sloping eaves, print wallpapers, and scenic views of the hills and fields from the windows.

The centerpiece of the living room is the fieldstone fireplace, which is always lit when the weather is chilly. In back of the house are the dining room and sun porch with views of the stone walls and back field. Breakfasts and dinners are served to guests only. House specialties include veal, steaks, and chicken cordon bleu. The home-made apple desserts are especially popular. The inn is just minutes from eight of Vermont's major ski areas and many other recreational offerings, such as hiking, horseback riding, and fishing and rafting in mountain streams. It is part of the "Cycle Inn Vermont" tour for intermediate to experienced cyclists.

*Accommodations:* 10 rooms, 4 with bath. *Pets:* Not permitted. *Driving Instructions:* The inn is a mile west of the green in Chester, on Route 11.

## *Craftsbury, Vermont*

**CRAFTSBURY INN**

Craftsbury, VT 05826. 802-586-2848. *Innkeepers:* John and Susan McCarthy. Open all year except April and November.

The Craftsbury Inn is a handsome columned inn that was built as a private home about 1850 by Amasa Scott for his family. Scott spared no expense building a sturdy house that would stand the test of time well. He proudly installed one of the first central heating systems in the region.

One of the great joys of visiting this inn derives from its abundance of original, lovingly cared-for woodwork. Its tones have mellowed with the patina of the years, having been spared the coats of paint that so often were applied in other buildings. There are numerous built-in cabinets, handsome door and window trims, and random-width spruce floors.

Upstairs are nine guest rooms, of which two have full and two have half bathrooms. The rooms have an old-fashioned look, with Colonial wallpapers, flowers, hand-made quilts, and antique touches such as old wicker. Rooms in the front of the inn are sunny, overlooking the roofs of the houses and stores of the tiny Vermont village.

In summer, when the main dining room is in full operation, it is festooned with hanging plants. Picture windows overlook the gardens, which are illuminated at night. Every table is set with white linen and a bouquet of fresh flowers from the gardens. All food served at the inn is made from scratch and finished to order. Steak au poivre, coquilles Saint-Jacques, veal Marsala, and desserts such as chocolate mousse, crème caramel, and ice creams made at the inn are among the specialties.

*Accommodations:* 9 rooms, 2 with private bath. *Pets:* If small, permitted after advance arrangements. *Children:* Under 12 not permitted. *Driving Instructions:* Take Route 14 north of Hardwick for 7 miles to the turnoff for Craftsbury. Take the Craftsbury Road 2 miles to the town. The inn is on the main street, across from the general store.

## Craftsbury Common, Vermont

## THE INN ON THE COMMON

Main Street, Craftsbury Common, VT 05827. 802-586-9619.
*Innkeepers:* Penny and Michael Schmitt. Open all year.

The Inn on the Common consists of two restored Federal buildings (originally a private house and a cabinet and sleigh shop, respectively), currently filled with a mixture of antiques and contemporary furniture. The Schmitts take great pride in their antiques, many of which are heirlooms, and in the extensive art work on the walls. Several of the inn's luxurious guest rooms have working fireplaces. All are individually decorated with quilts, print wallpapers, and antiques. Two of the most popular bedrooms are in the annex and have Jotul wood-burning stoves, exposed beams, and bold colors contrasting with a Victorian loveseat and a brick hearth. A sitting room full of antiques contains the inn's sole television set. Some of the guest rooms share hall bathrooms, of which there are several; but, for the sake of privacy, the Schmitts provide terry robes.

Guests eat together at three large tables under the watchful eyes of ancestral portraits. The menu reflects the Schmitts' travels in France and Italy. Meals feature vegetables and herbs grown in the inn's gardens and at the Schmitts' farm nearby. The inn has its own crafts shop, The Uncommon Market, where you can purchase colorful quilts.

Behind the main house are the lighted formal rose garden and a herb garden, as well as an English-style croquet court, a bocce court, a clay tennis court, and a solar-heated swimming pool disguised as a pond. The Schmitts are affiliated with the nearby Craftsbury Sports Center, where cross-country skiing is available on 50 miles of trails. Big Hosmer Pond offers boating and lake swimming in summer and skating in winter.

*Accommodations:* 16 rooms — 6 with private bath, 10 sharing 5 baths. *Driving Instructions:* Take Route 14 from the Montpelier-Barre area north to the village of Craftsbury Common. The inn is on the hill before the common.

*Dorset, Vermont*

## BARROWS HOUSE

Dorset, VT 05251. 802-867-4455. *Innkeepers:* Charles and Marilyn Schubert. Open all year except November 1 through December 10. Barrows House is actually a collection of buildings in the center of Dorset. The inn's property includes a number of early buildings carefully renovated and redecorated by the Schuberts and offering a variety of accommodations, from singles to arrangements for large families. Ten of the guest rooms are in Barrows House, with the remainder in the other buildings. Larger families can stay in Truffle House, where they can share three twin-bedded rooms and a common living room with a fireplace. The Stable has rooms with exposed beams and is the most expensive lodging at the inn. Most rooms have wall-to-wall carpeting, and many have coordinated drapes, quilts, and wallpaper. There are two new dormered suites.

Popular dinner entrées here are filet of beef, steak marchand de vin, scrod Florentine, and veal scallops with mustard cream.

Recreational facilities at Barrows House are excellent. Many cross-country skiers start right at the door (rentals are available at the inn's cross-country ski shop), and the inn has its own swimming pool, tennis courts, and sauna. There is a gazebo for relaxing.

*Accommodations:* 29 rooms, 27 with private bath. *Pets:* Not permitted. *Driving Instructions:* From Route 7 in Vermont, take Route 30 northeast to Dorset.

## DORSET INN

Church and Main streets, Dorset, Vermont. Mailing address: Box 8, Dorset, VT 05251. 802-867-5500. *Innkeeper:* Fred G. Russell. Open late May to October and late December to late March.

The Dorset Inn was built in two sections. The first section, dating from 1796, makes it the oldest inn in the state; the second, built in 1850, now houses the living room and dining room. The inn is characterized by old-fashioned decorations as well as wide-board floors and four-poster beds, antiques, and more recent solid country furniture. Most of the fifty-five rooms have been renovated to include private baths, although some still share baths.

The inn has a swimming pool and is within walking distance of the Dorset Field Club. Cookouts are held every Wednesday evening in the warmer months. The dining room has an intimate feeling with its papered walls and simple curtained windows. Meals are described as "authentic New England menus, prepared to delicious Yankee perfection." The dinner menu is kept small and includes four or five simple selections, such as steak, chicken, or haddock. Appetizer, salad, and dessert are included in the dinner price.

*Accommodations:* 55 rooms, 41 with bath. *Driving Instructions:* From Route 7, just north of Manchester, take Route 30 into Dorset.

# THE LITTLE LODGE AT DORSET

Route 30, Dorset, VT 05251. 802-869-4040. *Innkeepers:* Allan and Nancy Norris. Open all year except for short spring and fall vacations.

This bed-and-breakfast country inn stands on a hillside overlooking its own trout pond. The building's white clapboarding stands out sharply against the greens of the pines on the wooded mountainside behind it. Twelve-over-twelve windows are topped by second-story "belly" windows, so named because one has to lie on one's belly to look out of them.

The Norrises opened their inn in 1981, and their enjoyment of this new venture is clearly evident from the friendly and relaxed informality here. The guest rooms, with wide-board pine floors, are decorated with patchwork quilts and lots of calico. Beds are turned down at night and little mints placed on each pillow.

A barnboard den has a bring-your-own-bottle wet bar, a fireplace, and wonderful mountain views through the picture windows. Breakfast is served in the formal dining room or out on the sunporch. Everyone eats together family style and plots the day's adventures. There is much to do right here, with ice skating and cross-country skiing on the grounds and a golf course across the street. Downhill skiing is nearby, and the Norrises will be happy to steer guests to a variety of restaurants in the area.

*Accommodations:* 5 rooms, 3 with private bath. *Pets:* Rarely permitted. *Driving Instructions:* Take Route 30 to Dorset. The inn is the sixth house north of the village green.

## VILLAGE AUBERGE

Route 30, Dorset, Vermont. Mailing address: RD 1, Box 53, Dorset, VT 05251. 802-867-5715. *Innkeeper:* Alex Koks. Open May 15 through November 15 and December 15 through April 15. Village Auberge is an old clapboard Vermont farmhouse with a full-fledged European restaurant complete with formal table settings and a menu interesting and extravagant enough for the fussiest gourmet. Chef-owner Alex Koks is from Holland, where he trained at a hotel school in The Hague and operated several restaurants before coming to Vermont. The dining room is decorated with distinction, as is the rest of the house, thanks to Hanneke Koks's training as an interior decorator and fashion designer. The dining room with its large bay window can seat about fifty guests. A small sampling from a regularly

changing menu includes cold lobster and white asparagus with mayonnaise, sweetbreads Village Auberge, beef Wellington, sirloin flambéed with Calvados, veal sautéed with morels, and sole en papillote. Popular starters are quenelles with lobster sauce, crab claws in cocktail sauce, herring in mustard cream, and a terrine de campagne. For dessert, Alex often prepares baba au rhum and crème caramel. Just off the dining room is an intimate cocktail lounge papered with antique newspapers found in a forgotten corner of the attic.

The six guest rooms are individually done with miniature-print wallpapers and comfortable antique and contemporary furnishings. Each has its own private bath. Downstairs, the sitting room has a fireplace and lots of reading material, including magazines and books from Holland. The inn's lawns are shaded by maples, and there is an old-fashioned porch to relax on and view the Vermont scenery. Out back, by the kitchen door, is a very European herb garden. Hanneke operates a small antique shop in one of the outbuildings here.

Village Auberge is ideally located in the heart of southern Vermont. It is minutes away from the Dorset Playhouse, tennis courts, golf, and swimming. In winter three large ski areas, Bromley, Stratton, and Magic Mountain, are a short drive away, and cross-country skiing is available very near to the inn.

*Accommodations:* 6 rooms with bath. *Driving Instructions:* The inn is 6 miles north of Manchester on Route 30.

## INWOOD MANOR

Route 5, East Barnet, VT 05821. 802-633-4047. *Innkeepers:* Peter J. Embarrato and Ron Kaczor. Open all year.

Near a Vermont waterfall are the remains of the foundation of what was once a croquet-equipment factory. To provide housing for workers in the factory the main house at Inwood Manor was constructed in 1925. The innkeepers' living quarters are in a second building on the property, dating from 1840 and once a stagecoach stop.

At Inwood Manor many of the decorative pieces and much of the furniture are what innkeepers Peter and Ron like to call "early attic." The building's attic was, in fact, crammed with furniture from many periods, and they gradually repaired and refurbished these pieces and created a number of pleasing guest rooms. By grouping different kinds of furniture, they have been able to name their rooms after the dominant decorative features. Thus there are a Maple Room, a Pine Room, and even a Feudal Room. The last has a number of handsome oaken and bird's-eye maple pieces. Bouquets of dried local wildflowers are used skillfully throughout the inn.

Dinner is served in the same spirit of informal elegance, with candlelight and Baroque music setting the mood for each Continental-style supper. One entrée is served each evening. Typical offerings include manicotti Bolognese, pork chops with cannelini beans and fresh escarole, or beef rollatine stuffed with garlic, eggs, cheese, and raisins.

Inwood Manor is on about 20 acres of plateau overlooking the Passumpsic River on two sides, waterfalls, and the tiny town of East Barnet. The inn has a hiking trail that takes you to the highest point overlooking the falls. The Connecticut River is nearby, and Inwood Manor is part of a "canoe inn to inn" program.

*Accommodations:* 9 rooms with shared baths. *Pets and children:* Call first. *Driving Instructions:* Inwood Manor is 5 miles south of Saint Johnsbury on Route 5.

## Fair Haven, Vermont

## VICTORIAN MARBLE INN

12 West Park Place, Fair Haven, VT 05743. 802-265-4736. *Innkeepers:* Sue Cooper and Jan Jones. Open all year.

In 1867, Ira C. Allen built a mansard-roofed home faced with yellow marble hewn in Proctor, Vermont. The inn's exterior is made even more distinctive by the sets of paired columns that wrap around two sides of the inn. The Victorian Marble Inn, which faces the village green, is surrounded by 5 acres of grounds including stately trees, gardens, stone walls, and the river.

Both the public and guest rooms have been meticulously restored using warm colors and an eclectic blend of antique and occasional modern pieces. There are seven working carved marble fireplaces, including three in guest rooms. The wicker breakfast room is light, with plants in every corner. The dining room has a gold ceiling, and the candle and firelight is reflected in dark wooden floors. Light suppers, available with advance notice, include homemade soup, a simple entrée, salad, bread, and dessert. Main-dish specialties include Vermont cheddar soufflé and spinach and sausage quiche.

The inn's guest rooms have brass and iron or high-backed wooden beds, antique quilts and crocheted coverlets, and rocking or easy chairs. Also on the grounds is a brick and slate carriage house, which serves in warmer months as a gallery of antiques and crafts.

*Accommodations:* 8 rooms with shared baths. *Driving Instructions:* Take Route 4 to Route 22A and drive south 1½ miles.

## Gassetts, Vermont

## THE OLDE TOWNE FARM LODGE

Route 10, Gassetts, Vermont. Mailing address: RD 4, Chester, VT 05143. 802-875-2346. *Innkeepers:* Fred and Jan Baldwin and family. Open all year except Thanksgiving and Christmas.

This large white farmhouse is noted for a handmade spiral staircase, a testimony to early craftsmanship. There are wide-board floors throughout, and the rooms are partially furnished with antiques.

The farm was built more than a century ago as the Chester Towne Farm. The indigent of the town were given food and lodging in return for a hard day's work there. A new brick patio overlooks the inn's spring-fed pond, which guests use for swimming, fishing, and winter ice skating.

The lodge is heated by a wood furnace whose fragrant smoke greets travelers during the winter. Meals at this inn vary from traditional Yankee-style to gourmet, featuring Jan's Roast Royale, Ham al Vermont, breast of chicken with cranberry glaze, quiches, and colonial desserts. In summer, Fred's garden provides spinach and lettuce and tomatoes for the salads.

*Accommodations:* 10 rooms, 2 with private bath. *Pets:* Not permitted. *Driving Instructions:* Take Route 103 north through Chester to Route 10. Turn east on Route 10 and drive ½ mile to the inn.

## Goshen, Vermont

### BLUEBERRY HILL

Goshen, VT 05733. 802-247-6735. *Innkeepers:* Tony and Martha Clark. Open December through March and May through October. Many people first find Blueberry Hill during the ski season; for it is as a cross-country ski center that the inn has gained most of its fame. Thirty miles of groomed trails, a complete retail and rental ski shop, and an expert staff keep the inn's guest rooms full all winter. Each of these rooms is fitted out with numerous antiques and with homemade quilts. At almost any time of day during the ski season, Martha Clark keeps her soup pot boiling. By evening the inn fills with the tantalizing aroma of a dinner that might center around a dish such as beef Bourguignon, roast pork, or chicken cordon bleu. Breakfast is often served in the inn's greenhouse.

During the skiing season, the Clarks organize waxing clinics, ski seminars, picnic tours, night tours, and inn-to-inn ski tours and participate in the Bill Koch Races and the American Hennessy Marathon. In the warmer months, the inn continues to welcome guests who appreciate the quiet of its mid-Vermont location.

*Accommodations:* 8 rooms with private bath. *Pets:* Not permitted. *Driving Instructions:* Take Route 73 east of Brandon, and follow signs to the inn, north of Route 73.

*Grafton, Vermont*

## THE OLD TAVERN AT GRAFTON

Grafton, VT 05146. 802-843-2231. *Innkeeper:* Lois Copping.
Open all year except Christmas Eve, Christmas Day, and April.
The Old Tavern at Grafton is by far the most impressive piece of restoration as yet performed by the craftsmen at the disposal of the Windham Foundation. The Old Tavern, an imposing, shuttered, brick-and-clapboard white building, is distinguished by its seven two-story columns. The main inn, noted for its fine paneling, pumpkin-pine floors, and collection of antiques, is joined by a breezeway to the original barn, which now serves as the lounge for the inn's guests. Its exposed beams and ample use of board paneling give the barn a warm feeling.

The Old Tavern is our candidate for the most perfectly re-created inn in the northeast. Here no detail has been overlooked. This feeling of perfection, of every panel perfectly painted, of every piece of furniture perfectly placed, gives the inn a formality that would not appeal to those seeking the casual atmosphere of some Vermont inns. This is no feet-on-a-stool-in-front-of-the-fire inn, nor does it intend to be. This is an inn that makes few mistakes.

The Old Tavern has thirty-five guest rooms, all with private bath.

Of these, fourteen are in the Old Tavern building, and the remainder are in an assemblage of two old houses and a barn directly across the street. Known as The Homestead and The Windham Cottage, this complex also has function rooms that host meetings of business groups from all over New England. Each guest room has a collection of antiques including canopied or four-poster beds, interesting rugs, and comfortable furniture.

The inn has a natural swimming pond, tennis courts, and indoor-games rooms. There are well-marked hiking trails and, nearby, horseback riding and golf. Several miles of cross-country ski trails are maintained by the inn, and they can provide snowshoes, sleds, and toboggans for winter guests. Lunch and dinner are served at the inn for guests and the public, and breakfast is served for guests only. The menu has surprises like cold blueberry soup or cheese-and-bacon pie to augment some of its more standard items.

Woodrow Wilson, Theodore Roosevelt, General Ulysses Grant, Henry David Thoreau, Oliver Wendell Holmes, and Rudyard Kipling have all stayed at the Old Tavern. This is an extraordinarily well-thought-out inn for those guests who enjoy the ambience of this very special place. The secret is long since out, so plan to make reservations early. Families with children and pets are placed in one of several guest houses maintained by the Old Tavern.

*Accommodations:* 35 rooms and 5 guest houses, all with bath. *Pets and children:* Permitted in guest houses only. *Driving Instructions:* Take Route I-91 to exit 5, then Route 121 to Grafton.

## WOODCHUCK HILL FARM

Middletown Road, Grafton, VT 05146. 802-843-2398. *Innkeepers:* Anne and Frank Gabriel. Open May through October.

Woodchuck Hill Farm is the oldest house in Grafton, built about 1780. Originally built for the town's first minister, the inn has been completely restored. During the 1930s, a porch and other additions were built. On a hilltop with outstanding views, the inn is a comfortable place where the guests are joined in a family spirit. The living room has a big fireplace with a fire going on cooler days. In summer the large porch is a favorite gathering place before dinner.

In addition to the guest rooms in the main house, the Gabriels have created two new guest facilities: A studio apartment overlooking the fields and woods has its own entrance, kitchen, and large sliding-

glass door opening onto a deck. The barn apartment, with a loft bedroom, a large living room, and a modern kitchen with a wood stove, overlooks the apple orchard and farm pond where guests enjoy swimming, canoeing, and sunbathing in summer.

Each evening the Gabriels prepare a single-entrée meal served family-style with all the guests at a single large table. A recent dinner included Tomato Vintage, a spiced tomato bouillon; home-baked bread and muffins; pickled beets and caponata, a salad of home-grown greens; a mixed grill of filet mignon, loin lamb chop, kidney, and tomato served with mushrooms; and fresh vegetables and roast potatoes.

Although liquor is not served at the inn, setups are furnished with cheese and crackers in the lounge or porch area. The Gabriels also have an antique shop in a nearby outbuilding.

*Accommodations:* 4 rooms in the main house, 1 with private bath, and 2 apartments with kitchens. *Pets:* Not permitted. *Children:* Under eight not permitted. *Driving Instructions:* The inn is 2 miles west of Grafton on Middletown Road.

## HIGHLAND LODGE

Craftsbury Road, Greensboro, VT 05841. 802-533-2647. *Innkeepers:* David and Willie Smith. Open Memorial Day weekend to mid-October and December to April.

The Highland Lodge is a wide, two-story lakefront inn with a full-length porch. Most of the inn dates from 1926, although one part was a farmhouse for a sheep farm before that. Nonhousekeeping cottages were added to the 180-acre property on Caspian Lake.

The lodge's public rooms include a large dining room with wood-burning stove, a pine-paneled breakfast room with hand-braided rugs, and several sitting rooms including a library with grand piano and grandfather clock. One of the nicest rooms in the main lodge takes up the entire end of the house. It has two new brass beds, carpeting, traditional mahogany furniture, and striped floral wallpaper in soft blues and tans.

At dinner the menu includes veal, seafood, chicken, pork, and locally raised lamb.

At the lakefront there is a private sandy beach where a beach house affords guests a place to change their clothes and enjoy the fireplace when engaging in cookout grills and other lake activities.

The inn has a complete cross-country ski center with 30 miles of trails.

*Accommodations:* 11 rooms in the lodge, all with bath; 12 cottages, each with 2 bedrooms, living room–kitchen, and fireplace. *Pets:* Not permitted. *Driving Instructions:* Take Route 15 to Route 16 (east of Hardwick), where you turn north. Take Route 16 to East Hardwick and follow the signs to Caspian Lake.

## Jamaica, Vermont

*Jamaica State Park* offers swimming and kayaking in the West River, which is the site of many kayak races. The town is quite small and old-fashioned–looking. It is located 4 miles northwest of West Townshend and 14 miles from Newfane.

### THREE MOUNTAIN INN

Route 30, Jamaica, VT 05343. 802-874-4140. *Innkeepers:* Elaine and Charles Murray. Open all year except April.

Three Mountain Inn is a small inn built in the late eighteenth century. The white clapboard house with its original twelve-over-twelve windows and big center chimney has been carefully restored by the Murrays, and there is nothing they like better than showing off their handiwork. The living room's wide-planked floors and walls and its original Dutch-oven fireplace set the colonial tone. Some of these planks are the widest we have seen. A long, low sofa before the hearth is the favorite spot for before- and after-dinner drinks. Beyond this low-ceilinged room are the dining room and library, both used as dining rooms. They are candlelit at dinner and, on chilly evenings, have fires in their hearths. The library is well stocked with reading materials to help while away the wintry Vermont evenings. The inn's main entrance is through the low back door that opens directly into a little pub-lounge.

The guest rooms in the inn's wing are decorated with antiques and print wallpapers on one wall contrasting with stripes and floral prints on another. These rooms are unique, fashioned from the inn's former stable, whose old beams can still be seen. Upstairs in the main house is the "honeymoon suite." The third floor contains a family bunk room.

The dining rooms, open to guests and public alike, offer a menu that changes frequently. Elaine Murray's specialties are her vegetable quiche, a variety of hearty soups, and her desserts. Entrées usually include a fresh seafood dish and perhaps a beef Stroganoff or a chicken Jacques with a garlicky sour cream sauce. The evening we were there, fresh scallops, blue fish, and rainbow trout were on the menu. A selection of wines is available. For breakfast, you can choose a light Continental style with fresh-from-the-oven muffins, dough-nuts, or rolls; or you can take the heartier country route with locally smoked bacon or ham, pancakes with Vermont maple syrup, and eggs.

*Accommodations:* 8 rooms, 4 with private bath. *Pets:* Not per-mitted. *Driving Instructions:* Take I-91 to Brattleboro, second exit; then take Route 30 to Jamaica's Main Street.

## *Killington, Vermont*

## THE VERMONT INN
Route 4, Killington, VT 05751. 802-773-9847. *Innkeepers:* Judy and Alan Carmasin. Open all year except May and two weeks in November.

The Vermont Inn began life in the early nineteenth century as a farmhouse. It is set on an open rise of land overlooking the high peaks of the Green Mountains. Off to one side a woodland stream rushes past. Judy and Alan Carmasin have extensively renovated the farmhouse-inn, recently adding wall-to-wall carpeting in many of the rooms and polishing the hardwood floors in others. Today the inn's rooms have a contemporary look that sets off its antiques and green plants, which grow just about everywhere.

Just off the living room–lobby is the inn's cocktail lounge; beyond that, in what was formerly the barn, is the popular wood-paneled dining room. Here guests and the public dine by candlelight, warmed by a fire in the large fieldstone fireplace — the focal point of the room. The menu of New England and Continental cuisine features veal and fresh seafood that is trucked in from the New England coast. In addition to the full-service bar there is a well-thought-out wine list.

A new swimming pool, a sauna, and an all-weather tennis court are available at the inn for guests' recreation, and the Killington and Pico ski areas are just across the highway.

*Accommodations:* 14 rooms, 8 with private bath. *Pets:* Not permitted. *Driving Instructions:* The inn is set back off Route 4, 6 miles east of Rutland and 4 miles west of Killington.

## NORDIC INN

Route 11, Landgrove, VT 05148. 802-824-6444. *Innkeepers:* Filippo Pagano and Inger Johansson. Open Memorial Day weekend to mid-April.

The Nordic Inn is a converted New England residence built in 1940 and now housing a small inn steeped in Scandinavian tradition. There are four fireplaces in public rooms in the inn, as well as one bedroom with its own fireplace. In 1978, the innkeepers added a new ski shop and did other renovation work using rough-sawn lumber milled from trees cut on their own property. The cross-country ski area now has 14 miles of trails, with 16 more miles planned for the near future. Equipment rentals and instruction are available. Although cross-country skiing is the focus of many guests in the winter, the proximity of several fine downhill areas brings other skiers as well. The Nordic Inn recently started a new ski school program at Bromley. Innkeeper Pagano will be directing and teaching the Telemark method.

The inn is equally popular in the warmer months among those who seek the rural beauty of this area. In all seasons, guests are drawn to the inn to sample Inger's extraordinary dinners with her unmistakable Swedish touch. She is a professional who was head chef for the consul general of Sweden. Guests dine in an oak, brick, and glass solarium overlooking a brick terrace. The menu is an extensive one, including such popular Scandinavian specialties as smorrebrod and gravad lax med sas, salmon baked on a bed of dill. In 1981, the Nordic Inn won the "Taste of Vermont" culinary competition.

Each guest room is decorated differently, many with Scandinavian antiques brought here from the Johansson family farm in Kisa, Sweden. The rooms are named Sweden, Norway, Finland, Denmark, and Vermont. Each is decorated in the bright colors of the particular country's flag. If you want the room with the fireplace, ask to stay in Sweden. The lower level of the inn contains the ski shop and a fully licensed après-ski tavern.

*Accommodations:* 5 rooms, 3 with private bath. *Pets:* Not permitted. *Driving Instructions:* The inn is between Londonderry and Peru on Route 11.

## THE VILLAGE INN

RFD Landgrove, VT 05148. 802-824-6673. *Innkeeper:* D. Jay Snyder. Open December 20 through April 1 and early July through October 15.

The first part of the Village Inn was constructed in 1810 and has had various additions over the years. The most recent was made in 1976. The result is a series of low, interconnected buildings, mostly of clapboard, that has come to serve as a small resort rather than a country inn. On the property are private tennis courts, a heated outdoor pool, and a three-hole pitch-and-putt golf course. Inn guests who enjoy cross-country skiing can use trails that originate there, while downhill skiers have only short drives to Bromley, Stratton, Magic Mountain, Snow Valley, or Okemo. There is a Rafter Room Cocktail Lounge, a whirlpool spa, and a new game room. Guests can enjoy hayrides and sleigh rides for which the inn has horses.

The guest rooms are large, with curtains, comforters, and an old-fashioned look. Of the twenty rooms available, fourteen have private baths. Dinners at the inn are simple affairs featuring such main courses as roast beef with Bordelaise sauce or a seafood dish. Fresh breads and rolls are baked daily in the kitchen. The dining room is open to the public for breakfast and dinner.

*Accommodations:* 20 rooms, 14 with private bath. *Pets:* Not permitted. *Driving Instructions:* From Manchester, take Route 11 past the Bromley ski area and turn left into Peru. At the fork in Peru bear left and continue 4½ miles through the national forest to the crossroads in Landgrove. Turn left toward Weston; the inn is on the right.

*Londonderry, Vermont*

## HIGHLAND HOUSE

Route 100, Londonderry, VT 05148. 802-824-3019. *Innkeepers:* Chris and Tim Hill. Open all year except three weeks in April.

Highland House, built in 1840, has been providing lodging for travelers through southern Vermont for more than a century. The farmhouse-inn sits on a knoll under Vermont maples and other tall shade trees. Its intimate sitting room is warmed by a Franklin stove on chilly days. The dining room offers a traditional continental menu and is open to guests and the public for dinners and generous New England breakfasts.

Highland House is an informal rural inn where guests can take off their shoes and relax after a day of cross-country skiing or hiking the surrounding Vermont hills. At the patio around the 52-foot swimming pool, guests can enjoy a warm-weather cocktail after a swim.

*Accommodations:* 7 rooms with shared bath and a 2-bedroom cottage. *Pets:* Not permitted. *Driving Instructions:* On Route 100, go 1.7 miles north of Route 11.

## Lower Waterford, Vermont

### RABBIT HILL INN

Pucker Street, Lower Waterford, VT 05848. 802-748-5168. *Innkeepers:* Eric and Beryl Charlton. Open all year, except first three weeks of both April and November.

The four large, hand-hewn Doric columns that support the front porch of the Rabbit Hill give it a somewhat imposing look that is quickly forgotten within the relaxed atmosphere of the inn. The property consists of a main inn built in 1827 and enlarged about fifteen years later to its present size. It has always served as an inn, except for a short period when it was used as a private home. In its early days it served the active logging community in the area, and the floors still bear the marks of the spiked boots of the drovers and lumberjacks.

Guests who stay in this inviting inn can choose their accommodations according to their preference for more contemporary or old-fashioned surroundings. The guest rooms in the main house are upstairs off a sitting area. The "Briar Patch," a smaller building put up in 1795, currently houses a cross-country ski center below and some old-fashioned guest rooms above. In the mid-1850s an annex was constructed containing a ballroom that has since been subdivided into a number of rooms.

Everywhere one looks — in nooks and crannies, on antique end tables, and scattered on shelves and windowsills — are rabbits: ceramic, wooden, every sort of rabbit. A large wood-burning Defiant stove warms the sitting room–lobby and one of the dining rooms, while another dining room has a working fireplace hung with brass and copper buckets. Breakfasts and Continental menus at dinner are available to guests and the public.

*Accommodations:* 20 rooms with bath. *Driving Instructions:* The inn is on Route 18 about 9 miles north of Littleton, New Hampshire.

## THE COMBES FAMILY INN

RFD 1, Ludlow, Vermont. Mailing address: Box 43 TC, Ludlow, VT 05149. 802-228-8799. *Innkeepers:* Ruth, Bill, and Nancy Combes. Open all year except April 15 to May 15.

As the name indicates, this is a true family inn on a quiet country back road in the heart of Vermont's mountains and lakes region. There are 50 acres of rolling meadows and woods to explore and to ski cross-country in winter. Cupcake and Brownie, reported to be the friendliest goats around, share the farm with lots of equally friendly cats, dogs, innkeepers, and guests. The inn itself is a century-old farmhouse that the Combeses have recently renovated. The dining room has exposed beams and a big bay window overlooking pastures and Okemo Mountain. The lounge area is paneled in Vermont barnboards and is furnished with turn-of-the-century oak. Cocktails (bring your own bottle), card games, and conversation are the specialties here.

There are four guest rooms in the old farmhouse, all with shared baths. Five other guest rooms in an attached motel unit come with private baths. The Vermont-style meals here consist of cream soups, turkey, lamb, or pork roasts, fresh vegetables, and home-baked breads and desserts. The coffeepot is always on, and guests help themselves to Nancy Combes's homemade cakes and cookies.

*Accommodations:* 9 rooms, 5 with bath. *Pets:* Not permitted. *Driving Instructions:* From Ludlow, proceed north on Route 103 about 3 miles. Follow state signs for the inn.

## THE GOVERNOR'S INN

86 Main Street, Ludlow, VT 05149. 802-228-8830. *Innkeepers:* Charlie and Deedy Marble. Open all year.

One enthusiast for the town of Ludlow was Governor William Stickney. His farm was in Tyson, 10 miles away, and at the turn of the century he decided to build a townhouse for himself on Ludlow's main street. Today his house has been restored and converted into The Governor's Inn.

The inn's intricately carved oak woodwork exemplifies the careful attention paid to every detail. Furnishings in each guest room include Vermont country antiques and pieces from the Marble family collection. Comforters and towels are in abundance, as are baskets of fresh fruit and flowers.

The highlights of the inn's interior are its handsome woodwork and the marbleized-slate fireplace mantels that display an art that is virtually lost and is certainly worth seeing. The inn's five-course dinners often start with one of Deedy's unusual soups, such as blueberry Chablis soup, and end with the dessert of the day, which might be apricot Victorian or chocolate walnut pie. The Marble's teen-age daughter, Alison, makes all the inn's breads including a tasty strawberry tea bread.

*Accommodations:* 8 rooms, 6 with private bath. *Driving Instructions:* Take Route I-91 to exit 6 (Route 103) to Ludlow and the inn.

## THE OKEMO INN

Route 103, Box 4, Ludlow, VT 05149. 802-228-2031. *Innkeepers:* Ron and Toni Parry. Open all year.

The Okemo Inn is an 1810 Vermont home that was a private residence in the nineteenth century. It became the Locust Hill Inn in the early 1900s and has been under its present name since 1962. The inn's interior is distinguished by hand-hewn beams, wide-board pine flooring, and a diversified collection of Vermont antiques. Two of the inn's eight fireplaces are still functioning, offering warmth and atmosphere in the cooler seasons. Meals at the Okemo, available in fall and winter, are served family-style with a single entrée prepared each evening. Meals frequently start with homemade soup and fresh salad and end with a freshly baked dessert. Main dishes that are old-time favorites at the Okemo are roast beef, chicken saltimbocca, and pork schnitzel. The inn has a fully licensed lounge, which has the home's original cooking fireplace. A parlor affords a place for quiet reading and games and has a second fireplace. The inn's only television set is in what the Parrys call their "Public Room."

Among the inn's more modern amenities are its large coed sauna room and an outdoor pool for summer guests. Most winter guests are drawn to the Okemo because the Okemo Mountain Ski Area, with its twenty-two trails and nine major lifts, is virtually in the inn's backyard. Cross-country skiing trails start from the inn's door, and major Nordic skiing centers are nearby.

*Accommodations:* 12 rooms, 10 with bath. *Pets:* Not permitted. *Driving Instructions:* Take Route I-91 north to exit 6 (Route 103). Take Route 103 for 23 miles northwest to Ludlow. The inn is 1½ miles north of the village.

## Manchester, Vermont

## BIRCH HILL INN

West Road, Manchester, VT 05254. 802-362-2761. *Innkeepers:*
Jim and Pat Lee. Open late December to early April and late May
to late October.

Built in 1790, with an addition dating from just after the turn of the
century, Birch Hill has been part of innkeeper Pat Lee's family since
1917. The family large, homey New England house was a family
summer home until Pat and Jim bought it and transformed it to a
country inn in 1981. Its spacious, sunny rooms contain woodburning
stoves and fireplaces as well as the Lee's many antiques and house-
plants. The living room, with its extensive library, opens onto a
marble terrace that offers panoramic views of the Green Mountains.
The living room is a popular spot in the evening.

Guest rooms are decorated with antiques and have exposed-beam
ceilings. Meals are served family style near the big wood stove.

The grounds, with vegetable and flower gardens and a trout pond,
are surrounded by beautifully crafted stone walls and fences; 15
kilometers of cross-country skiing trails begin at the inn and wind
through open fields and peaceful woods.

*Accommodations:* 5 rooms, 3 with private bath, and a summer
cottage. *Pets:* Not permitted. *Children:* Under six not permitted.
*Driving Instructions:* West Road joins U.S. 7 to the south and
Vermont 30 to the north.

## THE 1811 HOUSE

On the Green, Manchester, Vermont. Mailing address: Box 207, Manchester Village, VT 05254. 802-362-1811. *Innkeepers:* Mary and Jack Hirst. Open May through March.

The 1811 House is a New England frame home built in the early nineteenth century, its later additions in keeping with the character of the original building. From 1905 to 1935, the 1811 House was the home of Mary Lincoln Isham, granddaughter of Abraham Lincoln. Mary and Jack Hirst bought the inn in 1982, completely restoring and furnishing it in keeping with its Federal-period origin. Twelve-over-twelve windows were installed, and it received a fresh coat of earth-brown paint. In back 2½ acres of lawn and gardens afford views of Equinox Golf Course and the mountains beyond. Inside redecoration included extensive repainting, papering, and stenciling. The innkeepers' collection of paintings, English and American antiques, and Oriental rugs is represented in every room. There are fireplaces in all public rooms, including the dining room, where a full English-style breakfast is served, ranging from bacon and eggs to fried tomatoes with mushrooms.

*Accommodations:* 10 rooms with bath. *Children:* Under thirteen not permitted. *Driving Instructions:* The inn is on Route 7 in Manchester, a mile south of Manchester Center.

## RELUCTANT PANTHER INN

West Road (just off Route 7), Manchester Village, VT 05254. 802-362-2568. *Innkeepers:* Ed and Loretta Friihauf. Open Memorial Day to October 30 and early December to early April.

The Reluctant Panther was fashioned out of an imposing clapboard home built in 1850. It is well landscaped and is painted in the unusual hues of mauve and purple. The decor inside, equally daring, shows a decorator's flair. The public rooms blend modern and antique furnishings. One dining room is a greenhouse with healthy plants everywhere, another has a Colonial motif, and the third has a display of wood carvings from old furniture. The cocktail lounge is a good place to relax on chilly evenings when innkeeper Ed Friihauf lights a fire in its hearth. The dining rooms are open to the public. Hors d'oeuvres include broiled trout and bacon-wrapped asparagus with Vermont cheddar cheese sauce. Nine entrées include roast loin of smoked pork, duckling à l'orange, and trout stuffed with shrimp and crabmeat.

The bedroom decor is imaginative. Some rooms have carpeting that continues up the wall. Four feature working fireplaces, and all have color television, room phones, and oversize bath towels.

*Accommodations:* 7 rooms with private bath. *Pets and children:* Not permitted. *Driving Instructions:* The inn is in the center of Manchester Village, about 20 miles north of Bennington on Route 7.

## *Marlboro, Vermont*

### LONGWOOD INN

Route 9, Marlboro, Vermont. Mailing address: Box 86, Marlboro, VT 05344. 802-257-1545 and 802-257-7272. *Innkeepers:* Thomas and Janet Durkin. Open all year.

Longwood Inn was already getting along in years as a dairy farmhouse when the Revolutionary War broke out. The clapboard inn was built in 1729 and, in addition to serving the milk-drinking public, spent a few years as a college dormitory for the nearby Marlboro College. The building has been lovingly restored and now welcomes travelers. Two of the inn's nine guest rooms feature wood-burning fireplaces that are still in use, a rarity in old country inns today. Throughout the inn hearths are kept going twenty-four hours a day in the winter months. There are two sitting rooms for guests. The grounds contain an old red barn that houses a summer theater, and a carriage house that has been converted into four studio apartments. The farm pond is a perfect spot for fishing or swimming in summer or for skating on when the ice isn't covered with a foot of snow. The land is crisscrossed with horse trails for hiking and jogging, and Alpine skiing is available just minutes away at three major sites. In 1961 an addition was built to house the inn's restaurant.

*Accommodations:* 9 rooms, 7 with private bath, and 4 studio apartments. *Pets and children:* Not permitted. *Driving Instructions:* Take I-91 north to exit 2 at Brattleboro. Take Route 9 to Marlboro, approximately 10 miles. The inn will be on the right.

## RED CLOVER INN

Woodward Road, Mendon, VT 05701. 802-775-2290. *Innkeepers:* Dennis and Bonnie Rae Tallagnon. Open Thanksgiving to mid-April and mid-June to mid-October.

The Red Clover Inn, named for the Vermont state flower, is a small farm whose main lodge was built about 1840. In 1923 the property was bought by General J. E. Woodward of Washington, D.C., who dreamed of creating a miniature working farm. It is in a hidden mountain valley just minutes from Killington and Pico.

The inn today consists of the lodge, a separate carriage house now called the Plum Tree House, and the farm barn. In the main lodge there is a sunny dining room facing the front of the building overlooking the distant hills. Here, and in a second room, Dennis's Continental meals are served.

Bonnie Rae painstakingly restored each of the inn's fourteen guest rooms, some of which are in the main inn and some in the Plum Tree House. The old-fashioned rooms in the inn are small, have print wallpapers, and are furnished with a mixture of antiques and more recent maple pieces. Some of the rooms in the inn share hall bathrooms with old-fashioned tubs. Rooms in the Plum Tree House are more spacious—several are suites—and done in a more modern decor. Recent additions include a new tennis court and billiard room.

*Accommodations:* 15 rooms, 8 with private bath. *Pets:* Permitted in the Plum Tree House only. *Driving Instructions:* From Rutland, take Route 4 east for 5.2 miles; turn right on Woodward Road.

## Middlebury, Vermont

## THE MIDDLEBURY INN

17 Pleasant Street, Middlebury, Vermont. Mailing address: Box 631, Middlebury, VT 05753. 802-388-4961. *Innkeepers:* Frank and Jane Emanuel. Open all year.

The Middlebury Inn, overlooking the village green, consists of a large brick building constructed in 1827, the 1825 Porter House Mansion, and a motel unit behind the main inn. The Middlebury is a fine example of a dignified college-campus inn. The Emanuels have undertaken the task of a major facelift for the old inn, with the help of a grant from Vermont's Division of Historic Preservation. The outside of the building and the public rooms on the ground floor have all been freshened up. The rooms were redecorated and wallpapered. The two floors above the lobby offer guest rooms of assorted sizes and shapes (most with private or connecting baths). Most of these guest rooms have been carefully redone, including such details as wallpapering the sprinkler pipes.

The old ballroom houses the Country Pedlar Cafe and Gift Shop. The Morgan Room Cocktail Lounge and the inn's dining room are open to both guests and the public for breakfast, lunch, and dinner.

*Accommodations:* 61 rooms with private bath. *Driving Instructions:* The inn is on Route 7 in the town of Middlebury.

## Middletown Springs, Vermont

### MIDDLETOWN SPRINGS INN

On-the-Green, Middletown Springs, VT 05757. 802-235-2198. *Innkeepers:* Jean and Mel Hendrickson. Open all year.

The Middletown Springs Inn is an 1879 Victorian mansion with Italianate overtones. Downstairs are a welcoming country kitchen and two high-ceilinged dining rooms where breakfast is served every morning; in the Music Room on this floor, a grand piano awaits a guest's talents, and in the library a wood stove adds its warmth. A doll-and-miniature collection, assembled by three generations of collectors, is on display at the inn. The guest rooms upstairs include the Honeymoon Suite, with its private bath. The Hendricksons provide velour robes for the rooms with shared baths. At night, covers are turned down and mints are placed on guests' pillows.

Dinner, by advance reservation only, is preceded by complimentary sherry or cocktails. A typical meal might start with snapper soup and proceed to Rock Cornish game hen, ending with Mile-High strawberry pie.

*Accommodations:* 7 rooms, 1 with private bath. *Pets:* Not permitted. *Driving Instructions:* From Rutland, take Route 4 west and then Route 133 south to the inn.

## BLACK LANTERN INN

Route 118, Montgomery Village, VT 05470. 802-326-4507. *Innkeepers:* Rita and Allan Kalsmith. Open all year.

The Black Lantern Inn was built as a stagecoach stop at the turn of the nineteenth century. The old brick building is located fewer than 10 miles from the Canadian border and minutes from the big Jay Peak Ski Area to the east. The inn has eleven guest rooms, nine with private baths, each individually decorated with antiques. There is a television room, and a sitting room warmed by an open wood-burning stove. A dining room and a taproom are open to guests and the public and are popular with skiers from Jay. The bar has exposed beams and a casual atmosphere. The candlelit dining room offers a continental menu featuring such entrées as lamb Marguerite, veal tarragon, and fresh seafood, all served with salads, fresh vegetables, and homemade breads and desserts.

In winter the area offers a variety of skiing choices in addition to Jay Peak. Cross-country skiing is excellent right out the door of the inn, and for downhill skiers there are four nearby Canadian ski mountains. Spring and summer bring numerous recreational activities, including fishing in many nearby streams and swimming in the old swimming hole.

*Accommodations:* 11 rooms, 9 with bath. *Pets:* Not permitted. *Driving Instructions:* Take Route 100 north to Route 118 in Eden. Follow Route 118 through Montgomery Center to Montgomery.

## THE FOUR COLUMNS INN

230 West Street, Newfane, VT 05345. 802-365-7713. *Innkeepers:* Sandy and Jacques Allembert. Open early May to November and early December to April.

The Four Columns Inn is a handsome white structure that looks out over the picturesque little town of Newfane and its green. The guest rooms feature brass and spool antique beds. On the tree-shaded grounds guests enjoy trout ponds and a pool. The restaurant, which is closed Tuesdays, has many seasonal specialties including fresh trout, breast of duck with rhubarb or raspberries, and pheasant raised on the premises. Luncheon is not served in winter.

*Accommodations:* 12 rooms with bath. *Driving Instructions:* The inn is 100 yards off Route 30 in the center of Newfane.

## OLD NEWFANE INN

Route 30 and the Common, Newfane, VT 05345. 802-365-4427. *Innkeeper:* Eric Weindl. Open May to October and December to April.

Built in 1787, the Old Newfane is filled with early American antiques and retains the wide-board floors, beamed ceilings, and red-brick fireplaces characteristic of this period. It was built on Newfane Hill and moved to the present location on the Common in 1825. The extensive and expensive French menu in the dining room lists more than a dozen appetizers and even more entrées, including such specialties as medallion de veau aux champignons, frogs' legs Provençal, rack of lamb, duckling à l'orange, and veal Gismonda. The ten papered guest rooms are decorated in traditional old New England style. Eight of the rooms have private baths; the remaining two have a connecting bath. This inn is highly recommended to travelers who enjoy excellent food in a somewhat formal atmosphere.

*Accommodations:* 10 rooms, 8 with bath. *Pets and children:* Not permitted. *Driving Instructions:* Take Route 30 to Newfane. The inn is in the center of town.

## North Hero, Vermont

### NORTH HERO HOUSE

Champlain Islands, North Hero, VT 05474. 802-372-8237. *Innkeepers:* Roger and Caroline Sorg. Open mid-June to Labor Day. The North Hero House is actually a group of buildings dating from the last century. The Champlain Island inn, built in 1890, has been completely renovated to contain guest rooms with private baths, dining rooms, a craft shop, and the Green Mountain Lounge. There are waterfront accommodations in the granite-walled Wadsworth House and Store. A suite has been fashioned out of the old cobbbler's shop, which now has a bedroom, a bath, a sitting room with the original fireplace, and a screened porch. Rooms are decorated with sturdy modern country-style furniture and attractive wallpapers or paneling. The waterfront area provides a carefully preserved steamship dock, as well as swimming, boating, waterskiing, and canoeing. A different menu offered each evening in the dining room includes a Friday-evening dockside lobster picnic. Dinner guests are welcome to select a wine from the wine cellar personally.

*Accommodations:* 24 rooms, 22 with private bath. *Pets:* Not permitted. *Driving Instructions:* The Champlain Islands are reached by ferry from Plattsburgh, New York, or by bridge 35 miles northwest of Burlington on Route 2. On the islands, follow Route 2 to North Hero.

## North Thetford, Vermont

### STONE HOUSE INN

Route 5, North Thetford, Vermont. *Mailing address:* P.O. Box 47, North Thetford, VT 05054. 802-333-9124. *Innkeepers:* Art and Dianne Sharkey. Open mid-April to mid-March.

The Stone House Inn is just feet from the Connecticut River, and guests can arrive by canoe, landing at the public boat-launch just behind the inn. Railroad buffs will be happy to note that the B & M (Boston and Maine) line also runs just behind the inn.

The Sharkeys were once schoolteachers. They recently decided to become innkeepers and were delighted to find that all their family furniture fitted perfectly in the inn. The living room has a tiled-hearth fireplace; over its mantel is an oak-framed mirror bearing a carved lion's head. In summer the Sharkeys serve country-style meals on the sun porch at the rear of the house overlooking a 2-acre pond. When we were there, meals were served in the dining room, which has a pressed-tin ceiling. The room had such touches as fresh flowers on the tables, napkins gracefully placed in the wine goblets, and Oriental rugs on the polished hardwood floor. Meals are served in one seating, and dinners are served on Fridays and Saturdays only. The bright guest rooms upstairs continue the country atmosphere of the inn. The inn is part of the "canoe inn to inn" program.

*Accommodations:* 6 rooms with shared bath. *Pets:* Not permitted. *Driving Instructions:* Take I-91 north of White River to exit 14. Take a right on Route 113 to Route 5. Turn left on Route 5, and drive 2 miles. The inn is next to a red barn by a sharp curve.

## *Peru, Vermont*

### JOHNNY SEESAW'S

Route 11, Peru, VT 05152. 802-824-5533. *Innkeepers:* Gary and Nancy Okun. Open Thanksgiving through March and July 4 through October 19.

This Vermont log country inn offers lodging and fine food with a special "houseguest" atmosphere. Originally built as a dance hall in 1926, Johnny Seesaw's has undergone renovation and expansion while still maintaining a very special rustic ambience. Accommodations range from a room in the inn with private bath to one of several large cottages complete with king-size bed, fireplace, and television. Bunk rooms are also available.

During the summer the inn's Olympic-size, marble-edged pool is inviting, and a clay tennis court beckons nearby. Bromley Mountain's Alpine Slide is only 500 yards away. Nearby are excellent golfing, horseback riding, and antiquing.

Nightly, the inn's chef prepares country fare, served by candlelight. All soups, breads, and desserts are homemade; special dishes will be prepared for vegetarians or those on a restricted diet. Children are served early, allowing the adults to enjoy a more leisurely meal. After their dinner, youngsters may enjoy the game room.

*Accommodations:* 30 rooms, 24 with private bath. *Driving Instructions:* Peru is midway between Manchester and Londonderry on Route 11. The inn is ¼ mile east of Bromley Mountain.

## *Plymouth Union, Vermont*

### SALT ASH INN

Plymouth Union, VT 05056. 802-672-3748. *Innkeepers:* Ginny and Don Kroitzsh. Open in the summer, fall, and winter.

The Salt Ash Inn has had a history as, at various times, a stagecoach stop, post office, inn, and general store. Most of the antiques in the building were originally used there. The new lounge is paneled with barnboard, and its walls are decorated with skis, crutches, and other wintry memorabilia. A large circular fireplace is the room's focal point, a pleasant spot to relax by the fire and look out at the hillside through the big picture window. A small pub adjacent to this room is very popular with local skiers. The old post-office boxes remain here, and if you look carefully you can see the Coolidge family name still on their mailbox. Nearby Plymouth is the birthplace of President Calvin Coolidge, and the Calvin Coolidge National Historic Restoration and family homestead are there.

The guest rooms are country casual, their pine beds covered with colorful homemade quilts. Some of the rooms are skiers' dorms with bright plaid blankets on the beds and rough-sawn wooden walls. This casual family inn appeals to active people who love the outdoors. The dining room with its old stove serves family-style meals including home-baked breads and a salad bar. The inn serves breakfast and dinner to guests and public alike.

*Accommodations:* 12 rooms, 4 with bath. *Pets:* Not permitted. *Driving Instructions:* The inn is at the junction of 100 and 100A.

## *Proctorsville, Vermont*

### CASTLE INN

Junction of routes 103 and 131, Proctorsville, Vermont. Mailing
address: Box 157, Proctorsville, VT 05153. 802-226-7222. *Inn-keepers:* Michael and Sheryl Fratino. Open mid-May to the end of
October and mid-December to the end of March.

A great variety of inns dot the countryside in this state, but far and
away the most unusual we have run across is the Castle Inn. As its
name indicates, guests here are treated to a night at a small stone
castle complete with mahogany and oak paneling, carved plaster ceilings, an oval dining room, library, and ten fireplaces scattered
throughout the building, many with elaborate carved mantels.

The inn, once a governor's mansion, offers ten guest rooms with a
distinct baronial feeling in keeping with the public rooms of the
estate. Eight of these rooms have private baths. A hot-tub and a sauna
are also available. Breakfast is served to guests, and dinner is available
to guests and the general public, featuring duck, shrimp, and veal
specialties.

*Accommodations:* 10 rooms, 8 with bath. *Pets:* Not permitted.
*Driving Instructions:* Take Route 103 north through Chester to Proctorsville; the inn is 2 miles south of Ludlow on Route 103.

## THE GOLDEN STAGE INN

Route 103, Proctorsville, Vermont. Mailing address: Box 218, Proctorsville, VT 05153. 802-226-7744. *Innkeepers:* Tom and Wende Schaaff. Open mid-May to mid-April.

Built in 1796, the Golden Stage has been a stagecoach stop and private home for 180 years. Once a link in the underground railroad, the inn has been completely redone by the Schaaffs. It is a rambling clapboard building with wraparound porches and an attached barn on 5 acres of lawns and gardens.

There are ten guest rooms, two with private baths; the others share four baths. The rooms are spacious, with comfortable beds, quilted bedspreads, wide-pine floors, and Colonial wallpaper and ruffled curtains.

A plant-filled living room with a fireplace provides enough space for guests to relax. The dining room (open to the public with advance reservations) serves traditional New England dishes and Continental cuisine. The menu features homemade soups, crepes, quiches, breads, and fish trucked in fresh from the sea. During the summer and fall, the vegetables come straight from the Schaaffs' own garden. Breakfast and dinner are served.

This inn is one of the most attractive ones we've encountered. The family horse grazing on the hillside and the inn's samoyeds add to the pastoral quality.

*Accommodations:* 10 rooms, 2 with private bath. *Pets:* Not permitted. *Driving Instructions:* Take Route 91 to exit 6, then go north on Route 103 for 18 miles to the inn.

## OKEMO LANTERN LODGE

Route 131, Proctorsville, Vermont. Mailing address: Box 247, Proctorsville, VT 05153. 802-226-7770. *Innkeepers:* Charles and Joan Racicot. Open all year.

Okemo Lantern Lodge has welcomed guests since the late 1940s. Built early in the nineteenth century, the house has many Victorian touches. Within, its natural butternut woodwork and stained-glass windows give the inn a warmth. In its kitchen, an old-fashioned Model Stewart wood cookstove often has a kettle of soup simmering on its top. Comfortable couches, chairs, and even a chaise longue in a bay window invite guests to linger and relax. The guest rooms are on the second floor. They contain antiques, wall-to-wall carpeting, and — in some cases — beds with canopies. The one suite has its own sitting area and a large private bath. Fresh flowers grace the rooms in summer.

Dinner and breakfast are served family-style at Okemo Lantern Lodge. Joan Racicot bakes all her own breads and often serves corn-cob–smoked bacon and homemade jams for breakfast.

*Accommodations:* 7 rooms, including a 2-room suite with bath; other rooms share baths. *Pets:* Not permitted. *Driving Instructions:* Take Route 91 north to Route 103. Go 18 miles northwest on Route 103 to the intersection with Route 131. Turn right to the inn, the ninth house on the left.

*Quechee, Vermont*

## THE QUECHEE INN AT MARSHLAND FARM

Clubhouse Road, Quechee, Vermont. Mailing address: Box 747, Quechee, VT 05059. 802-295-3133. *Innkeepers:* Michael and Barbara Yaroschuk. Open all year except three weeks in both April and early December.

Colonel Joseph Marsh, the first lieutenant governor of Vermont, built his home, known as Marshland, in 1793. The farmhouse and associated barns were used as a private residence until the mid-1970s, when they were restored and converted.

The renovation of the inn was done with care so as to maintain the original feeling of the guest rooms while providing fully modern private bathrooms and color cable television for the rooms. Furnishings are largely Queen Anne in style, with most rooms featuring wide-board pine floors, braided rugs, and old-fashioned print curtains.

There are two dining rooms: one small room with French doors overlooking the lake and a larger room warmed by an antique stove. Dinners are served to the public Wednesday through Sunday.

Guests at the inn are given passes for the Quechee Club recreational facilities. For a nominal fee, inn guests have access to boating, racquet ball, squash, skiing, tennis, golf, indoor and outdoor swimming, riding, and the exercise room, all according to season.

*Accommodations:* 22 rooms with private bath. *Pets:* Not permitted. *Driving Instructions:* From Route I-91, take I-89 north to exit 1—Route 4. Take 4 west about 1 mile; turn right on Clubhouse Road and proceed 1 mile.

## THREE STALLION INN

Stock Farm Road, Randolph, VT 05060. 802-728-5575. *Innkeepers:* Thomas and Roxanne Sejerman.

The Three Stallion Inn is a part of the Green Mountain Stock Farm, a 1,500-acre estate once occupied by Robert Lippitt Knight, the originator of the Lippitt strain of the Morgan horse. The inn's second and third floors date from the early eighteenth century; the first floor was built beneath the upper stories sometime in the first part of the nineteenth.

The Three Stallion Inn, offering overnight accommodations, is the focal point of a popular cross-country skiing center. Although some of the surrounding acreage has been reserved for private house lots and a small number of condominiums, the rest is available for skiing on groomed and tracked trails including one lighted night trail. There is a wood-fired Finnish sauna for after-skiing, or anytime. Other resort activities include tennis, horseback riding, golfing at the Montague Golf Course, and hiking and bicycling throughout the Stock Farm. Horse shows are held on the property each summer, and there is an active dairy farm on the land.

The inn has three floors. On the first floor are the dining room, entrance parlor, and two sitting rooms, all with working fireplaces. An oaken staircase leads to the upper floors, which house several antique-furnished guest rooms. At the back of the inn is an appealing two-floor suite with bedroom over the first-floor living room. Views from the guest rooms include large meadows, a horse paddock, and the Third Branch of the White River. During the ski season, home-cooked family-style single-entrée dinners are served to guests.

*Accommodations:* 13 rooms, 3 with private bath. *Pets:* Not permitted. *Driving Instructions:* From I-89, take exit 4 and proceed west for 2 miles.

## Ripton, Vermont

### CHIPMAN INN

Route 125, Ripton, Vermont. Mailing address: Box 37, Ripton, VT 05766. 802-388-2390. *Innkeeper:* Joan Bullock. Open all year except April and November.

The Chipman Inn was the first home built in Ripton by Daniel Chipman. He improved the local road and then charged tolls for its use. This small, fully restored 1828 farmhouse offers guests overnight accommodations in ten bedrooms, of which six have private baths. The Tavern Room sports a Dutch-ovened fireplace and a bar-lounge. Other public rooms include a music-and-game room and the dining room. Guests enjoy a five-course meal served family style with the emphasis on country cooking. During the ski season there is a "pot of the day" meal featuring kettle cooking with perhaps a hearty stew, soup, or chili dinner. Salads and homemade breads round out this popular winter meal. Alpine and Nordic skiing are available nearby.

*Accommodations:* 10 rooms, 6 with private bath. *Pets:* Not permitted. *Driving Instructions:* Take Route 125 to the inn.

## Saxtons River, Vermont

### SAXTONS RIVER INN

Main Street, Saxtons River, VT 05154. 802-869-2110. *Innkeeper:* Averill Campbell Larsen. Open April through December.

The current Saxtons River Inn was built in 1903. The Campbell family, with help from friends and neighbors, revived and restored it. The inn is now run with energy and talent by Averill Campbell Larsen, who not only cooks all the meals but is equally at home with a hammer and saw or a swatch of wallpaper.

The inn has a spacious public dining room, a bar with a copper top, and several public sitting rooms in addition to individually decorated guest rooms. Throughout the inn Ms. Larsen has shown tireless care in taking wood to its natural state and augmenting that look with a novel selection of wallpapers.

Saxtons River Inn serves dinner to the public and offers breakfast to overnight guests. The dinner menu changes twice a week and often includes exotic gourmet specialties. Desserts may be selected from a display on the inn's former coal-burning cookstove. The restaurant is closed on Tuesdays.

*Accommodations:* 20 rooms, 11 with private bath. *Pets:* Not permitted. *Driving Instructions:* From I-91, take exit 5 to Route 121 (left). Take Route 121 to 4 miles west of Bellows Falls.

## *Shoreham, Vermont*

## THE SHOREHAM INN AND COUNTRY STORE

Shoreham, VT 05770. 802-897-5081. *Innkeepers:* Cleo and Fred Alter. Open all year.

The Shoreham is a small, informal, family-run inn that dates back to 1799. Unlike many inns in Vermont, the Shoreham has always been an inn serving this small community. As you enter, you are greeted by the old stairway leading to the guest rooms above. The balustrade is actually from a church in Shoreham. The dining room and especially the guest rooms are furnished with comfortable "country auction" antiques. The dining room, with its exposed beams, is currently used only for guest breakfasts, often served before a fire in the fireplace. Cleo and Fred strive to emphasize the informal atmosphere here — guests share tables for breakfast and often strike up friendships. Adjacent to the inn is the Shoreham Country Store, also run by the Alters. This store is more than 150 years old. Cleo has stocked the shelves with a selection of local Vermont crafts, as well as wines and cheese and maple-sugar products of the state. The store also offers simple lunches for travelers, who often choose to eat them on picnic tables provided by the inn and located on a small green across the street. Be sure to try the ice cream!

*Accommodations:* 8 rooms sharing baths. *Driving Instructions:* The inn is on Route 74 West, 22 miles north of Fair Haven and 12 miles southwest of Middlebury, across Lake Champlain from New York State's Fort Ticonderoga.

## Stowe, Vermont

### EDSON HILL MANOR

RD 1, Edson Hill Road, Stowe, VT 05672. 802-253-7371. *Innkeeper:* Robert A. Brody. Open all year.

This brick manor was built as a private ski lodge in 1939. No expense was spared, as evidenced by Delft tiles on some of the inn's many fireplaces and big beams in the main living room. Much of the inn's interior is paneled in pine, and most of the guest rooms have working fireplaces. There is a comfortable mixture of antique and functional furniture. The guest rooms are in newer additions to the manor: the Wing, added in 1952, and the Annex, built in 1957.

The Edson Hill Manor is on 400 acres of woods and pasture. Below the inn are a secluded swimming pool, a terrace, and lawns. A cross-country ski center in winter, the inn has many trails with outstanding views. There is a cross-country ski school at the inn, with certified instruction and a ski shop. Downhill skiing is available at the popular Mount Mansfield nearby. The inn's dining room is open to the public except for lunch in summer.

*Accommodations:* 16 rooms, 10 with private bath. *Pets:* Not permitted. *Driving Instructions:* From Stowe, take Route 108N (the Mountain Road) for 3½ miles to the Buccaneer Motel. Immediately after the motel on the right, take the right fork and go 1.7 miles, following the signs to the Edson Hill Manor.

## FOXFIRE INN

Route 100, Stowe, Vermont. Mailing address: R.R. 2, Stowe, VT 05672. 802-253-4887. *Innkeepers:* Art and Irene Segreto. Open all year.

The main section of the Foxfire was built early in the nineteenth century as a farmhouse and later served as a stagecoach stop. It is one of the oldest frame houses in Stowe. Modified over the years, it has served as a guesthouse, a summer resort, and even a Chinese restaurant. Despite its diverse heritage the building still retains what is best described as the "Vermont look." The inn is set against a 70-acre wooded hillside.

The guest rooms with their wide-board floors, truncated ceilings, and nook-and-cranny layout have been carefully renovated, and several have exposed hand-hewn wood beams. Each room has its own bath: some big, some small, and one across the hall.

Probably the most distinctive feature of Foxfire is its fine Italian restaurant. It offers a classically structured menu—antipastos followed by prima (pasta) and secundi (entrée) courses followed by salad and cheese or sweets and fruit. A cross section of antipastos includes rolled eggplant, stuffed mushrooms, prosciutto and melon, and assorted antipasto. A selection of pasta dishes includes all the expected ones plus special treats like baked ziti with ricotta and eggplant, or baked ziti with broccoli, tomato, and ricotta. Entrée choices include veal prepared seven different ways, five kinds of chicken, steak, eggplant, and shrimp.

Many dinner guests complete their meal by having their dessert and coffee in the living room by the open fire. Foxfire coffee, a popular after-dinner drink, is a blend of frangelica (hazelnut liqueur) and Italian brandy with coffee, served in a snifter and topped with whipped cream and an Italian flag.

*Accommodations:* 5 rooms with private bath. *Driving Instructions:* The inn is on Route 100, 1½ miles north of Stowe village.

## THE GABLES INN

Mountain Road, Stowe, VT 05672. 802-253-7730. *Innkeepers:*
Lynn and Sol Baumrind. Open all year.

The Gables Inn consists of a 120-year-old house to which additions
were made in the 1930s. A motel was added in 1977. This many-
dormered inn is a place where you feel comfortable relaxing with your
feet up on the coffee table enjoying the warmth of the fire and good
conversation with new friends. The ground floor contains the main
dining room, which seats forty, and the living room with its paneled
fireplace, upholstered furniture, and coffee table–bench. Family-style
candlelight dinners feature such dishes as spadini, veal, baked chick-
en, homemade manicotti, and a dish whimsically called toothache
stew (a beef stew redolent of cloves).

Several of the guest rooms are tucked into the eaves and dormers
upstairs. Each is papered with a different print, carefully selected. We
especially like the one that has a canopy bed, a cranberry-colored
Oriental rug, and floral-print papers. A new solarium overlooks the
inn's swimming pool.

The Gables has one of the most interesting breakfast menus we
have seen in a country inn. In addition to the standard breakfast of
eggs and bacon or pancakes, one can order kippers with onion, cur-
ried poached eggs with chutney, sautéed chicken livers and scrambled
eggs, corned beef hash, or matzo brei. These meals are served in summer on the lawn or the inn's front porch overlooking the valley and
Mount Mansfield.

*Accommodations:* 16 rooms with bath. *Pets:* Permitted in the
motel only. *Driving Instructions:* The inn is 1.6 miles northwest of
Stowe, on Route 108.

## *Tyson, Vermont*

### ECHO LAKE INN

Route 100, Box 154, Ludlow, VT 05149. 802-228-8602. *Innkeeper:* Mark H. Brown, Jr. Open all year.

Echo Lake Inn, built in the last decade of the eighteenth century, has over the years been host to Presidents McKinley and Coolidge, Andrew Mellon, and other dignitaries. The inn's old-fashioned living room is lighted by hanging hurricane lamps. A grandfather clock ticks quietly next to the fireplace, and braided rugs add a touch of warmth. Two dining rooms serve meals to guests and the public. In addition to the regular menu, which features steaks, chops, and ribs, there are such evening specials as smoked Nantucket salmon, bay scallops paprika or breast of chicken tarragon, and blueberry meringue. The recently redecorated guest rooms have print wallpapers and reproduction colonial furnishings. There are also dorm rooms, which appeal to families or groups that use the inn in all four seasons. The inn's grounds include a tennis court and a heated swimming pool, and there are swimming and boating across the street at Echo Lake.

*Accommodations:* 20 rooms, 4 with private bath. *Pets:* Not permitted. *Driving Instructions:* The inn is 5 miles north of Ludlow on Route 100.

## KNOLL FARM COUNTRY INN

Bragg Hill Road, RFD Box 179, Waitsfield, VT 05673. 802-496-3939. *Innkeepers:* Bill and Ann Day Heinzerling. Open all year except April and November.

The Knoll Farm Inn, on 150 acres of hillside pasture and woods, is a converted farmhouse with four guest rooms, a large family kitchen with an old wood stove, dining room, study, and living room. The farm has a red barn and a smaller barn-shop. The barn is used to hold the thirty tons of hay needed to maintain the farm's twenty animals. This was a working farm in the last century and was converted to a combination farm and inn in 1937. It continues to produce its own meats, vegetables, fruits, eggs, butter, and breads. Dinners feature these ingredients in hearty meals including pot roasts, pork roasts, stews, bacon, sausage, apple desserts, and jams and jellies. The Heinzerlings serve what may be the biggest breakfast in any Vermont inn, using their own fresh ingredients and featuring blueberry pancakes with Vermont maple syrup on Sunday mornings.

The inn has its own pond with a dock and a rowboat in the summer and good skating in the winter. Ann is an accomplished naturalist, known in the area for her nature talks and slide shows; she is happy to guide the inn's guests on various nature walks. Riding horses and horsemanship clinics are available. The inn has a collection of old buggies and sleighs, which are used for rides. Guests are welcome to help with any chores, from milking to mending fences. Tennis, golf, canoeing, soaring, and Nordic and Alpine skiing are all nearby.

Beyond all this there is a special feeling here that is difficult to communicate. Innkeepers and guests all eat together, meet and talk together, and gradually a special relationship of friendship evolves. In Ann's words, "As you walk on our hill in any season, in solitude or companionship, you will find renewal and inner re-creation. The vital activities of the farm become meaningful to the basic life they represent." If this appeals to you, reserve early. The inn can be booked for the summer months a year in advance.

*Accommodations:* 4 rooms. *Pets and children under six years:* Not permitted. *Driving Instructions:* The farm is half a mile up the hill (Bragg Hill Road) from the junction of routes 100 and 17.

## MOUNTAIN VIEW INN

Route 17, Waitsfield, Vermont. Mailing address: RFD Box 69, Waitsfield, VT 05673. 802-496-2426. *Innkeepers:* Fred and Suzy Spencer. Open all year.

Built early in the nineteenth century as a farmhouse, the building became one of Mad River's first ski lodges in the 1940s. The Mountain View today is an attractive New England inn, with many heirloom antiques and green plants. A favorite spot is the couch by the wood-burning Vigilant stove in the living room, where guests may share space with an old cat or a handmade quilted pillow. A piano awaits talented visitors. Innkeepers Fred and Suzy Spencer serve skiers mugs of hot mulled cider by the fire. The inn accommodates up to twelve guests, who dine together family-style around the large pumpkin-pine harvest table. Fred and Suzy grow their own vegetables, serve eggs laid by their pet chickens, and top off the meals with homemade breads and desserts. Dinners are served to the public, but only with advance arrangements.

The guest rooms are decorated with braided rugs and handmade quilts. One room has a bird's-eye–maple canopied bed, while another is done up with colorful quilts and stenciled walls.

*Accommodations:* 4 rooms, 1 with private bath. *Pets:* Not permitted. *Driving Instructions:* From the junction of Route 100 and Route 17 near Waitsfield, take Route 17 west for 2 miles.

## TUCKER HILL LODGE

Route 17, Waitsfield, VT 05673. 802-496-3983. *Innkeepers:* Zeke and Emily Church. Open all year.

Tucker Hill Lodge was built in 1948 by the Martin family, although many who first come to the lodge are under the impression that it is more than a hundred years old. On 14 acres on a wooded hillside away from the road, the lodge is popular in all seasons. Many people use it for their wedding receptions and country retreats. It is an attractive place with clean, tidy lines. The living room's focal point is a large fieldstone fireplace. The lounge and dining room are also enhanced by fires in open hearths. Emily and Zeke are from North Carolina and pride themselves on the inn's "southern hospitality that has been transplanted to Vermont."

Tucker Hill is also a very popular dining spot, with good reason. Their chef's expertise is in nouvelle cuisine, and among the unusual dishes offered are golden bass en papillote, halibut Maltese, sole stuffed with broccoli and shrimp, veal Eduardo, and roast loin of pork with mustard sauce.

The guest rooms have fresh flowers on the bureaus and old-fashioned quilts on the beds. This inn is popular with skiers, who come for the 40 miles of mountainous cross-country trails offered by the Tucker Hill Ski Touring Center. In warmer months there are tennis on the inn's clay courts, swimming in its pool, nearby golf, and plenty of hiking, biking, and horseback riding.

*Accommodations:* 20 rooms, 12 with private bath. *Pets:* Not permitted. *Driving Instructions:* The inn is 1 ½ miles from the junction of Routes 100 and 17 in Waitsfield.

## Wallingford, Vermont

### THE WALLINGFORD INN

9 North Main Street, Wallingford, Vermont. Mailing address: P.O. Box 404, Wallingford, VT 05773. 802-446-2849. *Innkeepers:* Al Bruce and Kathleen Knowlton. Open all year except for short vacation periods.

A mansarded Victorian building built in 1876, the inn retains most of its original details, including fine oaken woodwork, arched marble fireplaces, elegant chandeliers, and polished wood floors. One reason that the Wallingford still has so many of its original features is that until 1969 the mansion was owned by the family that built it. That family's holdings included a small company that was to grow to become the True Temper Corporation. The son of the original owner of the building invented the pneumatic mailing tube, once a mainstay of virtually every department store in America.

The Wallingford Inn's high-ceilinged dining rooms offer candlelight meals with a number of seafood specialties, including shrimp scampi and broiled trout amandine. In addition to meat, poultry, and Italian specialties, the inn's creamy Caesar salad is a favorite of many diners'. The guest rooms are spacious and furnished with antiques, including many from the Victorian period.

*Accommodations:* 6 rooms with bath. *Pets:* Not permitted. *Driving Instructions:* The inn is about 7 miles south of Rutland on Route 7.

*Weathersfield, Vermont*

## THE INN AT WEATHERSFIELD

Route 106, Box 165, Weathersfield, VT 05151. 802-263-9217. *Inn-keepers:* Mary Louise and Ron Thorburn. Open all year.

The initial six rooms of what became the Inn at Weathersfield were built from 1795 to 1798 by Thomas Prentis, a Revolutionary War veteran. A carriage house was attached three decades later, and finally an antebellum-style columned gallery was added to the front of the building. Over the years the building has been a homestead, a tavern and stagecoach stop, a stop on the Underground Railroad, and, until its restoration in the 1960s, a summer estate.

The inn is set well back from the road on a 12-acre site. Its dining room has exposed beams, a stone fireplace, and antique furnishings. Menu highlights include sole with lemon, dill and caper butter, lamb cutlets in puff pastry, and chicken Weathersfield. Guest rooms have brass and canopy beds and antique furnishings and quilts. Several rooms have working fireplaces. Even a rainy day can be a blessing at the inn, whose library has more than thirty-five hundred books and forty current magazine subscriptions.

*Accommodations:* 8 rooms, 6 with private bath. *Pets and children:* Not permitted. *Driving Instructions:* Take Route 106 from Springfield 1 mile past the airport to the inn.

## West Dover, Vermont

### INN AT SAWMILL FARM

Route 100, West Dover, Vermont. 802-464-8131. Mailing address: Box 8, West Dover, VT 05356. *Innkeeper:* Rodney C. Williams. Open all year.

This 1779 property has undergone a renovation that has completely transformed the interior of the buildings into facilities with modern conveniences, while still retaining the old Vermont feeling. The buildings use the original structure with exposed beams and time-softened barnboard in an effective way. Many of the guest rooms and suites have fireplaces for added comfort. The inn is filled with brass, copper, and other antiques. A pond on the property provides swimming and trout fishing in summer and skating in winter.

The restaurant, with its exposed timbers and old mill tools on display, features an array of dishes. Appetizers include Irish smoked salmon, coquille of lobster; escargots, and the famed Vermont appetizer asparagus tips wrapped in ham and baked with Vermont cheddar cheese. Dinner entrées include scallopini à l'Anglaise, roast duck au poivre vert, frogs' legs Provençal, and breast of chicken.

*Accommodations:* 20 rooms including 8 fireplace suites, all with private bath. *Pets:* Not permitted. *Children:* Under ten not permitted. *Driving Instructions:* Take Route 100 north of Wilmington 5 miles to the inn.

## WINDHAM HILL FARM

West Townshend, VT 05359. 802-874-4896 and 874-4080. *Innkeepers:* Ken and Linda Busteed. Open all year except November and April.

The road from Windham Road to the inn borders a deeply cleft valley, and the effect is rather like arriving at Shangri-La. Windham Hill Inn, fashioned out of a 135-year-old farmhouse on the edge of a steep hill, is a happy place where innkeepers Ken and Linda Busteed are joined in their family effort by their three sons. The feeling here is that of being a houseguest rather than a transient. The Busteeds often call their inn the "best-kept secret in Vermont."

Meals are served by candlelight. Inn specialties include beef bearnaise, coquilles St. Jacques à la Provençal, and breast of chicken tarragon. Meals often begin with a soup such as potage St. Germain, made from peas grown in the inn's garden, or hearty mushroom bisque. Linzertorte, frozen chocolate cheesecake, or pineapple Romanoff are typical desserts. Windham Hill is fully licensed, and a wine list is available.

Each guest room is decorated in a different way, and all have pleasing views of the woods, valley, or mountains. One of the most popular is the Wicker Room with its collection of Victorian wicker pieces.

*Accommodations:* 10 rooms, most with private bath. *Pets:* Not permitted. *Driving Instructions:* West Townshend is 21 miles northwest of Brattleboro. In West Townshend, turn up Windham Road, and go 1¼ miles to the inn sign on the right.

## Wilmington, Vermont

## THE HERMITAGE INN

Coldbrook Road, Wilmington, VT 05363. 802-464-3759. *Innkeeper:* Jim McGovern. Open all year.

The Hermitage has been developed from a farmhouse that dates back to the early eighteenth century. At one time it was the residence of Bertha Eastman, editor of the famed Social Register, the "Blue Book" of society. The building and its grounds have since been renovated by its present owner, Jim McGovern.

The reputation of the Hermitage Inn rests primarily on cuisine. The restaurant, which received much praise from the press, is one of those most frequently recommended by innkeepers in the area. The inn has four separate intimate dining rooms. Among the specialties are an assortment of homemade soups, Wiener schnitzel, frogs' legs Provençal, fillet of sole Veronique, shrimps scampi, and chicken amandine. Daily specials are special indeed: game birds, pheasant, and quail all raised on the property. Saturdays and Sundays brunch is offered.

Each guest room at the Hermitage Inn is individually decorated and furnished with antiques. Eleven have working fireplaces. The carriage house contains a sauna.

The grounds were once the site of one of the largest maple-sugar operations in the state, and Jim McGovern has revived the business in the old sugar house. The maple-sugaring started out as a hobby for Jim, but it is now a full-scale operation.

*Accommodations:* 16 rooms with bath. *Driving Instructions:* Take Route 9 to Wilmington. At the traffic light, turn right onto Route 100. Go about 3 miles to Coldbrook Road on your left. The inn is another 3 miles down Coldbrook Road.

## NUTMEG INN

West Main Street (Route 9), Wilmington, Vermont. Mailing address: P.O. Box 818, Wilmington, VT 05363. 802-464-3351. *Innkeepers:* Joan and Richard Combes. Open late December to mid-April and Memorial Day to November.

The Nutmeg Inn is a little Green Mountain farmhouse with a brook nearby. The red and white inn consists of a late-eighteenth-century main house with connecting carriage house and barn from a later date. In summer the Nutmeg Inn is ringed with beds of flowering annuals and perennials. In 1957 the farmhouse was restored, its beams were exposed, and in combination with the carriage house, it was opened as an inn. The connected barn is the family home. The carriage house is now the lounge, with a piano, television set, and reading area. Books are available for guests, as are games and a bar (bring your own bottle). In summer, lawn games are set up.

Meals are available to guests only. In the morning there is an à la carte menu as well as a combination eggs, bacon, and muffin breakfast available. In the evening a family-style dinner with a single entrée is served. A typical dinner might start with onion soup followed by tossed salad and roast beef with gravy, potato, and green beans, along with rolls and butter and dessert. Typical desserts are chocolate fudge cake, apple pie, and "Nutmeg smile."

*Accommodations:* 9 rooms, 4 with private bath. *Pets:* Not permitted. *Children:* Under 9 not permitted. *Driving Instructions:* The inn is on Route 9, a mile west of the traffic light in Wilmington.

## THE WHITE HOUSE OF WILMINGTON

Routes 9 and 100, Wilmington, Vermont. Mailing address: Box 757, Wilmington, VT 05363. 802-464-2135. *Innkeeper:* Robert Grinold. Open May through March.

The White House of Wilmington was built in 1915 as the summer estate of a lumber baron, who mysteriously ordered a staircase hidden in the mansion's innards. A popular pastime with new guests is attempting to discover the whereabouts of the staircase.

The inn is surrounded by landscaped grounds, fountains, and formal gardens. A 60-foot swimming pool is in this attractive setting. In winter there is a complete cross-country ski-touring center with a dozen miles of well-marked and groomed trails.

The central section of the inn's ground floor features elaborate French doors topped by fan-shaped windows flanked on two sides by symmetrical two-story porches. Some rooms have large working fireplaces and views of the village and mountains. Three of the twelve guest rooms have fireplaces that work, as do the main dining rooms and lobby–living room. One favorite retreat for guests is the Patio Lounge, where drinks are served accompanied by views of sunsets over the Deerfield Valley and the crisscross of ski trails.

The inn's dining rooms are popular with skiers for lunches of hot chili and stews. The dinner menu offers Continental cuisine such as duck à l'orange and saltimbocca. This inn combines hospitality with the elegance of a turn-of-the-century mansion.

*Accommodations:* 12 rooms, 8 with bath. *Pets:* Not permitted. *Driving Instructions:* Take Route 9 West from Brattleboro 16 miles to Wilmington. In Wilmington, take Route 9 East for ½ mile.

## Woodstock, Vermont

### THREE CHURCH STREET

3 Church Street, Woodstock, VT 05091. 802-457-1925. *Innkeeper:*
Eleanor Cole Paine. Open May through early November and late
December to mid-March.

Three Church Street was built near the end of the first quarter of the
nineteenth century. There is some evidence that the Marquis de Lafayette may have lodged at the inn on his visit to Woodstock in 1825.
William Howard Taft dined here in 1912. (A special chair had to be
built by a local craftsman to seat the portly president.) Each of the
inn's guest rooms is differently decorated, most with at least one piece
of antique furniture. The several guest sitting rooms have either a fireplace or a wood stove. There is a drawing room with a piano and a set
of six chairs that were at one time given to Queen Victoria, as well as a
library and a small, informal sitting room and a larger living room. In
the attic is a small room that was probably used to hide runaway
slaves.

The breakfast menu here offers juice, hot cereal, sausages,
chicken livers, corned-beef hash, eggs of any style, and pancakes with
Vermont maple syrup.

*Accommodations:* 10 rooms, 5 with bath. *Driving Instructions:*
Take Route 4 to the center of Woodstock; the inn is next to the Town
Hall.

## THE VILLAGE INN OF WOODSTOCK

41 Pleasant Street, Woodstock, VT 05091. 802-457-9804. *Inn-keepers:* Anita and Kevin Clark. Open all year except two weeks each in April and November.

The Village Inn, until recently known as the New England Inn, was built in 1899 as a private home and office for a wealthy doctor and his family. The Victorian house, now the inn, its carriage house, and the caretaker's cottage are all that remain of what was once a 40-acre estate. Decorations in the restored house recapture the long-lost qualities of the turn of the century. The oaken wainscoting and moldings, beveled glass, and ornate tin ceilings were in the original house. Antiques were gathered from all over New England, and an intimate cocktail lounge was added downstairs. Here one finds stained-glass windows and an antique oaken bar with brass and nickle-plated fittings. The inn's dining room is open to the public for breakfasts and dinners by the fireside. Specialties include prime ribs of beef and rack of lamb.

The guest rooms, done in the Victorian manner, include two that now occupy Dr. Merrill's former billiard room on the third floor. Some guest rooms retain their original marble-topped washstands.

The inn is just a quarter mile from the historic town green and Woodstock's many craft and antique shops. Skiing is the primary winter attraction here, with Suicide Six in Woodstock and the Killington ski area just twenty-five minutes away. In warmer months there are auctions, festivals and a number of water attractions including swimming, fishing, and canoeing in the nearby lake and Ottauquechee River.

*Accommodations:* 5 rooms, 1 with private bath. *Driving Instructions:* The inn is a quarter mile east of the village on Route 4.

# Index of Inns

WITH ROOM-RATE AND CREDIT-CARD INFORMATION

# Index of Inns

WITH ROOM-RATE AND CREDIT-CARD INFORMATION

Inns are listed in the chart that follows. In general, rates given are for two persons unless otherwise stated. Single travelers should inquire about special rates. The following abbreviations are used throughout the chart:

dbl. = double. These rates are for two persons in a room.

dbl. oc. = double occupancy. These rates depend on two persons being registered for the room. Rentals of the room by a single guest will usually involve a different rate basis.

EP = European Plan: no meals.

MAP = Modified American Plan: rates include dinner and breakfast. Readers should confirm if stated rates are per person or per couple.

AP = American Plan: rates include all meals. Readers should confirm if stated rates are per person or per couple.

BB = Bed and Breakfast: rates include full or Continental breakfast.

## Credit-Card Abbreviations

| | | | |
|---|---|---|---|
| AE = | American Express | MC = | MasterCard |
| CB = | Carte Blanche | V = | Visa |
| DC = | Diners Club | | |

**Important:** All rates are the most recent available but are subject to change. Check with the inn before making reservations.

Addison Choate Inn, 122; rates: $48 to $60 dbl. BB

Admiral Benbow Inn, 198; rates: $65 to $85 dbl. BB; MC, V

Altenhofen House, 35; rates: $60 to $135 dbl. BB, less off season; MC, V

Arlington Inn, 203; rates: $45 to $65 dbl. BB; MC, V

Asheton House, 115; rates: summer $30 to $53 dbl. EP, winter $23 to $37, suite available

Aubergine, 40; rates: $40 to $55 dbl. BB

Barrows House, 217; rates: $105 to $132 dbl. MAP

Beal House Inn, 173; rates on request; AE, DC, MC, V

Bee and Thistle Inn, 19; rates: $48 to $66 dbl. EP; AE, MC, V

Bernerhof Inn, 165; rates: $25 per person BB; AE, MC, V

Bethel Inn and Country Club, 32; rates: $36 to $69 per person MAP; AE, DC, MC, V

Birch Hill Inn, 239; rates: $25 to $31 per person dbl. oc. BB, $32 to $38 MAP

Bishop's Gate, 7; rates: $44 to $50 dbl. BB

Black Lantern Inn, 246; rates: $35 dbl. EP; MC, V

Blue Hill Inn, 35; rates: $38 dbl. EP; MC, V

Blueberry Hill, 224; rates: $65 per person MAP; MC, V

Boulders Inn, 17; rates: $98 dbl. MAP; MC, V

Bradford Gardens Inn, 116; rates: $54 to $59 dbl. BB; AE, MC, V

Bradford Inn, 156; rates: $40 per person MAP (EP on request); MC, V

Bramble Inn, 77; rates: $44 to $58 dbl. BB

Brannon-Bunker Inn, 69; rates: $35 to $40 dbl. BB; MC, V

Breezemere Farm Inn, 38; rates: $42 per person dbl. oc. MAP; MC, V

Butternut Farm, 11; rates: $35 dbl. BB

Nauset House Inn, 86; rates: $42 to $55 dbl. EP; MC, V
Nereledge Inn, 183; rates: $40 dbl. BB; MC, V
New England Inn, 169; rates: $50 to $76 dbl. MAP; AE, MC, V
New London Inn, 179; rates: $30 to $40 dbl. EP; MC, V
Newcastle Inn, 63; rates: from $29 dbl. EP
Nordic Inn, 232; rates: $59 per person dbl. oc. MAP; AE, MC, V
Norseman Inn, 33; rates: $80 dbl. MAP
North Hero House, 248; rates: $28 to $70 dbl. EP
Northfield Country House, 113; rates: $30 dbl. BB
Nutmeg Inn, 272; rates: summer and fall $40 to $55 dbl. BB, winter $35 to $48
    per person MAP
Okemo Inn, 238; rates on request
Okemo Lantern Lodge, 254; rates: $38 per person MAP; MC, V
Old Farm Inn, 125; rates: $32 dbl. BB; AE, DC
Old Manse Inn, 81; rates: $26 to $48 dbl. BB; AE, MC, V
Old Newfane Inn, 247; rates on request
Old Riverton Inn, 23; rates: $35 to $40 dbl. BB; AE, DC, MC, TRADEX, V
Old Sea Pines Inn, 82; rates: $26 to $38 dbl. BB; MC, V
Old Tavern at Grafton, 225; rates: $40 to $75 dbl. EP
Old Village Inn, 65; rates: winter $30 dbl. EP, summer $55; MC, V
Old Yarmouth Inn, 151; rates: $55 to $75 dbl. BB; DC, MC, V
Olde Rowley Inn, 73; rates: $36 dbl. BB; MC, V
Olde Towne Farm Lodge, 223; rates: $35 to $40 per person MAP; MC, V
Palmer House, 161; rates: $24 per person BB; $34 MAP
Park Square Village, 92; rates: $14 to $42 dbl. EP; AE, CB, MC, V
Pasquaney Inn, 157; rates: $20 per person dbl. oc. EP, $38 per person MAP; MC, V
Perkins Cove Inn, 66; rates: $35 to $50 dbl. EP (lower off season)
Philbrook Farm Inn, 190; rates: $60 to $68 MAP
Pilgrim's Inn, 50; rates: $53 to $60 per person MAP
Pitcher Mountain Inn, 192; rates on request; MC, V
Pleasant Lake Inn, 180; rates: $32 to $37 dbl. EP
Point Way Inn, 103; rates: $35 to $65 dbl. EP; AE, MC, V
Publick House, 140; rates: $47 to $72 dbl. EP; AE, CB, DC, MC, V
Quechee Inn at Marshland Farm, 255; rates: $55 to $80 dbl. BB (less off season);
    MC, V
Queen Anne Inn (Chatham, MA), 83; rates: $85 dbl. BB; MC, V
Queen Anne Inn (Newport, RI), 201; rates: $35 to $55 dbl. BB
Rabbit Hill Inn, 235; rates: $31 to $60 dbl. EP; MC, V
Red Clover Inn, 243; rates: $35 to $40 per person MAP; AE, CB, DC, MC, V
Red Lion Inn, 138; rates: $36 to $67 dbl. EP (Pet $10); AE, DC, MC, V
Reluctant Panther Inn, 241; rates: $45 to $55 dbl. EP; AE, MC, V
Rocky Shores Inn and Cottages, 126; rates: $42 to $57 dbl. BB
Rose and Crown Guest House, 119; rates: $50 to $70 dbl. BB
Salt Ash Inn, 251; rates: $26 to $50 per person dbl. MAP (EP off season); MC, V
Saxtons River Inn, 258; rates: $28 to $55 dbl. BB
Seacrest Manor, 127; rates: $42 to $58 dbl. EP (less off season)
Seafarer, 128; rates: $34 to $48 dbl. BB
Seaward Inn, 129; rates: $42 to $55 per person MAP
1780 Egremont Inn, 134; rates: $100 to $120 dbl. MAP, EP available midweek;
    MC, V
Shelter Harbor Inn, 202; rates: $42 to $58 dbl. BB; AE, MC, V
Ships Inn, 109; rates: $65 dbl. EP; AE, MC, V
Ship's Knees Inn, 87; rates: $30 to $60 dbl. BB
Shire Inn, 211; rates: $30 to $45 dbl. BB
Shore Inne, 13; rates: $32 to $40 dbl. BB; MC, V
Shoreham Inn and Country Store, 259; rates on request
Silvermine Tavern, 18; rates: $48 to $53 dbl. BB; AE, DC, MC, V
Snowvillage Lodge, 191; rates: $95 dbl. MAP; AE, DC, MC, V

## THE COMPLEAT TRAVELER'S READER REPORT

To: *The Compleat Traveler*
c/o Burt Franklin & Co., Inc.
235 East 44th Street
New York, New York 10017 U.S.A.

Dear Compleat Traveler:

I have used your book in _____ (country or region).
I would like to offer the following ☐ new recommendation, ☐ comment,
☐ suggestion, ☐ criticism, ☐ or complaint about:

Name of Country Inn or Hotel:

_____

Address: _____

_____

Comments:

Day of my visit: _____ Length of stay: _____

From (name): _____

Address _____

_____ Telephone: _____